IN SERVICE TO AMERICA

VISTA nurses, Sherry Prozzo (left) and Carol Brage (right) make a home visit to a multiple sclerosis patient in Newton County. The Volunteers served with Ozark Opportunities in 1972. (Note the Winthrop Rockefeller poster on the wall of the home.) *Photo courtesy of ACTION*

IN SERVICE TO AMERICA

A History of VISTA in Arkansas
1965–1985

Marvin Schwartz
Preface by Governor Bill Clinton

The University of Arkansas Press
Fayetteville 1988 London

Manufactured in the United States
97 96 95 94 93 5 4 3 2

DESIGNER: Chiquita Babb
TYPEFACE: Linotron 202 Baskerville

The paper used in this publication meets the minimum requirements of the American National Standard for Permanence of Paper for Printed Library Materials Z39.48–1984. ♾

LIBRARY OF CONGRESS CATALOGING-IN-PUBLICATION DATA

Schwartz, Marvin, 1948–
In service to America.

Bibliography: p.
1. Volunteers in Service to America 2. Volunteer workers in social service—Arkansas. 3. Volunteer workers in community development—Arkansas. I. Title.
HC110.P63S34 1988 361.6′09767 87-19440
ISBN 1-55728-005-3
ISBN 1-55728-006-1 (pbk.)

Dedicated to Suzanne
for her patience and support

Acknowledgements

The completion of this work has been made possible by the generous assistance of the following individuals and organizations:

Ms. Lily Peter
Dr. F. Hampton Roy
Winthrop Rockefeller Foundation
Arkansas Community Foundation
Arkansas Endowment for the Humanities
Arkansas ACTION Office
CCX Network, Inc.

Photographs have been donated by Gene Richards and Andrew Kilgore.
Unless otherwise noted, all other photos are by Marvin Schwartz.
In Service to America *is a sanctioned Arkansas Sesquicentennial project.*

Contents

List of Illustrations *xi*
Preface *xiii*
Introduction *3*
National VISTA History *7*
VISTA Policy and Concepts *31*
ARVAC: Poverty and Local Culture *59*
"The Life and Times of a VISTA Warrior" by Bob Gorman *89*
Community Action Agencies *97*
Texarkana: Poverty and the Status Quo *111*
A Conversation with Bobby Morgan *159*
National Volunteers *171*
East Arkansas: Poverty and Civil Rights *185*
Laughing at Trouble: Jerry Cronin in South Arkansas *265*
Local Volunteers *279*
Summer Associate Volunteers *289*
Pulaski County: Poverty and Local Politics *305*
A VISTA Diary: John Lewis in Little Rock *353*
Mrs. Zelma Miller: "Soul" of Sweet Home *363*
Warren: Poverty and Community Values *371*
Arkansas VISTA Achievement *381*
A Letter from Bill Bookheim *407*
"Willie" Ferguson: The Arkansas Food Stamps Lady *415*
Post-Service Psychology *423*
VISTA Life Values *437*
Arkansas Impressions *455*
Bibliographies and Index *467*

Bibliography *469*
Individuals Interviewed *471*
Arkansas VISTA Project Files Reviewed *477*
Index *481*

List of Illustrations

Sherry Prozo and Carol Brage
Joe Bruch, Arkansas program officer
Freeman McKindra, Arkansas program officer
VISTA recruiting poster from 1970s
Goforth Coleman, Volunteer supervisor, Pulaski County EOA
Bob Torvestad, Director, Arkansas ACTION office
Lou Vitale, Volunteer and ARVAC administrator
Volunteer Joe Edelman
Volunteer Bruce Neft and Model Cities community organizer Willie B. Berry
Volunteers Joann and Tom Utterback
Texarkana Volunteers, September 1970
South Texarkana family assisted by VISTA
Texarkana Model Cities sign at street improvement project
Cover from March 1970 issue of *A Different Drummer*
Page from March 1970 issue of *A Different Drummer*
Stanley Kozinsky, Gilbert Bullaksen, and Bill Peters
Bobby Morgan, VISTA trainer and Summer Associate program administrator
Homes and outhouse in the Black neighborhood at Osceola
Young girl in east Arkansas
Corrine Cass
Volunteer Sandy Smegelsky
Volunteer and Respect member Gene Richards
Four photos by Gene Richards
Volunteers and Respect members Cheri and Earl Anthes
Charlie Imhoff, Dorothea Lynch, and Gene Richards
Bumper sticker created by Respect, Inc.
Booklet published by United People's Co-operative

Volunteer Frances Woods
Volunteer Christel Brellochs
Recruiting poster for the Lee County Co-operative Medical Clinic
Letter to Arkansas Governor Dale Bumpers from Joan Baez
Dr. Blumenthal examining a Lee County patient
Dr. Blumenthal making house calls in Lee County
Two illustrations by Ron Meyer, the *Benton Courier,* 1971
Ollie Neal, initial director of the Lee County Co-operative Clinic
Volunteer Jerry Cronin with Jesse Ware of Hampton
Volunteer Katherine Knight
Volunteer Estella Morris
Memorial to Jim Ranchino
VISTA workers meet the press at Little Rock
Volunteers Linda Patrick and Mary Potter
Volunteer Mike Watts
Photograph and article in 1975 issue of *Interaction*
Three photos of children in playground at Sweet Home Community Center
Brochure published by the Design Co-operative
Volunteers at the Design Co-operative
Pamphlet published by the Design Co-operative
A Pulaski County home before renovation
The same home following work by Volunteers
Volunteer Joann Rose and son Chris
Volunteer Tony Bozynski
Sweet Home community leader Mrs. Zelma Miller
Volunteer and Crowley's Ridge VISTA supervisor Loren Ivener
Volunteer Steve Anderson
Volunteers Rex and Neva Erickson (two photos)
Volunteer Mrs. "Willie" Ferguson

Preface

By Governor Bill Clinton

The progress of history is not limited to the grand sweep of major events or milestone occurrences. History is linked to the progress of people—to the slow and sometimes imperceptible changes that pass from one generation to the next. Arkansas has achieved great progress in the past and our people reflect an established heritage that projects Arkansas as the "Land of Opportunity" where any individual with the desire for self-improvement can succeed.

The federal anti-poverty program, VISTA, brought an influx of dedicated Volunteers to Arkansas. Young and old, VISTA Volunteers believed in self-help and self-advancement, but they also accepted the challenge of initiating that progress in others. VISTA Volunteers motivated Arkansas for positive change—change which is still evident today as we continue to urge communities to work together. I have seen time and time again the success that occurs when a community decides to help itself by pulling together its resources to provide jobs for its people and solve other problems.

Contemporary Arkansas history owes much to the groundbreaking efforts of VISTA Volunteers. Some of our major economic development programs today bear a striking similarity to the community development efforts initiated by VISTA some ten to twenty years ago.

The VISTA concept was ingenious. Its goal was great social advancements, but it began its work in what we now see as the obvious place: in the communities where that need was the greatest. VISTA taught us about the importance and power of people building from within.

VISTA projects relied on the essential dignity and hard work of people within poverty communities and demonstrated that the effective use of resources and planning would produce positive results, but only if the people themselves maintained the effort. VISTA Volunteers did more than just teach; they inspired others to learn.

Of course VISTA workers were not free of controversy. Change in those days was often accompanied by strife, but the work on balance had a very positive impact.

I am pleased to see this volume bringing due recognition to the dedicated individuals and communities that were involved in the first twenty years of Arkansas VISTA programs. As the first book of its kind in the nation, *In Service To America: A History of VISTA in Arkansas* should inspire other states to support written histories of their VISTA experiences.

In the largest sense, this book may rekindle an awareness and provide new vigor to public service programs weakened by budget cutbacks and anti-government rhetoric in recent years. Marvin Schwartz has written a historical and inspirational work whose value will likely increase with the passage of time.

IN SERVICE TO AMERICA

Introduction

VISTA, Volunteers in Service To America, has been called the most radical of all anti-poverty programs to emerge from President Johnson's War on Poverty and the Economic Opportunity Act of 1964. Depending on which side of the community power balance one placed oneself, the concept of radical action or in VISTA's case, government sponsored activities intended to change the nature of society, could be seen as either a threat or a source of unlimited pride.

For the have-nots, the impoverished, those at the depths of poverty, VISTA offered an unprecedented opportunity. It placed highly motivated and trained volunteers directly in the community to help local residents improve their lives. Volunteers brought needed skills to the poor. They were builders, teachers, lawyers, and nurses. They helped qualified individuals receive government services such as food stamps, welfare, and medical assistance. They brought about changes local communities had been unable to achieve on their own.

For those already in power, those who resisted change, VISTA was nothing short of subsidized anarchy. Unlike previous welfare programs that preserved the status quo with handouts only to those who remained in need, this was a government effort that altered society by turning need into constructive energy. Some politicians quickly realized that a new awareness growing from VISTA efforts could vote them out of office. Charges of every conceivable type were raised against the Volunteers, and state governors were pressured to remove them from projects.

VISTA projects have been part of Arkansas and national history since 1965. Through the focus of a state VISTA program, a detailed portrait can emerge that illustrates national culture, national character, self image, and the acceptance of change. This book will use the Arkansas VISTA experience as a mirror of an unwritten national history. The projects and personalities explored in these pages are distinctly Arkansan, but in a larger sense they are Southern, and in the largest sense they are unmistakably American.

More than 80,000 Americans had served as VISTA Volunteers by the program's twentieth anniversary in 1985, and approximately 1,300 of them served in Arkansas assignments. During their active service, Volunteers receive a subsistence wage, an income that generally qualifies them for food stamps. This was part of the plan—to have the anti-poverty change agents on the same economic level as the people being served, living among them and seeing the world from their perspective.

Originally conceived as a domestic Peace Corps, VISTA has survived federal budget cuts, policy changes, and specific attempts to kill the program. The human service work of VISTA continues in Arkansas and nationally, but in greatly reduced numbers than in previous years. In 1985, twenty active projects in Arkansas supported literacy tutoring, youth employment training, food banks, and other efforts.

An assessment of the long range results of VISTA must include the program's impact on the Volunteers themselves. To a large degree, many Volunteers conceded they gained more than they gave during VISTA service. Yet personal gain can be repaid by a lifetime of involvement.

For locally recruited Volunteers, a commitment to their home communities has been strengthened. Many national Volunteers found themselves absorbed into the local culture and have remained in Arkansas after their service.

Former Volunteers, both local and national, possess a distinct sense of community involvement. They can often be found in community affairs such as school boards, city planning, church activities, and youth programs. They are rarely involved in political office.

Human service is the distinct trademark of VISTA. Volunteers were trained according to program guidelines of helping people help themselves. In Arkansas, that often meant overcoming barriers of racism, mistrust of outsiders or anything that smacked of government, and the economic or political inertia of local power groups. VISTA was Arkansas' first concerted effort by outside organizers to bring about change, and many of its projects have achieved long range community improvements.

VISTA projects have directly related to the human need most evident in each environment. In Arkansas, that need has been partially met through recreational programs for urban youths in Pulaski County and medical and agricultural projects in eastern Delta counties. Through craft cooperatives for Ozark folk artists and literacy projects across the state, VISTA has served the people in the most personal means possible.

Arkansas has cause for pride in its VISTA program. The Lee County Co-operative Medical Clinic at Marianna, initiated by Volunteer efforts in 1970, is one of the finest institutions of its type in the nation. The Arkansas River Valley Area Council, a community action agency at Dardanelle, was until 1986 the nation's oldest ongoing VISTA sponsor, and ARVAC Rural Folk Crafts help preserve Arkansas culture by marketing the work of local folk artists and craftsmen.

VISTA also offers an understanding of the darker side of regionalism. Events in Marianna (Lee County) and Texarkana (Miller County) are comparable in the racial resistance each community brought against VISTA projects. In the east, Lee County's agricultural tradition created an atmosphere of violence and confrontation. In the southwest, Miller County had no Old South heritage to preserve, and there a level of doubletalk and diversion was used to hide true community feelings. In Marianna, Volunteers were directly insulted by county officials. In Texarkana, they were called "good boys and girls" whose efforts were said to be an unnecessary duplication of existing services.

Arkansas VISTA projects offer a unique understanding of the state identity and its position within a national perspective. VISTA is people. It is who we are and who we are becoming, an unseen and immeasurable reality. It is the premier of all poverty programs because it promotes the concept of loving your neighbor.

VISTA raises the question of morality and survival. It offers an understanding of why the "good" is necessary and what efforts must be undertaken to maintain that awareness. VISTA is a program of great resurrecting power. It has planted a seed from which later generations are reaping the harvest.

NATIONAL VISTA HISTORY

VISTA Origins and Initial Identity
1962–1969

The Nixon Years and Program Changes
1969–1976

From Carter to Current Status
1976–1985

VISTA Origins and Initial Identity 1962–1969

Initial federal interest in a domestic volunteer service program resulted from efforts by the Attorney General's office and the Justice Department to curb juvenile delinquency and adolescent street gangs in the early 1960s.

While the federal government was busy with domestic issues of desegregation lawsuits, forced school integration, and discrimination in federal jobs and housing, while civil rights activists were being routinely harassed, beaten and jailed in the South, the Peace Corps, already two years old, was achieving significant results overseas.

The realization that professionally trained personnel were least likely to work well in urban ghetto situations led federal planners to propose a "domestic Peace Corps," a service intended as more than just another well meaning intervention program. A key element in this early recognition was author Michael Harrington's *The Other America,* which awakened the nation to the existence of the "invisible poor."[1]

President Kennedy's 1963 State of the Union Address referred to the benefits of a domestic service program patterned after the Peace Corps, and early that year his proposal for a National Service Corps was issued. The program called for volunteers to serve for one year with minimum stipend. Local community agencies would plan their own projects and supervise the volunteer efforts. The only requirements were that Volunteers be eighteen years old, American residents, and have no dependents under eighteen years.

A bill was drafted for congressional consideration of the National Service Corps, yet despite widespread citizen support, the bill barely gained necessary approval in the Senate and never appeared for a vote in the House. Primary opposition to the bill was directed at what was considered creative federalism, direct grants to state and local projects that bypassed state-level veto power. In its original form, the NSC did not require state governors' approval of projects. That veto power was added later on, but following Kennedy's assassination in November 1963 discussion of the bill in the House ended.

One of President Johnson's first major domestic initiatives was the War on Poverty, and he selected Sargent Shriver, then director of the Peace Corps, to head the new program. Within a few months, passage of the 1964 Economic Opportunity Act created the Office of Economic Opportunity (OEO), an umbrella agency for a variety of anti-poverty programs such as the Job Corps, Upward Bound, Neighborhood Youth Corps, and Head Start. The National Service Corps concept, renamed Volunteers In Service To America, was included within OEO. Shriver, evidencing an enthusiasm as first OEO director, announced in 1965 that by 1976, the bicentennial year, there would be no more poverty in America.[2]

From the beginning, VISTA was unique among its colleagues. It offered neither job training nor funding. VISTA was people.[3] From the lofty OEO rhetoric—"the elimination of poverty in the midst of plenty by opening to everyone the opportunity to work and the opportunity to live in decency and dignity"—Johnson drew his remarks, now held as a VISTA anthem, addressed in December 1964 at a White House ceremony to the nation's first twenty Volunteers. Their job, he told them, would be:

> . . . to guide the young, to comfort the sick, to encourage the downtrodden, to teach the skills which may lead to a more satisfying and rewarding life. No aspect of the War on Poverty will be more important than the work you do. . .

> Your pay will be low; the conditions of your labor will often be difficult. But you will have the satisfaction of leading a great national effort and you will have the ultimate reward which comes to those who serve their fellow man.

The following month, the Volunteers, ranging in age from twenty to eighty-one, received six weeks of intensive training and were placed in year-long assignments in California migrant camps, in Arkansas rural communities, in the Hartford, Connecticut, ghetto, and in the hollows of eastern Kentucky.

Glen Ferguson, first national VISTA director, predicted a first year recruitment of 3,500 Volunteers, a group he described as "mentally alert, physically able men and women who would like to give a year of themselves to the poor."[4]

Material compensation for service would be a monthly stipend of fifty to seventy-five dollars and a termination stipend of fifty dollars for each month of service. Volunteers would also receive travel compensation, health insurance and other federal benefits though they were not strictly considered federal employees.

By the end of 1965, more than two thousand Volunteers were living and working among the nation's impoverished, and another one thousand Volunteers were preparing for placement. Despite some early growing pains, the program was flooded with applicants, a sense of mission demonstrated by young people in a response to the positive image of the program.

An alternate view of VISTA's early support suggests that the high public enthusiasm for Johnson's War on Poverty was the response of a guilt ridden populace, a "Great Society" embarrassed by its new-found affluence, wanting to assuage a middle class unease by helping.[5] This motivation, if it truly existed, may also have been a collective guilt resulting from the Kennedy assassination and a desire to shape a Kennedy legacy, which Johnson offered.

Padraic Kennedy, deputy and acting director of VISTA from 1966 to 1970, recalled the program's early years from a different perspective:

In the earliest days, from 1965, it was hard to get people to join, and VISTA was considered a poor relation of the Peace Corps. The things that changed that and hurt Peace Corps recruiting were the war in Viet Nam, which decreased the desire for international service, and the urban race riots which focused attention on American poverty in a dramatic way and made people want to serve at home rather than overseas.

National recognition of the program also grew as a result of organized promotional campaigns. Magazine and newspaper ads, radio programs and TV spots were run, and inserts were slipped into monthly mailings to millions of retired government workers. The 1967 VISTA film "A Year Toward Tomorrow," narrated by Paul Newman, won an Academy Award for best documentary. Additionally, Volunteers were allowed consideration for deferment from military service. Because of the universal allowance of such deferments, most Volunteers mistakenly believed VISTA service created an automatic deferment.

Adding to the misunderstanding were recruiting efforts held at college campuses across the nation. Some national Volunteers recalled large banners proclaiming "Get Your Draft Deferment Here!" hung above the VISTA recruitment table at their college student union. But local selective service boards still had to be notified of a man's VISTA status. This excerpt from a 1968 letter by Joe Bruch, OEO program officer for the southwest region and Arkansas, was part of many such letters to local draft boards:

> We feel that Mr. . . . will make a significant contribution to our efforts in the "domestic war." Please consider his VISTA application in classifying his draft status.

Training of VISTA Volunteers during the 1965–1969 period was modeled after training for Peace Corps Volunteers, even to the duration of the program. Because Peace Corps Volunteers received twelve weeks of training for a two-year service, VISTA Volunteers received six to eight weeks of training for their one-year service. Early VISTA training took place in contracted university centers in various parts of the country. Individuals were mostly nationally recruited, middle income college graduates, some with specific professional skills but most with basic liberal arts degrees.

A popular training model from this period began with a two week stay at a low-cost urban hotel or boarding house where trainees were introduced to the ideas of poverty through discussions, lectures, community walks and visits. This was followed by two weeks living in with an underprivileged family in a local community and two weeks back in the urban setting to review their experiences.

Where a person was recruited or trained had little or no connection with where he or she eventually served. A person could be recruited in New York, trained in Colorado, and serve in Florida. Volunteers rarely knew where they would be assigned until the last days of training, often because the position the trainee would fill hadn't previously existed. Program development and Volunteer training often occurred simultaneously.

Additional training programs of this time created two unique Volunteer types. One was the Program Development Planner (PDP), national Volunteers specially trained in community planning. The PDP Volunteer acted as a bridge between the VISTA-sponsoring agency and its community, helping them develop programs to resolve the area's problems. The PDP Volunteer laid the groundwork and helped design programs to be carried out by national Volunteers that followed. This was VISTA's attempt to assist Community Action Agencies in understanding and dealing with local problems.

The PDP Volunteers, with their quiet, orderly manner, left an impression in many communities that later Volunteers would conduct themselves with a similar decorum. In those cases, the aggressive, confrontational attitudes of some national Volunteers came as quite a surprise.

The other unique type of Volunteer trained during this time was the Summer Associate. These were college students who served in a special ten-week VISTA program during their summer break from school. Though they might be enrolled in a distant college, the students were often residents of the area or state they were assigned to serve. One purpose of the VISTA Associate program was to make potential sponsors aware of the value of the VISTA program and have them request more Volunteers in the fall.

In these early years, most volunteers were placed in local projects under the sponsorship of Community Action Programs (CAP), an OEO creation that enabled state and local non-profit agencies to receive federal funds for anti-poverty activities. With a federal budget of more than eighty-two million dollars to be dispersed in its first year, OEO encouraged the states to establish CAP agencies and many state OEO directors and technical assistants were quickly appointed.[6]

Volunteers could only be sent to an area at the request of the state or local agency or nonprofit organization, and they would work under the direction of the sponsoring agency. State governors were given veto power for the start up and continuation of all projects, but the primary Volunteer work was left to the CAP agency to decide. VISTA assignments shaped themselves into three distinct types:

1. Community Empowerment or Organizing—projects that attempt to raise group consciousness to social inequalities and develop the leadership to effect changes.

2. Basic Services—projects that provide direct assistance to individuals or communities through education, recreation, welfare counseling, transportation assistance and other services.

3. Physical Projects—projects that built or restored playgrounds, community centers, parks, that provided energy conservation services or other improvements to an individual or a community's physical environment.

Of these three project types, community empowerment or organizing efforts created the most resistance. Local power structures—the political, financial, and ethnic interests that shaped local societies—did not approve of Volunteers organizing low income communities to the point of changing the balance of power. Those complaints were made known by members of Congress, urban mayors, and governors.[7]

VISTA National Director William Crook recognized the lack of defined mission as early as 1967. In a staff memo that year he emphasized community organizing as a means and not an end. Social change could only be achieved within certain restraints, one of which was VISTA's ability to "take the heat," Crook wrote.[8]

According to Mimi Mager, former executive director of Friends of VISTA, a nonprofit organization that commemorates the program and lobbies for continuing federal support, the early Volunteers' political actions set up adversarial relations.

> VISTAS were involved in some controversial issues, and local politicians felt threatened by that. In issues such as strip mining legislation, VISTA was trying to address the root cause, not just band-aid assistance. This became very threatening to local officials.

Because OEO would not spell out proper behavior for the Volunteers, a fine line was drawn between legitimate VISTA goals and unacceptable militant action. Congress took the initiative and passed a series of restrictive amendments aimed at curtailing Volunteer and CAP employee activities. Most notable among these was the 1966 Hatch Act which prevented Volunteers from engaging in partisan politics and voter registration, prevented Volunteers from being involved in union organizing, and limited the use of the VISTA name for publicity.

Additionally, OEO trainers instilled in the Volunteers a sense of their being change agents who would help people help themselves. As criteria for project approval, Volunteers had to come in direct contact with the poor, and project activities had to produce an improvement in the lives of the poor.

In its first five years, VISTA had quickly established itself as a program where social education could easily be mistaken for social agitation. In its attempt to remedy the conditions that caused poverty by encouraging the poor to take action on their own, VISTA and the War on Poverty were seen by some as an example of the government financing a revolution against itself.[9]

If any such revolution was forthcoming, the next period of VISTA history decisively altered the program direction. Under a new presidential administration, VISTA struggled to survive yearly budget battles and federal mandates that altered and then attempted to eliminate the program.

The Nixon Years and Program Changes 1969–1976

VISTA had reached an impressive level of public support in its first few years. Applications received in 1968 were more than the OEO budget could absorb, up 120% from the preceding year. Federal analysts cited a new national awareness among youth, as three-fourths of newly assigned Volunteers chose VISTA over the Peace Corps because it served America first.[10]

The traditional Volunteer was still nationally recruited, college educated, and generally came from a comfortable economic level that made VISTA his first real involvement in poverty. Few Volunteers reflected a minority or low income background at this time. Those who had climbed up from poverty were, for the most part, not yet ready to return and help others do the same. Nor were there yet many older Volunteers in the program, a status probably influenced by the arbitrary assignment of training and project locations.

College campus recruiting efforts yielded the idealistic and energetic Volunteers for whom a one-year service period was their limited chance to change the world. It became rapidly apparent to them and to VISTA administrators that more than idealism and special skills were needed. Volunteers needed to be more sophisticated and capable because the problems they faced were more complex than had been realized.

Resistance to community empowerment and organizing projects was also great, and Volunteer efforts were often cut short by a local power base that viewed their work as unnecessary agitation by outside trouble makers. Recognition of a need for "inside leadership" led to a new direction in Volunteer recruitment, according to Kennedy.

> By late 1966 we had begun to rechannel our thinking. . . . We began to realize that to serve the proper communities justly we needed Volunteers who understood those communities—the residents themselves.[11]

A major shift in recruiting emphasis was begun in the late 1960s, and a larger effort was made to recruit older Volunteers and local residents of the low income communities. This shift would place locally recruited Volunteers (LRV) or community Volunteers in fifty-six percent of all Volunteer positions by 1975.

A VISTA team concept of national and local Volunteers was designed to appeal to two groups: the community Volunteers were expected to relate well to people in the poor community, and the national Volunteers were expected to have an impact on the middle class. The new recruitment drive was accompanied by a change in Volunteer training from the uniform national program of University-based training to a more regional focus.

An increasing emphasis was also placed on skills training at this time, and Volunteers who possessed skills associated with direct service projects—teachers, architects, lawyers, nurses, etc.—were highly valued. Though training now took place within the region or near the area of service, trainees rarely knew the location of their project sites until the last days of training.

Training contracts were offered nationally through a closed bidding system. Special divisions of major corporations such as General Electric, Westinghouse, Volt, and others, entered bids on the cost of the training programs and the six-week curriculum.

In many cases, state and project directors would come to the training event to review a new batch of Volunteers, seeking those with the skills their areas needed. The closing days of these training projects were often occupied with abrupt interview sessions in which directors tried to make personal assessments of the Volunteers.

This was often followed by prolonged bartering sessions among the directors for the individuals they believed could best serve their projects.

While many VISTA projects were still establishing an initial presence across the nation, the program as a whole was becoming more specialized. This was a forced change that came as a result of federal policy. Attitudes of the Nixon administration created the emphasis that brought in more local Volunteers, regionally based training, and a program shift from organizing to more direct service projects.

The 1968 election of Richard Nixon signified the beginning of the end for OEO as it was originally conceived. CAP agencies across the nation had been created under OEO guidelines and had sponsored the most controversial VISTA projects. According to Diana London, current federal branch chief of VISTA, the result—a natural tension between the agencies and the Volunteers—was both expected and welcomed by OEO leaders.

> OEO looked to the VISTA program to reform the CAPS and make them more responsive to the needs of the area. There were bound to be clashes between the power structure and what the Volunteers tried to do.

Community organizing activities by Volunteers contributed to controversy, but Nixon had other ideas about what OEO agencies should attempt and to whom they should be accountable. By mid 1969 he had reassigned Head Start to the Department of Health, Education, and Welfare and the Job Corps to the Labor Department. His reorganization plan would eventually place VISTA under a totally different guidance policy than it had with OEO, but until 1971 he took little action other than to lift the semi-official draft deferment on new and current Volunteers.[12]

C. R. Lane, acting VISTA director during this period, was more explicit about the new direction for the agency:

> VISTA is no longer going to be this place where you can do your own thing . . . especially if that means confronting the establishment. We hope, predict, and are striving for a new type of volunteer who will work within the system and lower the noise level.[13]

During this time, the Nixon administration was quietly preparing plans to eliminate VISTA altogether. David Pass, a former Volunteer doing research in Washington for a thesis on VISTA claims to have discovered these plans when a page outlining them was left behind at a copying machine by a federal cleric. Pass said he brought the information to Volunteer leaders giving them time to organize their reaction.

The response by national volunteers might have been predicted. On July 27, 1970, 350 Volunteers, carrying with them proxies for another 1,200, arrived in Washington, DC for a three-day conference. The trained community organizers held a rally and formed the National VISTA Alliance, a Volunteer organization that demanded VISTA and OEO be returned to their leadership positions in the War on Poverty.

Though a confrontation had begun, it was immediately clear which side had the upper hand. Nixon's response was to propose zero funding for VISTA in 1971, in effect kill the program.It was his way of dealing with the program after initial attempts had failed to bring it under stronger control. Congressional support kept VISTA intact, but executive influence brought on the next phase of the reorganization plan. In July 1971, the federal program ACTION was created to serve as an umbrella organization for all existing volunteer agencies.

On the surface level, it may have been time for VISTA to restructure its emphasis. The 1960s were over. Time was up for the period of consciousness building and social pride, the intangible results of empowerment projects. In the1970s, the emphasis was on achievement and economic results.

In the most simplistic terms, ACTION supporters might have defended the new federal emphasis as a change from making people feel good to making them do good. It also gave the Nixon administration a positive image by making the gesture of restructuring an existing volunteer program, thereby discrediting critics who held the Executive Office as an opponent to such programs.

Under its new ACTION guidance, VISTA began to slowly feel the restrictions placed on it by an unsympathetic administration. Yet some federal employees view this change as far more deliberate than it might appear. Bob Torvestad, current ACTION administrator for Arkansas and Oklahoma, said the 1970 VISTA rally and march in Washington reportedly infuriated Nixon.

That march was the single event that caused national recruiting to go downhill. National training contracts also ended about that time. The use of local Volunteers had nothing to do with the shift from OEO to ACTION. The march actually got Nixon mad. That was something.

Nixon's exaggerated concern over radicals created the paranoid atmosphere which distinctly characterized his administration. He perceived OEO as a haven for radicals and a symbol of change. His decisions to reform the War on Poverty could be considered a response to the voters who placed him in power, a voting block clearly not among the OEO clientele group.

Yet according to Bruch, the assignment of VISTA to ACTION was Nixon's reaction to not being able to phase out the program.

Because they couldn't beat it in Congress, they changed VISTA's direction. Nixon's people hated OEO and they tried to administer us to death. I was constantly in trouble. I screamed back a lot. Because mail directed to me would be intercepted by the regional director, I had my friends in Washington send it to my home. That was how I was able to get the training done.

Bruch also referred to an effective chain of command through which the Nixon administration made known to subordinates its approval of certain actions taken against the VISTA program. One of these may account for a difficulty in locating project and volunteer records from the program's early years.

Destruction of obsolete records is a standard government policy, and searching for fifteen- or twenty-year-old files from CAP agencies that had little or no administrative background may be a futile task. But critics of Republican attitudes toward VISTA have suggested another reason why pre-1971 records are now so difficult to locate. These critics believe that following the shift from OEO to ACTION, early VISTA records were deliberately destroyed by Republican zealots hoping to eliminate any future rallying of Democratic strength.

Speculation or fact, the truth may never be known. In a post-Watergate analysis of the political subversions carried out by Nixon appointees, the premise gains some credibility. It is further substantiated by Bruch, serving in the Austin, Texas office at the time, who recalled this scene:

> When OEO changed to ACTION, the Republicans went crazy. They tossed entire files into huge roller containers kept in the halls for incineration of materials. I climbed into those bins and saved many of the records. It was a maniacal attempt, malicious on their part, to do away with VISTA services.

In terms of specific projects, the shift from OEO to ACTION resulted in a decline of CAP agencies as VISTA sponsors and a gradual move toward more moderate and well established sponsors such as state departments of energy or social services, United Way agencies, and even municipal governments.

Volunteers were no longer simply assigned to an agency or an area where poverty existed. The mid-seventies emphasis on direct services called for specific projects and Volunteer assignments. Communities needed to identify their own problems and sponsors needed to establish Volunteer job descriptions with specific time-phased goals and objectives.

Accompanying the increasing use of low income, local Volunteers, training for specific skills was primarily assigned to the sponsoring agency. Federal training had diminished to six-to-ten day pre-service orientation programs which mainly emphasized the concepts of ACTION volunteerism.

Shriver voiced his objection to placing VISTA within the ACTION structure, stating that Volunteers would never "rally around an organization chart" and that the basic fault of the program, in the Volunteers' view, was an emphasis on "appearance of change rather than substance."[14]

Nixon's significant election victory in 1972 gave him the chance to further define VISTA according to his personal concepts of volunteerism. Michael Balzano, his appointee as ACTION director, implemented the idea that VISTA, originally intended to be a service organization, had been distorted by OEO, trainers and the Volunteers themselves.[15]

The Republican concept of volunteerism placed its support more in the private than the public sector. Nixon's attempts to restrict and gradually diminish VISTA were continued by President Gerald Ford. Ford planned for the program's complete elimination with a long range budget culminating in zero-funding for Fiscal year 1979. That plan was dramatically reversed when President Jimmy Carter took office in January 1976.

From Carter to Current Status
1976–1985

During the four years of the Carter administration, the VISTA program was redirected toward what was considered its original principles. Sam Brown, the 1960s activist appointed as ACTION director, was chosen to revive the program. One of his initial impressions was how close VISTA had come to not surviving.

> . . . there was no request in the federal budget for money for the next year and some of the Volunteers, all talented people, were being restricted more and more to administrative jobs in social service agencies. Gone was the emphasis on citizen participation. Gone was the idea of poor people helping themselves. VISTA, one of the government's most unusual programs, was on its way to becoming quite ordinary.[16]

Brown chose to return the program to an emphasis on community organizing. A national VISTA grants program began directing Volunteers and support resources to organized groups or networks. These groups allowed local problems to be addressed by small projects that otherwise would not have the structure to support Volunteers.

Some of these organized groups served as "umbrella agencies," placing Volunteers in local projects while the larger, more organized agencies provided administrative support. Other groups were national organizations such as the Federation of Southern Cooperatives, ACORN, and others.

The policies of this new approach were stated in the VISTA Guidance Papers, published in 1978 by the Office of the Program Director. The proper role of a Volunteer, the document stated, would be working to empower groups to influence the decisions that affect their lives. The goal of improved conditions for the poor would result from an increased access to decision making through cooperative efforts.

The basic concept of the Guidance Papers was that empowerment leads to decisions that provide control. In other words, the poor must develop the capacity to help themselves. Projects approved for VISTA sponsorship could, for example, work to create a library, but Volunteers could not serve as the librarian. Volunteers could create a mechanism for tutoring high school drop outs, but they could not themselves simply provide a tutoring service.[17]

For Marge Tabankin, VISTA director during this period, this was a reaffirmation of the principles which led to the program's creation—"assisting the poor to break the bonds of dependency by working through the democratic process."[18]

During the Carter years, the program weathered a renewed assault of criticism resulting from its return to community organizing, and in January 1981, a budget of thirty-four million dollars (highest in the program's history) supported nearly five thousand Volunteers nationwide at approximately nine hundred anti-poverty community projects.

But administrative support was soon to swing back in the other direction. Tabankin's assessment of the program's challenge in the 1980s, published six months before the Reagan adminstration took office, predicted that only positive, long range planning would be able to surmount a looming economic crisis.

> The 1980s will challenge grassroots organizations to take the initiative. Self-help groups . . . have to go on and develop positive alternatives, a vision of the kind of place the neighborhood ought to be a few years down the road. They have to put in place the structure and the programs necessary to fulfill their visions. . . . The challenge of the 1980s, both for VISTA

and the grassroots, self-help groups VISTA works with, is to keep working and innovating in the face of economic retrenchment.[19]

The challenge was issued in a more threatening manner by James Burnley, first VISTA director under the Reagan adminstration, who claimed the program had in recent years "funded and supplied Volunteers to numerous left-wing groups." He went on to state that VISTA "wasn't worth its cost, wasn't eliminating poverty, and isn't a proper function of the Federal Government." Burnley's tirade also included the boast that he was working as hard as he could to be "the last VISTA director."[20]

Those remarks are difficult to fathom in light of Volunteer ability to mobilize resources far above the costs of their training, placement, and support. Program analysts have estimated the average cost per Volunteer at approximately $7,700 with an average Volunteer mobilization of more than $26,500 in funds and services otherwise not available to low-income communities.

Nevertheless, VISTA's record budget of 1981 has been reduced to seventeen million dollars. As of June 1958, there were 2,400 Volunteers assigned to 450 anti-poverty projects across the nation. Public and Congressional support has again refused to allow the program to be abolished, but the Reagan administration has been attempting to change the agency's focus.

Current emphasis has been moving it away from advocacy and organizing and toward the provision of community services such as food banks and literacy programs. Suzanne Wise, VISTA director appointed in January 1985, said the program is trying to meet basic human needs but avoid having Volunteers involved in confrontation situations in communities.[21]

According to Mimi Mager, VISTA has been more changed by the Reagan adminsitration than by any other, especially by its appointment of people who are set on killing the program. Wise is the fifth VISTA director since 1981, and the program is suffering from a changing perspective of what it ought to be, Mager said.

In the past, local communities addressed the problem. Now this administration says unless you're working in A, B, or C, don't come looking for

VISTA assistance. Now Washington is telling local communities what the problems are. This is directly in conflict with the philosophy of VISTA.

The lack of administrative support is also reflected in reduced recruitment efforts that are ignoring a population base with a willingness to volunteer its services, Mager added.

The age of volunteerism has not passed, and the opportunities for service are different, not fewer, than what they once were, Diana London believes. She contends that VISTA has been a flexible program and able to adapt to changing trends. A need did not previously exist for current VISTA projects such as food banks and shelters for the homeless. Because these projects reflect how federal anti-poverty funds are spent, VISTA has had to follow where the poverty funds were allocated, London said.

For Bruch, though he continues as an ACTION employee, the current status of VISTA is too far removed from what he believes to be its most effective operation.

> I am for the elimination of the program now. Yet I love VISTA and my life has been significantly changed by it. But the times have changed too much. Various administrations have destroyed or gutted how it should work. Without the budget and philosophy to make it work, I see it now as almost fraudulent. You spend 90% of the time just fighting to keep it alive.

But VISTA continues, and more than eighty thousand Americans have served as Volunteers since the program began. In its present form and probable future transformations, it will continue to provide the "change agents" whose goal is simply to help people help themselves. Flexibility has been key to VISTA survival among changing political views.

At the program's core remains the commitment to place Volunteers directly in the poor communities, a placement that has created life-long dedication to fighting poverty. At the present time, the programs that seem to work best are those that exhibit the broadest base of community support.

For a state program director like Bob Torvestad, current policy requires he approach his job with a different attitude than exhibited by earlier staff. He sees himself as much less idealistic than earlier administrators.

I'm not so concerned about what could or should work, no pragmatism or wonderful objectivity. It's more a learning of things that do or don't work and who can do them. Programs need to know what they're about and have the continuity to wait on us. If you need immediate service, we're not your resource.

Notes

1. VISTA, *15th Anniversary Book,* June 1980, Pgs. 22–23.

2. David Pass, "The Politics of VISTA in the War on Poverty: A Study of Ideological Conflict," PhD thesis for Columbia University, 1976, Pg. 194.

3. VISTA, *15th Anniversary Book,* June 1980, Pg. 26.

4. *Arkansas Gazette,* January 31, 1965.

5. Ben Seligman, *Permanent poverty: An American Syndrome,* Pgs. 168–170.

6. *Arkansas Gazette,* December 17, 1964.

7. David Pass, "VISTA: 15 Years of Service," *Community Jobs,* June 1980.

8. Pass, "Politics of VISTA. . . ," Pg. 194.

9. Victor Ray, Pulaski County EOA executive director, *Arkansas Gazette,* April 6, 1966.

10. *Arkansas Gazette,* July 4, 1968.

11. VISTA, Pg. 26.

12. Pass, "VISTA, 15 Years. . ." Pg. 4.

13. Pass, "VISTA, 15 Years. . ." Pg. 4.

14. Sargent Shriver, *Congressional Record,* June 2, 1971, Pg. S8057.

15. Pass, "VISTA, 15 Years. . ." Pg. 4.

16. VISTA, Pg. 6.

17. *VISTA Guidance Papers,* Office of the VISTA Director, March 1978. Pgs. 3–6.

18. Pass, "VISTA, 15 Years. . ." Pg. 4.

19. VISTA, Pg. 62.

20. *The New York Times,* July 9, 1985.

21. *The New York Times,* July 9, 1985.

VISTA POLICY AND CONCEPTS

VISTA Service Philosophy

Volunteers as "Change Agents"

Training

OEO and ACTION Criticism

Empowerment vs. Direct Services

VISTA Service Philosophy

To view the essence of VISTA policy in the concept of self-help or maximum feasible participation of poor people in the decision-making process is to focus on the end result of VISTA service more than the service itself. This establishes the program as another "means to an end." VISTA certainly had the goal of readjusting economic levels in society, but it was the techniques VISTA brought to its mission and whom those techniques influenced that made the program so unique.

Social welfare programs that promote passive acceptance of handouts, that encourage people to be recipients rather than producers, are based on the concept of preserving the status quo. They are stop-gap measures that postpone a degeneration of conditions but do little to improve them.

W. L. "Sonny" Walker, a former Arkansas OEO director, has commented on the appeal of these types of programs to the American public.

> . . . [the programs] make us proud because we have temporarily kept the peace, stopped the fires, bandaged the wounded, hired and silenced the aggressive, and provided the sedative to put the poor to sleep and dream an impossible dream and then to awake to the reality that things haven't changed. . . . We must inject a spirit of honesty and sincerity of purpose into the programs.[1]

Joe Bruch, Arkansas program officer

VISTA's spirit of honesty and sincerity was embodied in the Volunteers living in poverty communities. Beyond the initial benefit of closing the gap between community values and the Volunteers' middle class backgrounds, VISTA living arrangements forced a Volunteer understanding and identification with the people served.

Many consider this the real genius of the program, for it is one of very few such arrangements that deliberately blurred the line between giving and receiving. In many cases, Volunteers spoke of gaining as much as they gave, of learning new values which have directed them far beyond their original year of service.

Most important to the community, however, was the personal level of communication the Volunteers could bring. Available assistance programs were no longer hidden within foreign environments of county courthouses or social services offices. The Volunteers, according to former Arkansas program officer Freeman McKindra, were like a walking resource to the community.

> People began to see the Volunteers as someone who could get help out. Available 24 hours a day, they became part of the institution. They made it easier because they were living there.

Most communities were very good at sifting out what they needed to do and what resources were required, but very few had knowledge of available programs to help them, McKindra said. This lack of knowledge was due in part to a lack of outreach staff among the agencies offering help.

Housing support, for example, was readily available through the Farmers Home Administration or Housing & Urban Development, but there was no way of making the connection between the federal agencies and the people. Volunteers who could bridge that gap became extremely valuable to their communities, McKindra said.

By living among the poor on their meager stipends, Volunteers had to rapidly shed any false motivation which might have brought them to their service, any "arms length" attitude about helping the poor but not getting personally involved. Self help was the ultimate goal, but personal involvement was the VISTA's unique contribution to national anti-poverty efforts.

Ted Wilson, former VISTA supervisor of a six-county area in east Arkansas, commented on his role of providing Volunteers and projects with administrational support.

> My approach was that I let the Volunteers find out for themselves what they were and weren't able to do. . . . I really did not have answers to the multitude of problems they encountered, which frustrated me as well, as I felt a responsibility to provide them. . . . I feel I made it possible for the Volunteers to develop and utilize what skills they had with the least amount of interference.

Personal involvement of Volunteers provided the motivation to poverty communities and individuals. In some cases, it was a young VISTA worker whose palms grew callused from working a chopping

Freeman McKindra, Arkansas program officer

hoe in the fields of Mississippi County, who sweated in a community cannery to store her harvest for later distribution. In other cases, it was an urban planner in Pulaski County helping to hoist a recycled railroad tie into place for part of a community playground.

The essence of VISTA service is more than self-help. It is the actions of Volunteers that encourage people to create self-help groups and vigorously pursue their goals despite the conditions that previously held them back. For Sam Brown, ACTION director during the Carter administration, this is a measure of a nation's commitment to justice and equity for people at the margin of society.

> VISTA Volunteers work at that margin. In doing so, they encourage the poor and give thousands of Americans a sense of shared commitment that by helping others to help themselves the moral dimensions of their own lives and the social dimensions of our society can be expanded.[2]

Volunteers as "Change Agents"

The role of Volunteers and the providing of leadership to a community involves another misunderstanding. Leadership does not always mean putting oneself at the head of a group. In poverty communities, the concept of leadership has to grow from within. It must crystallize in words, action, and character, and it must manifest itself as an integral part of that group.

VISTA leadership had to inspire communities and individuals to take their own first steps. It could not take that step for them. Volunteers had to influence community direction by revealing alternatives and choices, not by making the choices themselves.

Volunteers also had to exercise great personal diplomacy when motivating a community to tackle its problems. Saul Alinsky, the sociologist whose advice on establishing "people's organizations" greatly influenced Volunteers and trainers, wrote in *Reveille For Radicals* that organizers who try to initiate action by revealing to people the source of a problem are essentialy insulting those same people by implying they were too stupid to realize the cause of their own problems.

Organizers gain far more dedicated local support by allowing community members to express their own views on the cause of problems, views which Alinsky suggested were most often clearly on target. The message for Volunteers was that communities didn't need to be told what their problems were. They needed to be shown ways to solve them.

VISTA recruiting poster from 1970s

For Neal Blakely, a former VISTA trainer and Arkansas program consultant, the Volunteer place in community affairs was distinctly outside of the leadership role.

How to be a change agent? You let the people lead, and then you go on to something else. Then you were successful. I'd tell the Volunteer that the community didn't want him out there leading them. Teach them how to deliver a speech to the mayor. Let them handle that. You go home.

Blakely's advice was directed to the community as well as to the Volunteers. In many Arkansas poverty communities, the general state of affairs was so dismal that almost anything the Volunteers did was of some help. Blakely realized that many communities never understood the role of Volunteers. By letting Volunteers provide leadership, a dependent attitude was created, a community mind set that relied on a Volunteer always being around to handle the problems, he said.

We'd tell the community—you got to learn how to run this thing. Learn your skills from the Volunteer. You're strong, honest. The Volunteer is supposed to teach you these things, then move on out.

Volunteers originally had one year of service to accomplish their goals, though a second year extension was available and frequently requested. For the most part, the one-year service policy forced Volunteers involved in large-scale community projects to take extreme mesaures. It heightened their confrontational attitudes and reinforced their determination to proceed according to their own assessments of need. Pulaski County Volunteer Joann Rose commented on that determination.

There was an urgency among the Volunteers. Though poor people had a lifetime, we had only one year to make the changes. Our diplomacy was not very high, but we didn't care about diplomacy. A lot of us had problems with authority, but we weren't afraid of getting fired. We didn't care. I never had the ability to manipulate someone's ego to get what I wanted.

One year of service also revealed what some Arkansas Volunteers perceived as an inherent VISTA flaw. Christel Brellochs, whose VISTA year in Mississippi County has been followed by a career of community development work, saw little value resulting from a single year's service.

I wish I was then as sophisticated as I am now about how community decisions are made, how co-operative ventures are made, and how to stay with them. One year? Forget it. This is the delusion of VISTA. Change the face of poverty with people in a year's time? You're nuts.

Earl Anthes, a former Volunteer who continues to serve communities and non-profit ventures through a West Memphis consulting and training agency, spoke of the time restraint as VISTA's refusal to prepare for "the long haul."

Individual case work is a never ending series of band aids that requires an institutional response. There has to be a step in building that response, a tool to get into the community. My biggest complaint with VISTA was as a one- or two-year program. You can't make the institutional change.

Under ideal conditions, one year of VISTA service should have allowed Volunteers to work themselves out of a job. In that time, a project should have developed the long range goals that would eliminate reliance on any single Volunteer. A Volunteer who served for just one year would probably not see measurable results, but the continuity of one Volunteer following the next could carry the effort through. Yet many projects did not have a capable supervisor to provide continuity and many VISTA assignments did not allow an overlapping period for departing Volunteers to orient their incoming replacements.

As a result, some Volunteers took on community leadership roles that were not always in the overall best interest of the poor. The temporary Volunteer status encouraged some to be irresponsible change agents who pursued change for its own sake rather than community benefit.

Jim Crawford, a former Arkansas VISTA program officer, defined the Volunteers as "temporary agents of change" whose usefullness decreased over time as community members learned necessary skills.

> A lot of Volunteers may have tended to hang on too long, thinking they would stay in VISTA and play useful roles. Those who had lived through the experience and the hassles, those who had "spilled blood," you can see why they stuck it out and thought there would always be a place for them.

It was a rare national Volunteer who could remain in the small Arkansas town of his VISTA service and find a comfortable level of post-service involvement. This was not the case in Little Rock, and several former Volunteers continue to reside in the area, most doing community or human service type work. For the most part, they are extraordinary people who would enhance the social environment wherever they chose to live.

Some former national Volunteers still live in small Arkansas towns, but the majority have moved on. Their souvenirs of VISTA service are recollections of local people and Arkansas culture. Few keep in touch with each other and the community members with whom they once worked. Fewer still make return visits.

Training

As in any job, effective performance requires proper understanding of the problems to be faced and the resources at one's disposal. Most Volunteers entered VISTA with a commitment to helping people, but few had the specific skills to channel that motivation into real work.

The primary goal of VISTA training was to transform the Volunteers' general desire for social improvement into specific skills that could be applied in community situations. VISTA trainers knew the most effective tool they could provide to a community was a Volunteer with a keen awareness of the culture of poverty and community needs and a broad understanding of available government services.

VISTA training had to exploit the emotions that brought in Volunteers. Unlike military training, which systematically destroys individual identity and free thinking, VISTA training had to preserve individual personality. Because the program was based on personal contact and implemented mostly by solo Volunteers, VISTA trainers enlarged those roles to reinforce a group effort, Joe Bruch said.

> As motivation, I put us in the position of right and good, sort of a moral crusade attitude. We knew there was injustice and poor people in the midst of plenty. I told them the system sucks, but you don't.

Bruch also used historical perspective to heighten the Volunteers' understanding of their service. His comments reinforced the two prime VISTA concepts of personal fulfillment and community advancement.

I would say 15 or 20 years from now when you're faced with a judgment, what you do and see here will affect the choice you make. I would end every session pointing out that when all was over and history would look at this, they would look at what the Volunteers did. That would be the summation of VISTA history. That put a little pressure on them.

Having brought the Volunteers up to a high motivational level, trainers also had to keep them focused on achieving realistic goals. Idealism brought many Volunteers into service. Jim Ranchino, director of the VISTA Summer Associate program sponsored by Ouachita Baptist University at Arkadelphia, said one role of training was to break some of that idealism.

Many VISTAS are naive dreamers who enter the program because they think they can accomplish something. Many picture themselves as a kind of knight in shining armour on a white horse going out to save the world. You need some of this philosophy if you're going to achieve something, but you must be pretty realistic about what you're going to face.[3]

VISTA training left some national Volunteers with the feeling that they were educationally and emotionally equipped to change the world. Some of them brought about significant changes, but others were unable to make the transition from the fantasy of their expectations to the reality that awaited them. Sometime within his year of service, a Volunteer had to adjust from what he had hoped to do to what he actually could do.

Specialist Volunteers had a more difficult time making that transition. Many of them had joined VISTA with set expectations. They focused on their own needs and their own idea of what problems the community should address. Melvin Brown, a locally recruited Volunteer in Pulaski County, recalled the problems that resulted from such attitudes.

Some of them thought they was Jesus, here two years and gonna change the whole world. Their ideas were acceptable, but they wanted us to accept them like they knew it. Some got irritated because it took us too long to get an idea.

Goforth Coleman, Volunteer supervisor, Pulaski County EOA

Idealism tempered by reality—what brought a Volunteer into the program and what would allow him to succeed in his work. Trainers had to destroy preconceived notions of poverty among Volunteers who, in some cases, had never had close contact with poor blacks or whites. Bruch said he often used the word "dignity" in teaching Volunteers how to deal with people as individuals. Blakely said his key word in training was "honesty."

> The main thing I did was try to be honest, be honest with what you are and why you are there. What I knew about black people worked the same with white people. Poor people can see it in your eyes if you are there making fun of them or there to help.

Training, according to Blakely, was the chance for the Volunteers to learn how to act, how to dress, what church to go to, and how to choose their friends in the poverty community. Honest Volunteers could develop genuine relationships in the community just by sitting on their front porch and being friendly. There was no big training technique, no magic strategy for Volunteer success, just common sense, Blakely said.

> For example, how could some woman in the community sell bootleg Sunday whiskey, and everyone know it and she never get caught? Why, she got some connection with the "man." So for the Volunteer, you got to make her your friend and let her know you're no threat to her.

What the national Volunteers most lacked was direct exposure to poverty and awareness of the personal survival skills required under such conditions. Volunteer Charlie Deknatel said he gained this awareness under acclaimed VISTA trainer Howard Higman, who showed Volunteers how they could be resourceful despite not having immediate control over their lives.

> They would move us around abruptly to different locations or send us out to look for jobs without our resumes. One night they turned us out with only $1. They put up information on the day's agenda in Spanish, and it was our problem to find out what it meant.

Deknatel, a Program Development Planner, remembered being warned not to let himself become just a grant writer or to fall into the agency bureaucracy. Training emphasized planning and management tecniques, and engineering texts were used to illustrate how to establish and achieve clear objectives, Deknatel said.

Training sessions had to destroy the Volunteers' naive idealism yet preserve their determination to help people and their belief they could bring about change. Volunteer Charlie Imhoff recalled that balanced awareness as essential to VISTA success.

> Whatever grandiose expectations one might have had upon entering VISTA were dulled in training sessions. This was done not so much to discourage the Volunteer as it was to bring us back to the reality of the situation and make sure everyone went into the field with their eyes open.

Walker, a trainer at early sessions at the University of Oklahoma, said he tried to give Volunteers some knowledge of the social dynamics, the risks and dangers, of the communities in which they'd be working. Volunteers would have to deal with attempted sexual relations, sob stories, guilt trips, appeals for money, things which had little or no relation to their projects, Walker said.

> We did a lot of role playing to prepare them for the games people would play on them. A lot of the young, white female Volunteers were not aware of social restrictions on their involvement with black males. My approach was to prepare them emotionally and mentally for their assignment.

Walker used the language and techniques Volunteers would encounter in the community, such as sexual advances and appeals for money. Another level of community awareness was reflected in Volunteer appearances. Walker said some had the false notion they had to dress in ragged clothes to be accepted by the poor.

Trainers sometimes used those techniques themselves to prepare Volunteers for such encounters, to assess Volunteer reaction, and possibly for the trainer's self interest. One Arkansas Volunteer recalled her future project director interviewing her at the end of a University of Oregon training session. The Volunteer, an eighteen-year-old white, Irish Catholic, said she was a half hour into her initial conversation with the black man when he suddenly changed the conversation and leaned across the table.

> He looked me in the eye and said before the year was over he would "get" some of me. He said either he would or someone else would and he would know about it. I jumped up and said, "The hell you will." We made a bet on

> it. As his payoff, I said he had to buy me a bottle of the best Irish whiskey he could get. He lost that bet and later bought me two bottles of whiskey.

Arkansas program officers claimed they were able to get some of the best national Volunteers assigned to the state because of their preparation and bargaining techniques at training sessions. Bruch said his team would review the training project files and identify the specific Volunteers needed for Arkansas projects.

State officers who converged on training sessions were given lists of the available Volunteers and their perceived skills. McKindra said interviews were rapidly arranged in which Volunteers were subjected to various techniques to reveal their personalities.

> We didn't have long to size them up, so we had to pick up what we could. Were they articulate? Did they have strange beliefs? Were they so serious they would wipe out in two weeks? How did they handle the silence? Did they nervously chatter or take control? Did they stay silent?

Following the interviews, program officers' bargaining sessions sometimes lasted through the night, and the competition for talented Volunteers was strong. In an atmosphere he compared to a slave auction, McKindra admitted that some creative Volunteers may have been missed. When a Volunteer was offered that no one seemed to want, McKindra said the Arkansas team might take that person and use him to barter for getting the next good one.

Adding to the program officers' selection criteria was a knowledge of what kind of supervisor support was available at specific projects, McKindra said. Though all supervisors wanted the super Volunteers, some of them were too slow or bureaucratic to handle exceptionally creative types.

These types of bargaining sessions for Volunteer placement in the Southwest Region lasted until 1969 when a group being trained in Austin threatened to walk out of the program unless they were given a better role in the selection process. Volunteers were then allowed to choose their top three assignments.

Selecting projects in areas they knew something about, the Volunteers showed a strong preference for New Mexico. Because most didn't have a positive image of Arkansas, McKindra said his team tried to educate them about the state. Those who were assigned to Arkansas received one of the best state orientation and training programs in the nation, Bruch said.

> I would draw a picture map of Arkansas and talk about it as a third world nation with emerging power structures. I talked honestly about what was there. I told them they were not going to change the social and economic infrastructures. That only comes when middle class America, the true power brokers in the country, comes to an awareness.

During a week orientation program, Arkansas Volunteers learned about state economy, religion, education, and other social influences. They attended classes at the State History Commission, where Blakely said he made sure they asked questions. They also spent some time living with low-income families before being sent to their projects and specific assignments.

The idea behind the Arkansas training plan was to develop various levels of commitment. The commitment to VISTA service was followed by a commitment to Arkansas, which was then followed by a commitment to a project, McKindra explained. Each time a Volunteer made one of those commitments, he was involved at that stage. A Volunteer not committed to a specific project might still find effective work at another Arkansas assignment, McKindra said.

Arkansas VISTA training was effective because it was based on objectives. It let trainers measure what they wanted the Volunteers to know before being sent out on assignment, Blakely said.

> If they had that knowledge, it might stop them from asking some stupid question or making a mistake that would get them run out. The Volunteers would be going in to establish a program. We found they couldn't do that without a plan.

OEO and ACTION Criticism

In its earliest phase, OEO held the promise of the ultimate democratic social assistance program. Its concepts of self-help through direct involvement and reduction of social class barriers through interaction were buoyed up on the premise of a Great Society.

In addition to VISTA and other anti-poverty programs established as a result of the Economic Opportunity Act, OEO administrators put into place a mechanism through which those programs would be assured greater success. This was a training program designed for CAP employees and staff to assist them in understanding the dynamics of community improvement.

The OEO Training Program established one of its two national offices in Little Rock with Dr. Earl Evans as its director. Evans, a black appointee of Gov. Orville Faubus, was considered a safe person to lead the agency, someone who could avoid controversy administering the program and be counted on to take the proper side if a confrontation arose.

Evans displayed an ability to reduce complicated issues to meaningless social platitudes when he stated in 1966 that the interests of members of Arkansas' power structure were the same as the interests of the poor. Both groups, Evans claimed, desired basic human dignity. Evans went on to state that ninety-eight percent of the people don't understand the poverty program, mistakenly thinking it was only for blacks.[4]

Such oversimplifications were accompanied by a policy acceptance in sharp contrast to the Volunteers' refusal to compromise or play political games. Rev. M. W. Williams, OEO technical assistant to the governor's office from 1966 to 1972, said the entire OEO program missed the point because it refused to provide direct assistance to the poor.

Williams, who said his job was to visit state CAP agencies and trouble shoot for Volunteers, criticized OEO for its failure to overcome the defensive idea that giving money to the poor would encourage them to waste it. The poor are victims of an economy, they are sick and unemployed people, not drunkards or social parasites, Williams said.

Another criticism of OEO spending relates to the amount of money delivered in relation to results. George Ivory, VISTA supervisor of Mississippi County in 1969–70, believes a lot of federal money was wasted because little forethought was given to how it was to have been spent. Those who most needed the federal assistance were the least capable of handling it, he added.

Ivory's comment has relevance for the entire VISTA-OEO phase. Though he credits the VISTA program for making significant long range improvements in race relations in Mississippi County, Ivory said the overall program did not accomplish as much as was thought.

He blames a lot of the program's waste and imperfect understanding of southern poverty on Washington bureaucrats who designed programs without firsthand knowledge of how and where they would be implemented. The poverty program was a maverick that didn't integrate itself to local governments, Ivory said. This was primarily due to a recognition among people of power, people with the most to lose, that it was not to their advantage to be involved, he added.

Arkansas OEO director Robert Whitfield described the federal government's disenchantment with VISTA in terms of its immeasurable goals.

> It is difficult to measure success in something like this. You don't bring people out of poverty like a car on a finishing line. And this has been one

of the problems. The people in the Nixon administration want to see something for their money, and you can't see relief, hope, and that sort of thing.[5]

The Nixon administration worked to dismantle OEO and eliminate VISTA altogether. It was successful in the first part of those plans. Alvin Arnett, national OEO director of 1974, summarized the phasing out of the program by a changing administrational emphasis from the original service strategy.

OEO has never dealt with economic problems on a grand scale. . . . We've delivered health, housing, transportation services . . . been in the position of helping the poor endure their poverty a little better. OEO has not lifted a substantial number of people out of poverty. . . . You make people unpoor by laying money on them, whether through jobs or cash transfers, and OEO has never been in that business.[6]

The shift to ACTION brought VISTA projects under a much tighter government policy, one that approved projects only if they fell within specific guidelines. From Crawford's perspective, this change influenced many decisions on volunteer placement, decisions he believes were based more on politics than local need.

A lot of times, I would work with local projects, raise their hopes, and then get shot down for political reasons. I couldn't go back and face those people and tell them their programs were turned down. A lot of good people left ACTION because of that.

One example of a project with substantial community support that was denied Volunteers was the South Madison County Home Improvement Project. Crawford said that 1973 project had support from the county judge and local resources committed. The project even had a citation of praise passed in the Arkansas House of Representatives.

The ACTION refusal, based on a lack of training slots, was not a rational one, Crawford contends. He also criticized a lack of concern for the Arkansas program in the regional office. Crawford said he could not get a secretary for his Little Rock office and had

Bob Torvestad, director, Arkansas ACTION office

to send his letters to Dallas to be typed. These and other political manipulations made him leave the program with some bitterness, he added.

For the current Arkansas ACTION administrator, the program policy no longer creates those problems. With many proposals coming in, Bob Torvestad said VISTA is no longer directed by project emphasis. Current decisions are based on what an organization has asked for in resources as much as what it plans on doing with them, he said.

Torvestad gave the example of Robert Johnson, mayor of the small east Arkansas town of Birdsong (Mississippi County). Johnson, who had worked as farm manager on the VISTA-initiated United Peoples' Co-op fifteen years earlier, was assigned a local Volunter in 1985, Torvestad said.

> I was intrigued by this small town mayor and gave him time to talk. I had no idea he had previous involvement with the VISTA program. No other government agency would have approved his project.

Empowerment vs. Direct Services

Since the origin of the VISTA program, a comparison of community empowerment projects to those based on direct service has divided program administrators and influenced the course of VISTA history.

Direct service projects use Volunteers to provide tutoring programs, medical assistance, housing rennovation, child care, and a host of other specific services to individuals or a community. These types of projects most often result in positive VISTA memories because the Volunteer is able to assess his contribution.

Direct service projects also create immediate community goodwill, despite a relatively short term impact on any given problem. They primarily deal with symptoms of a problem, not with its root cause. They are easy to measure and generally raise little local resistance. Politicians and bureaucrats adore them.

Community empowerment or advocacy projects, on the other hand, attempt a more planned systemic change. Projects such as co-ops, tenant rights organizations, voter education, projects that increase a community or individual awareness of due process and civil rights—these and other empowerment projects look beyond immediate need and attempt to restructure the situations that cause problems.

Empowerment projects do not generally receive immediate or widespread support. Empowerment projects threaten the status quo. They are generally ignored for as long as possible by politicians and bureaucrats. When public pressure ultimately demands a political gesture, empowerment projects are often the first to feel the axe. Their results are difficult to measure, and their long range impact on Volunters is often one of frustration and doubt.

Arkansas VISTA personnel held different opinions on the proper place for empowerment and direct service projects in the poverty program. Blakely spoke of the inherent problems facing a Volunteer who entered a community to initiate an empowerment project.

> If the same jobs were out there, I'd apply for some direct services thing. You help a kid doing poor in school, you win momma and the whole family. Then those folks will go to the Volunteer to ask about voting or welfare rights. . . . Empowerment, that's hard. A co-op or such has got a lot of weak areas, so many ways the community could tear it down.
>
> You don't sell VISTA to a community, don't even mention it unless they ask about it. Just say it's a program to help you. You're just a human being come in to the community with some skills to share. Then you're going on. If we could get that over, that's direct service. You start off with a co-op, they'll say the Volunteer did it.

Empowerment situations may have developed from VISTA work, but more as an interpretation of OEO legislation than as a direct result of program policy, George Ellis, a personal services specialist for the southwest region, believes. The empowerment role naturally belonged to a community leader, and Volunteers involved in empowerment projects often lacked the broad understanding of complex social dynamics a local leader had, Ellis said.

> Empowerment is the long range goal of direct services. You don't give that responsibility to the Volunteers. You give it to the community leaders. The grass roots VISTA sponsor is what we should have had all along.

VISTA projects with a "storming the walls" attitude usually didn't work out in the long run, yet VISTA training emphasized a confrontational approach based largely on Alinsky and labor union models, Ellis said.

> I don't see again the possibility of the federal government paying for a project that would vote a Congressman out of office. Change does come

out of basic services and physical projects. Those can be done again, and they are probably more important than ever.

The success of Arkansas' most controversial VISTA empowerment project, the Lee County Co-operative Medical Clinic, was closely tied to the civil rights movement, Ellis said. The same Volunteer energy in a context outside the civil rights movement would not have similar results, he added.

For Joe Bruch, who described his commitment to VISTA as "burning your candle at three ends," the only problem with empowerment projects was of some potentially misused rhetoric, and he strongly disagreed that community development was a futile concept. Volunteers were one part of a large effort to change society, and almost everything they did had some value, Bruch believes.

> We knew the Volunteers would never achieve instant results, yet while they were doing their business, they were doing what they said could never be done. We had people going into situations that never occurred before. The Volunteers were creating empowerment. They just didn't know they were.

The most comprehensive position in this debate was taken by Freeman McKindra, who recognized the complementary nature of direct services and empowerment projects and saw the need for both in any single environment.

> You need the basic services to create an acceptable level of being there. There's a little child that can read, an old lady with new dentures. No one can argue with that apple pie image. On the other hand, you need to do something with the system that caused that to happen. Any need for direct services had an organizing base behind it.

McKindra raised the question of why so many Arkansas VISTA projects requested tutors and Head Start programs. The answer, he said, was because the public education system wasn't doing a good job. VISTA couldn't point that out because it would have forced local groups to admit they weren't doing what they were supposed to or reject the Volunteers, he said.

Another issue Volunteers worked on was a contradiction between poverty regulations and actual practice, McKindra said. Written regulations said a system of appeals existed, but the real issue was that the regulations weren't workable and too much discretion was left to local administrators. East Arkansas Volunteers learned that system so well they got the whole state welfare system turned around, McKindra claimed.

> Another area was health care, with a large request for VISTA nurses because local care wasn't available. So in lots of places we provided the service, deciding we were going to do a soft shoe on some and knock them on the head with others.

The plan was to look for Arkansas projects that identified a need, then attack those who were denying services, McKindra said. With many areas in the state having close to nothing in services, it was sometimes easy to fall in and deliver the services without looking at the higher level of what caused the need, he added.

McKindra agreed full scale organizing was the quickest way to get a program killed, but when the "power came down on OEO," he said no distinction was made between organizing or service projects.

The current VISTA environment uses Volunteers in planning and resource roles, and communities currently approved for VISTA projects are past the need for an organizing role, McKindra said. Such projects use Volunteers to impact the poverty community in a way that encourages participation by the community at large, McKindra believes.

Torvestad agreed, stating that decisions are no longer made on development vs. service projects. His criteria for successful projects are broad based local support and involvement.

> In serving the needs of the low-income, we are not just empowering them. That won't work for us now or ever again. The focus is changed. I'm here to provide a resource to a community program that relates to disadvantaged people. I don't say it's either development or services. That's fulfilling the dreams of your own rhetoric. If you do, you'll end up with a monoculture.

Notes

1. W. L. "Sonny" Walker, *Arkansas Gazette,* June 6, 1971.
2. VISTA, *15th Anniversary Book,* June 1980, Page 7.
3. Jim Ranchino, *Arkansas Gazette,* May 7, 1969.
4. Earl Evans, *Arkansas Gazette,* December 2, 1966.
5. Robert Whitfield, *Arkansas Gazette,* February 10, 1973.
6. Alvin Arnett, *Arkansas Gazette,* February 15, 1974.

ARVAC

POVERTY AND LOCAL CULTURE

ARVAC: Origin and Early Issues

Myrtle Cress

Volunteers and Projects

Frank Rudzik

Jon Pelkey

Major Projects and VISTA Support

Lou Vitale

ARVAC: Origin and Early Issues

In the west central portion of the state, the Arkansas River cuts between the Ouachita and Ozark Mountains on its journey from Fort Smith to Little Rock. Steamboat travel brought early settlers here while other areas in the state were still difficult to reach. Numerous towns and small communities grew, sustained by river and rail traffic and the state's earliest boom industry—timber.

Arkansas pioneer life flourished for generations, but by the 1920s the last of the virgin timber stands were gone and so was a livelihood for many river valley residents. The 1930s completed the devastation, forcing homesteaders from a self-sufficient lifestyle to a prolonged state of impoverished hopelessness.

With no work to do, with the hill soil rendered nearly useless by unrestricted cutting practices, with the fertile river bottom lands in the possession of wealthy landowners, the Arkansas hill resident began the cultural degeneration that has given way to much joking and laughter. The dilapidated cabin with leaky roof, hounds lazing beneath the porch, the country yokel with barefoot children and women—these and other overplayed images made up a widely held impression of Arkansas hill people.

By the 1960s, close to forty percent of the population lived below poverty level in the five thousand-square-mile service area of the Arkansas River Valley Area Council (ARVAC). Unemployment, illiteracy, and substandard housing were common in ARVAC's

Lou Vitale, Volunteer and ARVAC administrator

eight-county service area. The land was pretty as a post card—rolling hills and sweeping panoramas of river and distant mountains. But within that landscape were the "invisible poor," people that ARVAC Volunteer Supervisor Lou Vitale said he got to know well.

> The issue in these areas is the lack of definition or sight of poverty. But it's obviously here. The big house is seen, but the little house is back in the trees. There are white folks in both. Folks out there in the hills hurting. Poor whites over the years haven't had a voice. No controversy about them. So disenfranchised, they won't tell you they're hurting.

The area's VISTA history began in 1964 when the newly organized Yell County Economic Opportunity Program was selected as one of the first pilot progams in the nation to receive an OEO grant. By 1965, ARVAC had been established to provide a wider service area and the Yell County project was absorbed in it. During the next two decades, ARVAC was host agency to a number of national and local Volunteers. The agency initiated several important projects begun with Volunteer help, projects that have since become independent grass roots enterprises.

When a project's success can be credited to VISTA help and guidance, time will reveal that link only to those who stay close enough to be aware of it. ARVAC's success can be strongly attributed to the two men who have had the longest tenure with the agency—Vitale, with nineteen years experience, and Bob Adkison, executive director for twenty-one years.

From the earliest, ARVAC's plan has been to unite local leadership, yet it was regional economic development, not the War on Poverty, which led to initial cooperation. Adkison said flood control and navigation work on the Arkansas River and the completion of the Dardanelle (Yell County) Lock and Dam raised hopes for a multi-county development. Poverty was almost incidental in the minds of community leaders in the mid sixties, he said. They were aware, however, that sizable federal grants had been made to Appalachia, an area with poverty levels similar to Arkansas, Adkison said.

> The Appalachia regional program was formed, and we realized if they could get federal money, we had poverty here, too. Poverty became a key word here.

Local leadership, united by the concept of regionalism, founded Ozarka and the Ozark Regional Commission, organizations that gave the area an effective identity when applying for federal aid. Grants were approved in late 1964 to establish the Yell County CAP and place four Volunteers there. The Volunteers, assigned to help young people from rural life make a transition to modern education, mainly served as tutors.

One of the first Volunteers was Pamela Teggatz, twenty-three, of Milwaukee. Officially, she was to get drop-outs back in school, but her projects went far beyond that role. Teggatz helped enroll parents in basic education classes and children in Head Start programs. She visited homes across Yell County and helped families apply for low-interest housing loans. She started a clothing donation to aid needy families. In a 1965 interview Teggatz said:

> I was most concerned that I could do something useful, something worthwhile in conjunction with the program. I don't mind. All this doesn't seem like work in the first place.

Boss Mitchell, director of the Yell County program, recalled the good work of another Volunteer. Betty Burnett, assigned to Dardanelle in 1965, helped local blacks overcome nonqualification for FHA loans by organizing a housing co-op and borrowing money, Mitchell said.

The early Volunteers were pioneers whose work helped prepare the community to accept those that followed, Adkison said. They introduced the concept that the Volunteer should live and identify with the people served. Their effort was to convince both ARVAC and the local community that if VISTA was to be accepted, its mission was to be with the poor.

Fortunately, several of the agency's initial Volunteers had little trouble fitting into local community ife. Harry and Olive Heald, an older couple who tutored and taught remedial reading in Oark and other Johnson County schools in 1965, were well accepted and the couple was invited to speak at many social and civic clubs.

The Healds' most memorable achievement was a simple event. They arranged an art show at the Oark school, displaying the work of a local artist, post cards and ornaments from foreign countries, and unusual rocks. The display helped local children gain a new awareness of their state and other areas. This lack of exposure was also recognized by Myrtle Cress, an older Volunteer assigned to Ola (Yell County) in 1966.

Joe Edelman, an ARVAC Volunteer in 1972, discusses quilting with Mrs. Gothard of Perryville. *Photo courtesy of ACTION*

Myrtle Cress

Myrtle Cress had already raised eight children and been a teacher for fifty-six years when she joined VISTA. She had begun teaching when she was sixteen years old at a rural Kansas school, earning thirty-five dollars per month. That was in 1906. Sixty years later she was a Volunteer teaching at a rural Arkansas school for the standard federal stipend of fifty dollars per month.

The town of Ola had need of an experienced teacher. It needed many other things as well, as Myrtle's detailed class books and VISTA monthly reports reveal. Her notebooks refer to special children she called her "heartbreak groups." These were classes of children needing special education, medical or physical assistance, children with brain damage from rabies shots, shy children and roughnecks, many of them overaged and undersized for the classes.

The students' home environment, strongly influenced by illiteracy and alcoholism, offered them little more than the continuing problems faced by their parents. As a teacher, Myrtle related the problem to reading.

> Once the 4th grade is reached, the home vocabulary grows into a completely foreign language for the disadvantaged child. The middle class child faces this same challenge at the seventh grade level, at newspaper vocabulary where the average people in our county find a reading level.

Myrtle used this challenge to her advantage, using "book language" to lure her students into a larger perspective of their world and the opportunities it offered. But the problem was larger than she originally presumed, as these notebook entries show.

What is wrong is that the children have no idea what the books and their teachers are talking about. The teachers do not understand and call them dumb. The children are hurt and the teachers are frustrated.

Can you imagine fifth and sixth grade boys who never heard of Lou Gehrig and to whom Babe Ruth is a candy bar? I even had to draw a diamond and illustrate where each player worked and what a mound was.

This goes for about 200 of our 400 pupils here. But they are learning a lot about drinking, smoking, yes and sex, but not the truth. I am concerned because I fear that the things I have written are true of too wide an area. We are losing our heritage of a strong moral people, becoming a nation of curs. Half of these 200 disadvantaged children could be saved. Not by more taxes nor by more teachers, but by giving these children training they could take.

As a tutor, Myrtle taught problem learners from every grade and adult education in the evening. She joined a local church, a social club and the Chamber of Commerce. From her daughter's house in Fayetteville, Myrtle brought down boxes of her granddaughters' outgrown clothes and distributed them to families. She also kept VISTA and Job Corps literature prominently displayed at the post office and school library.

Her notebooks also offer brief glimpses into the community life she shared:

Learned of a family with nine children, six of school age. None have ever attended school nor have the parents. So I can soon expect to have a beginning class in reading.

Working with the seventh grade boys I feel my greatest contribution here is the behavior and citizenship talks which they just label as conversation.

The school year is over and my first reaction is definitely low blue. I have worked so hard and accomplished so little. Then I really work on evaluation and I feel better. I guess when you take a group of practically nonreaders and get them to the 3 or 5-year level, it isn't too bad.

Myrtle's assimilation into the community was total, and one of her VISTA reports hints at the understanding an older Volunteer such as she could bring to the program. Recounting her visits to an "old couple" (eighty-three and eighty-eight years), Myrtle wrote that she had seen what is bound to happen when "one has lived too long."

A tragedy and extra sorrow struck the family of one and two generations younger than they. They couldn't help. They couldn't go. They could only sit and wait and try not to worry each other by their worry that turned into fear and loneliness as they waited for the scanty reports the busy family had time to remember to give. I was glad to have the opportunity to be with them as much as I could. They were both panicky as only senile people can get. . . . Yes, they have children, all away from home here . . . and the old folk want to die where they have memories and a familiar location.

Myrtle Cress served more than two years in Ola. With no car of her own, Myrtle met other ARVAC Volunteers at agency parties and meetings. She wrote the following description of two Volunteers whose spirit apparently struck a common bond with her own.

TWO FACES OF VISTA

About 30 miles east of Ola as the hoot owl flies is Toad Suck where Pat Temeyer and Sharon Hyde are living and doing their bit as Volunteers. From different backgrounds and homes separated by half a continent, these girls are giving us a new look at the courage of Young America in Action.

Twenty miles from the comforts of even a small city, these girls found the necessities to furnish a living room, bed room and kitchen of the house they rented.

Pat, who comes from Iowa, seems so quiet, a bit on the smallish side and young, but don't let that fool you. She drives that GSA car with an efficiency that is most reassuring to this passenger. Her ten brothers and sisters have taught her things about handling children that no training school can instill but which make for efficiency in the Toad Suck project.

Sharon is taking a breather from college to complete a major in Experience. She is a little older than her VISTA partner and comes from Connecticut. Sharon is an attractive blonde who has learned to swing a mean axe since she came to Arkansas. "It's wonderful therapy for frustrations," says Sharon. "Besides, the appetite of our two stoves is never satisfied."

The girls have a tutoring project going there in Toad Suck commnity; the children are dropped off at their house by the school bus, then after an hour or so of remedial work with the girls, they are taken on to their homes.

Right now it is cotton picking time in Toad Suck, so school is closed while the children are in the fields and you will find Pat right there with them in the daytime. The girls visit in homes at other times and are starting an adult education project, also on a tutorial basis.

By attending auction sales and exploring second hand stores when they found themselves in larger cities, the girls have partly furnished their rented house. They do have electric lights—their only claim to anything modern. Water comes from a well in the yard. They have a cook stove and now a heater for the living room and "enough frustrations" to keep them both going, Sharon says.

Pioneers? Maybe," she added thoughtfully, "but these folks have lived this way all their lives. We should be able to take it for one year." And Pat agreed.

The girls can laugh about the difficulties they must meet, but being eighteen or twenty miles from a laundry or even a small store is more than a laughing matter, as is the big laundry tub in their bathroom. You carry the water from the well, you heat it on the stove, you carry it to the tub, take a restrictive bath, then you carry it outside somewhere and empty it bucketful by bucketful.

Some of us usually have dinner together after our VISTA meeting at Dardanelle. I enjoyed their joking about the hardships at the last one, but I also was remembering when I first came to Arkansas. Couldn't get it off my mind, so the next evening I called the girls and invited them to a Saturday party.

You don't know what a Saturday party is? Well, in those days ditching was mostly a hand and back job; the soil is very rocky upstate where we settled so pipes were mostly laid six or eight inches deep. When the bad storms came, the pipes froze up and stayed frozen sometimes for ten days or two weeks. Some parts of town would not be so exposed. It depended on which direction the storm came from. Friends got together and had a Saturday party. It usually meant a pot luck lunch and dinner, taking turns at a good soaking bath and just a generally good time.

The girls were a little late getting here for Pat had promised to take some children pecan hunting. We enjoyed being together for the few hours. Then with shining faces and arms full of already read newspaper to make fire starting easier, off they hurried to a six o'clock recreation meeting they had planned 30 miles back home.

Sharon says she is extending her part of their VISTA activities to include Sweet Home community while Pat concentrates on Toad Suck. They can do it now, for Pat has the GSA and Sharon has her own car with her.

Lucky Toad Suck and Sweet Home and three big cheers for Pat, Sharon, and VISTA.

Volunteers and Projects

The two Toad Suck Volunteers also impressed Lou Vitale, who recalled their bare wooden shack out in a field, a site so forlorn and empty the landlord gave them a choice—if they could stand living in the place for two months, he would let them have it rent free.

Temeyer and Hyde lived in the shack, but they had a few precarious moments. During a severe ice storm, Vitale said the girls telephoned for help, saying they were ill and out of firewood. On one occasion they called Mary Potter, a national Volunteer who had already served a year in Little Rock.

Potter, a VISTA leader in her second year, made monthly trips through the ARVAC counties to check on the scattered Volunteers. She had come to Arkansas as a confident eighteen-year-old. One year later she was no less adept at personal survival.

> I lived in Solgahachie (Conway County) in an old house way out in the country. I hauled water, cut and stacked my own wood and learned to cook on a wood stove. That winter I got a call from the two at Toad Suck. They were freezing in the cabin, no food, sick. I loaded up the car with wood and groceries. Stopped at Morrilton for beer, then drove four hours to get there. We partied all weekend.

Potter worked at her local community center when she was not traveling. She was critical, as were other early ARVAC Volunteers, of center staff for being too conscious of their own power and position. In a 1968 report, one Volunteer described her problems in trying to find a house for a poor family of eleven people.

When the aides [ARVAC community aides] found out what I was doing, one said they didn't want that family down here, that I should leave them out on the hill. . . . But I think this family needs a chance, especially the children.

ARVAC's early, older Volunteers were replaced by a new character type, the Hippie Volunteer, whose radical clothing style was a sufficient barrier to most local contact. Yet some of those second wave Volunteers helped start projects that attracted the attention of local power figures, Adkison recalled.

The Volunteers were having a field day with their idealism, and there was some struggle between them and the county judges. ARVAC had to convince the power structure to let the Volunteer come into the community and not put a muzzle on them. We had to tightrope that thing.

While the agency had to appease local power entities, it also allowed Volunteers to test local tolerances. The Volunteers had to stir the pot to get action, and they probably did more community organizing than the agency's paid outreach workers, Adkison said. The Volunteers, because they had no local allegiances, pushed those efforts in many new directions, but ARVAC never became as radical as other state projects, he added.

We accepted the realities of the situation and kept a low profile approach, a subtle use of power. We raised our issues through soft sell rather than overt use. We were probably not as aggressive as some cities, but for a rural area our thrust was assertive. We didn't accept the status quo.

To find a common thread, a cohesiveness for the poor whites in its region, ARVAC selected target areas, individual communities such as New South Hope, Grey Rock, and Union Chapel, on which to focus their poverty resources. The target groups taught the agency much, but they drew criticism from other area leaders whose communities had not been selected as targets.

Adkison suggested that by trying to be all things to all people,

ARVAC may not have best utilized its Volunteer expertise. Like other new CAP agencies, ARVAC may have had a difficult time in its start-up years. To overcome those early difficulties, ARVAC was assigned some excellent Volunteers, PDPs who influenced some long-standing successful projects.

Frank Rudzik

As a Program Development Planner, Frank Rudzik was taught to analyze CAP agency performance. His service to ARVAC was to sharpen agency skills and identify proper direction for its projects. In his first report, dated November 1968, Rudzik wrote that outreach capacity was key to ARVAC. What may seem an overly simple conclusion is the essence of ARVAC or any agency that deals with a sparse and widely scattered population. To succeed, the agency had to direct its energy outward, not attempt to draw people and activity into itself.

In Rudzik's time, the neighborhood center concept was in its first year. While he refrained from judging the value of the program, Rudzik commented that the centers were more like offices where the clerks could do paperwork than a place where people in the community could come together.

> Perhaps I am hung up now on nonoffensive tactics. Perhaps I have been overtrained on this soft sell approach and could end up accomplishing nothing this year, just waiting around for an assignment. . . . An essential part of being a Volunteer lies in creating your own job without being told to work on a specific assignment.

Further into his year of service, Rudzik positioned himself as working "for the people of the area and not the ARVAC agency." Agency staff, with a few exceptions, were possessive of "their" poverty program, he wrote, adding that the agency would have to be shaken up and rearranged it if were to continue to help solve rural poverty problems.

> I believe that a progressive and dynamic institution must support an optimum amount of conflict if it is not to become static and wallow in its own stagnation.

By the end of his service year, Rudzik was even more critical of ARVAC. He saw the agency as an ineffective provider of services, not knowing how to organize communities and covering its errors and idleness with unnecessary busy work. He was particularly critical of an order for all ARVAC committees to have a community meeting before the end of the month.

The request was an agency attempt to justify its own existence and paychecks, Rudzik wrote. Real community organizing was not achieved in forced meetings. A required meeting indicated no honest community organizing was being done. Nor did the agency have an idea of what honest community organizing was. Nothing positive could come from a meeting called for no reason, and where nothing is accomplished, Rudzik concluded.

> ARVAC must pull itself out of this stereotyped notion of what community organizing is. More emphasis must be put on organizing groups around smaller issues as a means of solving a particular problem.

As a PDP, Rudzik's advice to the agency was to put more emphasis on the special problems poor people have which make them poor, problems middle income people don't have to face.

> I think the gap is widening between the marginal and hard core poor, and ARVAC is part of the wedge separating the two. This agency has to stop and take a thorough look at itself. . . . Every dollar and energy has to be directed toward the hard core people, the people who are getting left behind.

Jon Pelkey

Jon Pelkey, a 1968 Volunteer from Oregon, had the usual cultural shocks when he began living with an Arkansas poverty family. Assigned to a small community near Russellville (Pope County), Pelkey experienced life in uninsulated wood shacks where large families lived in few rooms, where meals were mainly bread, beans and milk, and everyone rose at 5:30 a.m. and went to bed by eight o'clock.

Pelkey found it easy to identify with local problems, but it was harder than he expected to raise a community response. Pelkey soon learned an essential Volunteer lesson—one can only hope to organize people around issues *they* see as problems.

> To find the community priorities takes time, patience, a lot of talking and listening. It is difficult to determine if a community doesn't see an issue as a pressing problem or just haven't acted because nothing's been done in the past and they are afraid to take the first steps. Or perhaps they simply don't know the first steps or procedure to follow.

Pelkey, assigned as a tutor, formed a boys group and began meetings for those who had dropped out or were planning to leave school before graduation. His general goal in the club was to orient the youths to the future, he said.

> They live in the present now, only concerned with watching TV, eating and sleeping at home and maybe catching chickens. . . . I would like to create

an atmosphere in the club where the boys will have a concern about their future. . . . Hopefully they may realize group education and self betterment can be part of group cooperation as much as recreation.

Pelkey used the community center for group meetings and tutoring classes. From the beginning of his service, Pelkey said the center director and advisory board were apathetic about his work and provided limited support. A conflict ultimately developed and Pelkey was barred from the building.

In his year-end analysis, Pelkey identified these basic problems:

HOUSING—Outdoor bathrooms are the rule rather than the exception, and outhouses are very unsanitary. The houses are shacks with walls of merely one board and no insulation. Cardboard is nailed on the walls and ceiling. Broken windows and holes in the walls are not uncommon. Wood stove heat is a fire hazard. Garbage often fills the yard. Electricity is in the home but most wiring is unsafe. These shacks are rented for $30–40 per month. Owners have little concern other than collecting the rent.

EMPLOYMENT—Two main sources are the chicken industry and soybean/cotton farming. Chicken catchers work at night. They may travel up to three hours to get to a chicken house, a dirty tough job with not a great income. Often the father has done this job and the sons are following. In a few years, machines may have these jobs but the kids can't see that. . . . In the land known as the "bottoms," several families live as tenants in substandard houses provided by the landowner. A worker's wages may be $1 an hour, out of which the landowner takes 20 cents for Christmas bonus and 10 cents for rent. The Christmas bonus is merely money held back to hold the family there for the year.

CHURCH—The . . . Church is not geared toward solving problems in the community. It seems so wrapped up in spiritual religion that it does not even address itself to community problems. Members are mostly not from low income families. Some look down on low income families as trash beneath their feet. This is a Christianity of hate instead of love.

Educational problems in the town were at a critical level. Pelkey wrote that it was rare to find a high school graduate among boys who drove tractors or caught chickens for a living or to find a parent who had gone beyond the eighth grade. Pride In Education (PIE) was a special tutoring project he initiated to combat these problems. Having gained some support from local parents, Pelkey's program used college students from Arkansas Tech at Russellville for tutoring sessions. By the spring of 1969, more than forty-five tutors and sixty students were involved in PIE.

Despite that success, Pelkey questioned his community assistance and organizing. His involvement with a local family is a case study of endemic problems and the system's inability to deal with them on a logical and personal level. Commenting on the W. family, Pelkey described a fifty-six-year-old, unemployed ex-miner who lived in a homestead strewn with old junk cars and garbage, whose wife and daughter, both retarded, received welfare payments.

Pelkey became involved in the family's troubles when the mother and daughter were placed in a nursing home. Mr. W. seemed eager to get his family back, and at Pelkey's suggestion, he cleaned up his house. He got Pelkey to drive him to the nursing home for visits. Pelkey's reports tell how Mr. W. was misled by various agencies as to his visiting rights. They conclude with Mr. W. being arrested on an incest charge and sent to the state hospital for psychiatric testing. Pelkey's account of the ordeal ends with this comment.

> Let us just take a look at where we have taken the W.'s. Years ago they apparently lived together in something less than a shack. A culture perhaps close to animals, but surviving and surviving together. Along comes Community Service, Welfare, ARVAC and VISTA. Now where are the W's? In a nursing home and probably on the way to prison. Yes sir, they have clean sheets, a good roof and square meals. Surviving, but surviving separately. . . . We have failed them. How can we concentrate solely on the physical conditions and neglect to recognize the unit called family. Do we all not need to take a hard look at what we are doing?

Following these incidents, Pelkey found his own relations with the director of his community center growing increasingly difficult. He realized his time in the community was at an end.

In his final report, Pelkey described the community as one filled with hate, with clear divisions between the well-to-do and the poor, the church and non-church, the pro-ARVAC and anti-ARVAC. Critical of his own role, Pelkey finally realized the education projects he started would never have a life of their own until the community assumed leadership.

> I have learned responsibility. I need to learn now of humility. I can examine all the problems but I can't tell you the answers. . . . I am generally discouraged of late. Yet I am still open to the future. I am not through in. . . . I am still a kid and I am still learning.

Major Projects and Vista Support

In April 1986, the last four ARVAC VISTA slots were denied extension and the agency's twenty-one-year role as a Volunteer sponsor came to an end. It was the longest continuous sponsorship in the nation.

Over the years, ARVAC used national and local Volunteers in a range of community services. Early projects were generally more individual in nature, and Volunteers were placed in one-to-one situations. Later projects had the Volunteers coordinating larger group efforts, community-involvement programs that matched a maturing awareness in VISTA and in the agency about how to get things done.

In many cases, the distinct credit due ARVAC Volunteers is difficult to identify. Early ones directed their efforts toward somewhat intangible results, while later ones merged their energy with group efforts. The better ARVAC Volunteers kept themselves well in the background.

Yet major projects undertaken at ARVAC have had their impact on the region. In line with the essential VISTA philosophy, they have become true community efforts, on-going entities that continue to serve a need. Their spin-off from ARVAC was planned from the beginning.

Three such programs continue to serve the ARVAC region as independent non-profit corporations. They are involved with issues basic to the area—housing, mental health, and traditional Arkansas folkcrafts.

UNIVERSAL, INC.—Formerly known as the ARVAC Housing Development Corporation (HDC), this program enables low income families to secure decent housing in an affordable manner. It does so by adapting the old rural tradition of barnraising.

The HDC established groups of six to ten families who formed an association that could obtain federally subsidized financing. The groups then shared their labor to build the houses, staying together until each member/family had their house completed.

Through bulk purchases of materials and "sweat equity" labor, the HDC self help groups constructed full sized, energy efficient homes for almost half the price of comparative housing. More than two hundred homes were built in this manner in Johnson County, where the program began, and hundreds of others have been erected in communities throughout the ARVAC area.

The HDC started as a more traditional housing program, using its first two Volunteers for loan packaging and needs assessments. It was Volunteer Greg Haag who researched the concept of self-help housing, and wrote the initial proposal to the FHA for a $70,600 technical assistance grant.

That original request has grown to a three–four million dollar annual budget for Universal, which spun off from ARVAC as its own independent agency in October 1985. It is the largest self-help housing program in Arkansas and probably the most successful. After two years in VISTA, Haag served from 1974 until 1978 as HDC self-help project director.

COUNSELING ASSOCIATES—Established in 1968 as the ARVAC Community Mental Health Program, this project used Volunteers to help raise financial and community support to purchase medicine for the chronically mentally ill. Bob Ashcroft, a national PDP Volunteer from Vermont, provided early assistance in writing the program charter.

Overall, Volunteers were allowed only a limited involvement in the project because of the confidential nature of its services. The

Volunteer efforts were successful enough to gain the project a strong community base. By 1972, the planned spin off from ARVAC took place. Since that time, the agency has grown and expanded its multi-county human service efforts.

ARVAC RURAL FOLKCRAFTS—Few Arkansas VISTA projects offer the clear focus on regional identity and culture that is apparent in this crafts cooperative. Hand sewn quilts, sturdy white oak baskets, dolls and other items marketed through the co-op are the handiwork of native artisans. Their skills are some of the state's most cherished folk traditions.

But cherished traditions don't put food on a poor person's table. The Rural Folkcrafts project has taught its members an important lesson—how to reverse decades of hopelessness and despair by working together. It has shown them how vulnerable they are without that group support.

The crafts co-op, started in 1975 and incorporated as an independent agency five years later, also offers an understanding of a VISTA project's ultimate destiny—the race to achieve autonomy before Volunteer support is withdrawn.

The crafts co-op, one of ARVAC's most successful projects, functions on the concept of individual self-sufficiency applied to a group. Throughout the agency area, crafts people create artifacts. The co-op staff or volunteers make pickups and bring the goods to a central office for marketing. In some cases, the co-op staff help with purchases of new materials such as cloth for dolls or quilts.

At times, the co-op has brought in special instructors. Making baskets from strips of white oak is a craft native to the woodlands of Arkansas and similar areas across the nation, but it was a craft being lost as a result of generations of poverty. People who can barely survive have little opportunity to maintain tradition. They rarely have the skills to promote their work or judge adequate compensation.

The crafts co-op brings its producers into pricing, promoting, and marketing functions. It creates employment and brings real income to those involved in it. The co-op currently has a retail shop and distribution center at Russellville and a sales network across the nation and in foreign countries. It has generated more than one hundred thousand dollars per year in income, more than ninety percent of which is returned to the producers. In addition to the money, the success of the project has greatly improved client mental attitudes and self confidence.

The beauty of the crafts co-op is in more than its finished products. The hand made baskets and quilts are a reflection of native character. Few Arkansas VISTA projects have so accurately targeted the proper community strength on which to base their efforts.

Vitale initiated the crafts project, and over the years he has been a determined defender of its VISTA support. In a 1976 letter congratulating Vitale on an outstanding project profile, a VISTA deputy director wrote:

> As I read through the profile I could not help but visualize you in all your sincerity and devotion to helping poor people achieve an economic status that did not previously exist. It is supervisors like you that provide the leadership and understanding that can show America what can be done to assist the poor when the desire is there.

Despite the glowing reports, the VISTA budget was cut at ARVAC and other state programs through the 1970s. In a 1976 letter to the state ACTION director, Vitale commented on a recent sharp budget cut.

> When we talk about the "plight of the poor people," I try my best to keep away from a play on words and back up what I say with documented evidence. With the help of the VISTA Volunteers, we have built an economic development native crafts industry based on 165 crafts people. . . . They make money, money that is made by the sweat of their brow and not by the handout method. . . . No federal, state or local cash of any kind was used to start this program. To date, in excess of $300,000 has been returned directly to the crafts people. . . . This project is too valuable to the people in this area that have little or no voice whatsoever as to their destiny. There is no way this project is going to die, not while I am around.

The Arkansas ACTION office informed ARVAC that a phase out of its VISTA programs was scheduled for 1977. The phase out did not occur until much later, primarily because of Vitale's effective resistance.

In a 1982 report, Vitale wrote that no area program in the last 15 years has equaled the economic impact on the rural poor as ARVAC Rural Folk Crafts. Eliminating the program would do irreversible harm, he said.

> It is inconceivable that the present adminisration would want to eliminate a project which offers job opportunities and economic well being, not to mention therapeutic value, that poor people have derived from this project. . . . We are on the threshold of affecting the tourist and leisure industry, not only in this area but the entire state. . . . In the mildest of terms, it would be an injustice for a project that has gone so far to be stopped short of its goal, which is so near.

State program director Bob Torvestad backed Vitale's request for conitnued support. In a 1981 letter to the southwest regional office, Torvestad called the crafts co-op a model project that provided income for its producers and social interaction between the young and the old. Most of all, Torvestad wrote, the project provided a way of passing to the young the skills and culture of the old while producing at the same time a serviceable and safe item.

Such praise did little more than put off the inevitable end of VISTA support. Vitale seemed to recognize this in a 1981 Christmas letter to the state office.

> I don't imagine we can be facing any worse times, compounded by the flooding in our state, and it is probably a hell of a way of expressing a holiday message. However, I truly believe as I did sixteen years ago that in facing up to hard times, the seeds of hope will spring. You know, it's really not much different now than the time the good Lord came to us on this Earth almost two thousand years ago.

As with other ARVAC projects that became independent, the crafts co-op maintained its effective performance. The 1986 loss of its last four Volunteers will not significantly affect it. Vitale's "seeds of hope" have taken root and flourished.

Lou Vitale

With his city mannerisms and eastern dialect preserved after almost twenty years in the area, Lou Vitale, fast talking, streetwise, and wearing dark glasses, is one of those rare VISTA products that transformed a year of voluntary service into an on-going career and regional dedication. In his distinctive way, he became part of the community he was originally sent to serve. He has stayed on the scene ever since.

I am the same now as when I first came, a very practical, logical type person. I take things at face value until you prove it different. I never took on any radical causes, yet that didn't change my approach to poverty or what VISTA had taught me or how I thought things should be in Centerville, Arkansas. The only thing different I did was with the old VISTA statement—"To help people help themselves"—I added "but don't let them know who did it."

Vitale said he joined VISTA after being rejected by all branches of the armed forces because of his age. The twenty-eight-year-old Pittsburgh native had just lost both his parents and knew he had a decision to make. He said it may have been "the Kennedy pitch" heard on the radio—what you can do for your country—that made him consider VISTA. Or it may have been a previous trip through Appalachia that exposed him to the problems of American poverty, he said.

Entering VISTA service early in 1967, Vitale soon found himself in a demanding training session at the University of Oregon. The trainers' attention to detail effectively prepared him for the work to follow, Vitale said.

None of us knew what we were getting into, but we had some of the best trainers. During our initial community placement, they would follow us from door to door and evaluate our contact and pitch to each person to get them to a meeting. I was living in Fall City with a poor logging family. Rats running across the bed at night. All those war stories.

Assigned to the tiny Yell County community of Centerville, Vitale said he associated with all local elements and tried to build bridges between people. One of his first realizations was that he didn't have a firm understanding of how people were involved in decision making.

At one meeting, Vitale said he had an old church filled up and local people excitedly discussing the topic of incorporating the town. Toward the end of the meeting a local landlord walked in drunk and told the people that if they incorporated, the federal government would take their homes away. The people believed him and voted incorporation down, Vitale said.

I sat in the back of the meeting but I shouldn't even have been there. Afterwards in group discussions, one guy asked me, "Who are you?" In his eyes, I didn't exist. People knew me but didn't know why I was there. I tried to keep them guessing. Suppose they found out I was Italian, Catholic, a government worker, and worst of all, a Yankee. So I played it good. People knew me and identified with me as a person.

During his year in Centerville, Vitale said he had his share of trying experiences, including falling through the seat of the outhouse at his rented house and being shot at as he drove his van to isolated country homes. But Vitale also started successful youth recreation and adult educational programs. VISTA recognized his abilities and started putting labels on him, Vitale said, first as a VISTA leader, then as a trainer, and later as a supervisor.

As a supervisor, I'd scrutinize the Volunteers closely. They'd walk in here and after one meeting I could tell if they'd make it. I'd lay it right out, talk about adjustment, sex, drugs, and they'd open up to me. I was effective because I had been a Volunteer, out in the trenches. I was out there and knew what was going on. Our people were well screened. A lot of agencies wouldn't take the time to talk to their Volunteers.

ARVAC never encountered the social controversy that greeted VISTA projects in other areas of Arkansas. Because the ARVAC service area included so few blacks, racial issues were not a significant part of the agency's programs, Vitale said. Its problems were in dealing with the two cultures typical to the area—people of the river valley and those of the more isolated hill environment—and identifying the common degree of poverty they shared.

Vitale said his twenty years in Arkansas indicated his feeling for the state. His career VISTA service is an expression of another deeply held belief.

I believe every person in this country should do something for his fellow man. Should be in some kind of service. It will take the whole society to eliminate poverty. VISTA is that human element that's got to be expressed.

Vitale wrote the following essay for the VISTA 15th anniversary celebration. It is reprinted here in its entirety.

"I guess I've been here almost forever. I might have been in the third or fourth group in the country, for all I know. I spent a year as a Volunteer doing a little of everything, and then I moved on to supervisor. I saw some stuff that was really disillusioning. The hill folk would do some really good craft work and then someone would come along and steal it for almost nothing. Or, they'd put it in a little shop down the road on consignment and never get any money and never get the piece back. They were really getting ripped off.

What I saw that I liked was the talent that was evident. I felt that with that kind of talent, we could get a substantial return back to the people in the river valley if we provided proper guidance and direction.

We started with virtually nothing—something like a hundred dollars. Now we've got anywhere from 170 to 200 people making crafts. Outside salesmen, who work on commission, sell our three kinds of products in forty-five states and two foreign countries.

In the country, it's hard to gather groups of people around issues. "Scatteration," mileage—they all work against you. It can only come about if there is food on the table and clothes on your back. Without getting melodramatic, I'll just say that you can't do it unless you've got the bread. The incentive here is money. A constant flow, a return for a job done, a month to month regardless-of-whether-you-sell-the-product paycheck, returned to the producer. You can't come down here and try to organize without an objective in mind. That's just taking pot shots. And you can't take pot shots in the country.

It used to be when a person first came down here, he could buy a quilt for fifteen bucks. But you can't do that to these people now. They know what's going on. They get together in meetings and ask the right questions. And they've got the answers, too. There isn't anyone putting anything over on them anymore. That's something that VISTA's influence has done a lot to help.

In the crafts program, all the VISTAS are locally recruited and voted in by the whole group. One time we had a replacement for a Volunteer and then the original one wanted to come back. Hell, I thought there was no problem. They got in a meeting and . . . they came down on me like gangbusters! They said no way did they want that person back. And I said, "Well, you had that person for two years and it worked out fine." And they said, "In no way did it work out!" And they listed specifically what didn't work out—things that I had never been aware of.

I really like the old concept of working yourself out of a job. We did a self-help housing project in one county. Except for the first few families that came in, they wouldn't know VISTA from shmista. And there's a multimillion dollar health program over here we wrote and pulled off a few years back. If you told the people that are over there now that we were involved at the beginning, why, they might think that you were a liar. That's the only way to do this job. When you get done with something, you spin it off and go on to something else.

THE LIFE AND TIMES OF A VISTA WARRIOR

BY BOB GORMAN

Bob Gorman was twenty-one years old when he joined VISTA in 1968. Having grown up in the tenements of Boston, he brought with him to Arkansas a streetwise sophistication and an irreverent attitude that was totally foreign to most rural folks. Those qualities, coupled with the traditional Volunteer commitment to human service, made Gorman a distinct figure in the state program.

While other Volunteers were able to maintain a sense of humor about their work, few could match Gorman's level of personal freedom and wide range of activities. Some Volunteers are remembered for specific accomplishments. Others for the personal relationships they were able to build with community members. Gorman's legacy, like his self-appointed title for these recollections, may be one where fact and fantasy are inseparably mixed. Or in his words, "If I did a rain dance and it rained, who was I to say it wasn't my responsibility?"

Gorman left Arkansas to pursue a graduate degree in horticulture. He currently works with a county agency in Washington state.

I was impressed with Saul Alinsky, his idea that the real change agents of the future would not be paid but would be the meat cutter who comes home and organizes his neighborhood. At the University of Oklahoma where I was trained, the feds were there because then you needed FBI clearance to be a Volunteer. We had to pass physical endurance tests—rock climbing and rappelling. I thought that would be a good option for fighting poverty.

We had our three-day drop off in Oklahoma City. I got off the city bus with another Volunteer, a deranged Irish Catholic from the Bronx. We got jobs as day laborers. Hitching a ride, we got picked up by a black couple. We partied with them at all the black joints in Oklahoma City all night, then worked the next day. We finally stumbled into the YMCA more tired, less frustrated, and richer.

I got assigned to Newton County with Bob Darden from Memphis and Indulis Palmers, a Latvian who'd escaped from Russia and seen his father gunned down by the East Germans. Before we went to Newton County, Joe Bruch had us down in Austin, reading everything we could about the area. Bruch decided it needed organizers, not teachers anymore. We had been trained to community organize in urban black communities, so we were well prepared for that setting.*

Indy and Bob liked to party, so we needed a vehicle for unofficial business. We bought a 1948 Packard ambulance with no seats in it for $150. We put an old couch in the front. J. W. Waters, the school superintendent, at first perceived us in an adversarial role. The first time we saw him he was being chased by a swarm of bees from his hives. We drove up as he was being stung a lot. I got along well with him. Those folks like to drink.

I was supervisor for the kids in the Neighborhood Youth Corps. We'd cut firewood and sell it to old folks for $4 a pick up load. We had no money for recreational equipment and all we earned went for the saws and other tools. But that got us the money for the bootleg.

I had set up a bookmobile on the back of the GSA pick up, built a

*Newton County in North Arkansas is sparsely populated, mountainous, and has virtually no black population.

canopy and some shelves, borrowed the books from the library at Harrison. I used it as an entry to meeting people. Later I had false shelves behind the books for the bootleg. I'd drive up, the kids would come out to get their books and the adults would come out to buy the booze.

Once at Flat Rock Creek, I was fording the stream and the truck bottomed out. I started digging it out. Looking up, I saw the books floating away downstream. I got out my minnow seine and rescued them and later put them in the oven at home to dry out. A local fellow with a winch finally helped me out of the creek, but it took a long time. In return, I helped him get welfare rights for a 16-year old he'd knocked up.

I helped get electricity and phone lines to small communities. People in the mountains had signed up back in the 1940s for Rural Electric Association service. Their homes were wired but they hadn't the service. Organizing was not the bag of those Ozark folks, so we challenged the REA. We pushed it with Hammerschmidt (district Congressman J. P. Hammerschmidt) and he sent a good letter to the REA. They called me a radical and contacted VISTA. Bruch and Hammerschmidt stood up for me there.

We were on the leading edge of general decadence in the area. This was before the hippies and retirees moved in when the area still hadn't been exposed to a lot of outsiders. One time two bus loads of black kids came up from Upward Bound in Russellville. The looks on the locals' faces was like it was the end of the world. They realized they didn't even have enough rope in town to hang all those kids. It was a minor, silent victory.

Folks up there accepted me as sort of the village idiot. I talked funny, did crazy things. They tolerated me. I'd contact Lou Vitale in Dardanelle to line up some R&R. Trips to Little Rock, we'd carry back cases of beer. I really came into my own up there.

A week before I was to leave, Bruch called and asked if I'd like to work in training. At that time, the training contract was with the GE Management & Training Division—Apollo Systems, same outfit as in the space program. I headed down to Austin and found things between loose and disorganized. They had a lot more Volunteers that session than expected.

It was bartering for bodies at the training sessions. We worked as a team and were able to get the best Volunteers because there was no in-fighting among us. We did have a reputation of having a certain attitude—if you can't win fairly, then cheat. We came out with productive Volunteers, even the generalists.

At that time, most emphasis was on east and central Arkansas. I became a field trainer and assistant to Neal Blakely for the north and west parts of the state. I was left alone with no political pressure. That suited me fine. One time, the regional office warned me that an OEO national reviewer was coming to visit and I was to drive him around. Up in Jasper, I had arranged for the Newton County sheriff to arrest me. He pulled me out of the car, cuffed me and drove me away. We left this poor guy alone the whole day. Later he somehow lost his billfold and his "black book," his hit list for the whole southwest region. We mailed it back to him, but we made copies first.

My greatest involvement after Newton County was with projects for the Washington County EOA. The Boston Mountain Co-op was bringing in national Volunteers to provide special educational services in the public schools. Some of them started getting into community activism, and things got hot. A few resigned and the project sponsorship went to the County EOA.

I worked with a university professor who started VIEWS, Volunteers in Educational Work & Service, a special program to get black kids increased reading skills and give college kids credit for community work. We provided Volunteers for a youth home, senior centers, a community cannery and other projects. We also got into housing repair and renovation, going into demolished buildings and using the salvaged materials to rebuild needy homes.

One time we got permission from the city to demolish an old barn on the Highway 71 hill below the town square. It was on a steep incline just above the road. We had to drop it on the uphill side or it would fall on the highway. Some of the Volunteers were crazy. One of them found this huge winch at the local REA equipment yard. He cut the wire on the back fence, stole the heavy equipment, then painted it green and used it to tear down the barn. Everything we had was either borrowed, ripped off, or given to us.

Northern Arkansas projects were not as volatile or outwardly political as other parts of the state, yet there was a lot of behind the scenes stuff. All the Volunteers and projects in Fayetteville were involved in alternative lifestyles. We exposed a lot of Arkansas kids to issues that would come back into their own homes. They saw the relevance of human development and service to their community. We made an impact on people.

COMMUNITY ACTION AGENCIES

Established as a part of the original Office of Economic Opportunity (OEO), the Community Action Agency (CAA) was designed to support poverty projects through direct representation by local communities. The CAAs were planned as a conduit for distribution of funds through approved federal programs. VISTA, Head Start, weatherization, adult education, neighborhood councils, and other programs were implemented through the CAA agencies.

In concept, the idea had merit. The CAA would be a private, nonprofit organization governed by a local board of directors whose membership was subject to a strict quota. One-third of CAA board members had to be from major community groups such as business, religion, education, or labor; one-third elected officials or their representatives; and one third selected from low income residents. A CAA board makeup reflects the agency's community position and hints at the primary problem that plagued many of them.

With a local power base weighing heavily on one end and a relatively weak and politically inexperienced poverty community positioned on the other, it was logical that agency boards would side with those more adept at wielding power. CAA staff could not carry out programs without their board's approval, so they too became familiar with the compromises and concessions of local politics.

At best, the CAA staff recognized that time and committed effort could bring about change, that patience and diplomacy had long range benefits. At the worst, the agency staff became corrupt materialists who fattened their egos and their pocketbooks with federal resources designated for the poor.

Normally an Arkansas CAA board of directors reflected the concerns of a conservative community. Several agencies had impressions of Volunteers as a troublesome bunch. Peaceful rural communities learned of disruptive activities blamed on VISTA in east Arkansas, in Texarkana, and in Little Rock. Resolutions passed by the state Farm Bureau and county associations condemning VISTA and requesting its removal from the state added to those local fears. If not for CAA staff playing key intermediary roles as VISTA supervisors, it is doubtful more than a handful of the Arkansas agencies would have maintained their project sponsorships.

Ted Wilson, VISTA supervisor at the East Central Arkansas CAA, said his role gave him a better understanding of agency wishes and desires than the impressions Volunteers communicated throughout the counties. An awareness of agency intentions, however, did not lessen the fact that his heart and his thoughts were with the Volunteers.

> I can recall agency meetings where ideas were expressed that seemed very reasonable. Meeting later with the Volunteers, their reaction to the same ideas was derision and suspicion. My job was trying to broker those differences, trying to interpret from one to another so a suitable peace was established and the Volunteers could function. I had to keep us out of trouble with the agency because we were so dependent on it.

The rare CAA had a strong executive director or an enlightened board that understood what the Volunteers were capable of doing. According to Joe Bruch, that progressive attitude could gain a project its initial sponsorship, but Volunteers had to generate their own local support.

> From the beginning, the program was fighting for its life. The strong agency directors or boards had to balance the traditional pressure of the status quo against mandates of the program to directly attack things which some businessmen and the Chambers of Commerce supported.

Passage of the 1964 Economic Opportunity Act allocated approximately $4.7 million in immediate and direct benefits to Arkansas, with $3.4 million in grants for CAA jobs already organized. The amounts were based on state totals of welfare recipients, unemployed persons, and children in families earning less than one thousand dollars a year.[1]

Arkansas community leaders quickly became aware that large sums of federal money were available if they established the proper agencies and programs. By March 1966, Arkansas had received or been approved to receive $25.3 million through OEO and other federal subsidies. Of the state's seventy-five counties, fifty-six were included in CAA service areas, and other counties were expected to be included soon.[2]

Though it was ranked nineteenth in the nation on the basis of poverty population, Arkansas was thirteenth in the receipt of federal poverty funds. The Arkansas Gazette wrote that the state was getting more from OEO than other southern states with higher poverty levels because it had less initial resistance to the racial integration of program facilities and projects.[3]

The early expansion of CAAS in Arkansas can be attributed in some degree to two types of national Volunteers assigned between 1965 and 1970. A combination of older Volunteers and the restrained Program Development Planners gave communities the idea that VISTA was an easily managed program that would provide them with skilled workers and little or no controversy.

State support of CAA development included establishing the Rural Training Center in early 1965. The Center was a technical assistance resource which prepared agency staff for their upcoming work. It had little positive impact on state CAAS, according to Richard First, an experienced VISTA trainer who joined the faculty of the University of Arkansas at Little Rock in 1969 and served as a Center training coordinator. By that time, ineffective training and a growing disenchantment with the goals of some federal programs had made CAAS less hospitable to outside influences, First said.

The CAA directors were afraid for us to come. Though regional OEO would require them to have the training, they would sabotage our efforts while we were there or afterwards. Our job was to teach people how to increase citizen participation. The Volunteers in the areas stood on the sides and cheered us on, but our strategies for organizing were not well accepted.

First said a major accomplishment for his trainers was simply getting invited to an area where they weren't wanted. CAA board members and staff were new to the roles they had taken on and, like the Volunteers, required specialized direction and training. George Ivory, a VISTA supervisor at the Mississippi County CAA, said more time and money should have been given to training agency boards. Problems facing the agency were in many ways similar to the organizing problems experienced at the community level, Ivory said.

A lot of agency staff had to explain to the board what the projects were all about. There was a lack of accountability. The same applied to local projects. How do you get people not used to making decisions to do so within the time element?

According to Rev. M. W. Williams, state OEO technical advisor, the whole thing was more or less an experiment in which CAAS were not sure of their own roles or those of the Volunteers. Having Volunteers taught somewhere else was contrary to all CAA teaching, Williams said. The agencies perceived the Volunteers as feeling they had the answers to local problems, yet the CAAS didn't know what their own problems were, Williams added.

The PDPS were instrumental in helping community agencies understand and work toward solving their problems. Yet in a manner typical of Volunteers, they did it by disregarding official OEO policy whenever it seemed necessary. Bruch said PDPS were supposed to have nothing themselves to do with writing up or implementing long range Volunteer plans. The PDPS were to increase CAA staff ability by making them better planners and advisors. That wasn't how it happened in Arkansas, Bruch said, as PDP Volunteers became part of the overall VISTA plan.

Charlie Deknatel, a PDP who worked in east Arkansas, believed that as a result of the pressure put on CAAS by OEO field reps, agencies supported what would otherwise have been unacceptable projects.

> The OEO wanted the agencies to be effective and the Volunteers to be out raising hell, putting pressure on the agencies, too. I got into the planning role, helped with grant applications and planning paperwork. I also did the agency work, establishing youth centers and working with teenagers.

As more Volunteers arrived in Arkansas, the issues became clearer. There seemed to be distinct differences between what the agencies wanted from VISTA, what the Volunteers themselves hoped to accomplish, and what OEO staff urged them to try. The most effective Volunteer would be able to assess a growth environment and grow along with it. Yet some were not sensitive enough to see community opposition growing, and they made no effort to mollify all concerned parties.

Williams said the agencies didn't want certain Southern traditions changed. With many social influences coming at them at the same time, the agencies at times perceived Volunteers as militant hippies coming in to do what they felt was justice for the poor. VISTA represented an effort at mixing, organizing, and service roles. While no agency would be opposed to direct service projects such as youth recreation or Head Start, there was strong concern that Volunteers would quickly cross over into socially unacceptable areas.

Volunteers were not always skillful enough to work within an approved setting and still carry out the organizing goals that reflected their own values. State program officer Freeman McKindra said this had nothing to do with Volunteers doing a good job or serving a need. It was simply that the community wasn't ready for that kind of work.

> The fact was that Volunteers were there to work in situations where poverty existed. We can only agree their work was right and proper. The sponsors played a key role in ensuring community acceptance. They intervened in a lot of cases we didn't know about. A local CAA could go a long way in blunting blatant opposition to Volunteers being there.

Yet agencies could also take an opposite stand and reflect a community fear that national Volunteers were unnecessary trouble. Locally recruited Volunteers would have served well in such situations, but this did not happen for two reasons. First, there were few locally recruited Volunteers in service in the early years of the program. Second, local Volunteers very rarely had the training to challenge community values in the way national Volunteers did.

Charles Imhoff was a national Volunteer who recognized that not being raised locally was a drawback. The problem was not nearly as significant in his dealing with poverty communities as it was when dealing with middle and upper class land owners and power structures, Imhoff said.

> It seemed at times a Catch 22 situation. The Volunteer had to be invited into the area by a local power structure, usually the county judge. If a Volunteer worked toward getting a family or group off the plantation and into job training programs, it would mean the plantation owner would lose his source of cheap and dependable labor. The owner complains to the county judge, and the Volunteer is invited to leave. This may be an oversimplification, but you had to work within the system, and that often seemed like swimming upstream.

Some VISTA supervisors expressed amazement that CAAS agreed to bring in outsiders such as national Volunteers. The idea of bringing in large numbers of Volunteers had to have acceptable appeal so as not to encounter the ire of public officials, but agency staff generally viewed the Volunteers as an unknown entity it was best to stay away from, Wilson said.

> There was no real desire on the agency staff to become involved with the Volunteers. The CAA was in a very precarious position. Its governing body relied on support and endorsement from people in government positions for whom change was an anathema.

Wilson believes that the benefits derived by Volunteers through actual services or community changes had less impact than the conflict engendered by the presence of non-southerners living in small, rural southern communities. This was clearly not the case in all community agencies, but conflict or the fear of controversy definitely influenced many rural boards. Ozark Opportunities at Harrison (Boone County), a six-county agency in north central Arkansas, had no major conflicts result from Volunteer activities, yet the agency board was always extremely cautious about its Volunteers, supervisor Gary Watkins said.

> Once the community or board people heard there was a problem, they began looking for one. Our board wanted to keep a tight rein on the Volunteers because it was afraid of them. With bad publicity elsewhere, the board would get afraid. To keep the Volunteers here, we had to keep everyone aware of what was going on. I had the Volunteers go to board meetings. Good public relations was our survival tactic. That was how you had to work with the program.

Opposing factions in the average Arkansas community were at the core of the problem. Low income groups generally welcomed change and were willing to work with Volunteers to achieve it. Though white poverty communities were often more reserved and difficult to organize than blacks, support from any low income group could generally be counted on if Volunteers properly did their work.

In contrast, the community power group generally opposed change for a variety of personal, economic, and cultural reasons. The power group could also effectively influence the community middle class to take its side on the issue.

The CAA was caught between opposing forces. As a representative agency, it could not establish a position independent of its supporting community. But neither could it support one of the extreme positions. Taking the low-income/Volunteer position would quickly raise the ire of power groups who would seek to have the Volunteers removed. The CAA could also not subjugate VISTA policy and planning without eventually frustrating and losing its Volunteers and the federally funded community projects they arranged.

The trade off was obvious. A compromise of values would gain some community benefits. A compromise of community benefits would preserve some established values. Or as Bruch put it, "they were using us and we were using them." The standard question Bruch said he received from agency directors was how far to let the Volunteers go in their organizing work.

The question has no single answer other than "as far as possible." Each situation would be influenced by the specific projects Volunteers attempted, the community reaction to that effort, and the Volunteers' and the agencies' ability to bridge those differences. Volunteers had the more visible role in this effort, and their ability to compromise and be patient often made the difference. Saul Alinsky commented on the need for personal subordination in his book *Rules for Radicals.*

> If the real radical finds having long hair sets up psychological barriers to communicating and organizing, he cuts his hair. If I were organizing in an orthodox Jewish community, I would not walk in there eating a ham sandwich, unless I wanted to be rejected so I could have an excuse to cop out.[4]

The CAA could also create firmer community support by using locally recruited Volunteers. Through local people, the agency could more effectively reach community members who needed help but were hesitant to expose their problems to "outsiders." Similarly, the use of local Volunteers would refute the power group argument that problems caused by VISTA projects were the result of outside agitators.

A changing federal emphasis on VISTA gave the CAAS a different relationship with the program. Beginning with the Nixon administration's abrupt decision to cancel the program and the continuing decline of federal appropriations since that time, community action agencies found VISTA financing becoming less and less dependable. A decision in the early 1970s to allow other community organizations to sponsor VISTA projects also freed the CAAS from their role as primary sponsor. By 1985, only two of the twenty Arkansas VISTA projects were still sponsored by CAAS.

In a final assessment of the VISTA impact on community agencies, the distinction between Volunteer and community contribution to a successful project is difficult to determine. Agency directors across the state credit the Volunteers' role in initiating and implementing ongoing projects such as health clinics, marketing cooperatives, day care centers, and educational programs.

While community action agencies were a local place to begin in the early years of VISTA, the nature of those organizations kept them from being the best VISTA sponsor. Government entities are created to implement public policy. It is not the role of a public agency to foster social change until the call for change has the majority support. The CAAS were private organizations, but their government support and their attempt to unify community leadership gave them a role similar to a public or political entity.

The general public will not tolerate this type of leadership until it recognizes the value of a particular effort. Goforth Coleman, Volunteer supervisor at the Pulaski County EOA, said this logic was demonstrated in community response to VISTA projects and the current policy which regulates the program.

> Once you start making in-roads to a social activity, your funds will be cut off or you will be redirected. That happened with VISTA. The Volunteers were involved in bringing about changes that maybe were not in the best interest of the local power structure. They locked us into something else. Now the community has to tell us what they will do with the Volunteers. No more just turning them loose.

The bottom line for an agency receiving public support is what the public gets for its money. In the early years of the state CAA program, large sums were spent on administration with little more than advice going to the poor and needy. Williams recalled an early meeting in Mississippi County to establish the local CAA. Close to five hundred people attended the half-day session, and near its end a local farmer stood and addressed the presiding board.

> The man stood with tears in his eyes. He said "I'm a farmer, but I can't farm no more. I got two sons that need to go to college. I have no food. I came here thinking I could get relief." All we could offer him was advice.

At the present time, the nineteen community action agencies operating in Arkansas offer a great deal more than just advice. Administered by three state agencies—the Department of Human Services, the Division of Economic & Medical services, and the Office of Community Services—Arkansas CAAS support programs of self-help housing, Head Start, senior citizens, weatherization, and a variety of other social efforts that once were addressed almost exclusively by VISTA.

The current status of Arkansas CAAS is to function in a service role, and they are considerably more responsive to people than traditional bureaucratic agencies that have been around much longer. In this sense, some vestige of OEO remains, for the agencies try to help people regardless to their category or level of need.

Beyond the immediacy of being a service provider, the CAA offers a unique perspective on twenty years of assistance to Arkansas poverty communities. For veteran agency directors like Bob Adkison of ARVAC, the question of an agency's long term effectiveness has become a more pressing concern. The problem is most evident in a lack of jobs and the resulting out-migration of people, Adkison said.

> We can train people for jobs, but what are we doing in actual job creation? The jobs are not out there. So what do we do with our resources as an agency? What good is it to sit here and train our people for its own sake?
>
> We have become institutionalized and we're facing a crisis point in the existence of our organization and its future. After 20 years, what are we designed to do, settle down or take on more innovative programs?

Adkison had no answers for these questions. He believes the CAA was established to deal with poverty issues from a different approach than other agencies, that it has a continuing need to be creative and not settle into traditional roles. Adkison recognizes that bringing jobs into an area is outside the scope of his agency. Yet training people for jobs without having a local opportunity to put such training into practice seemed a poor way to put money into circulation, he said.

Notes

1. *Arkansas Gazette,* September 27, 1964.
2. *Arkansas Gazette,* March 27, 1966.
3. See note 2 above.
4. Saul Alinsky, *Rules for Radicals,* Random House, New York, 1971, Page XIX.

TEXARKANA

POVERTY AND THE STATUS QUO

A Texarkana Portrait

Bethel Church and Rev. David Stephens

The Model Cities Program

The Texarkana Volunteers

Project Sponsorship

VISTA Activities

Long Range Results

A Texarkana Portrait

The border town of Texarkana is divided by a long wide thoroughfare. State Line Boulevard has Arkansas on one side, Texas on the other. Past the rows of drive-in restaurants, motels, and convenience stores loom the downtown buildings, and a massive post office signals arrival at the center of town.*

At a popular tourist spot on the post office lawn, visitors stand with a foot in either state and have their photographs taken. The city motto is "Texarkana, Twice as Nice." But when the first VISTA Volunteers arrived in 1968, the city was marked by several other dividing lines.

The VISTA history in Texarkana is notable for its confrontations and dramatic reversals. It is the story of a city that had little idea of its identity and even less understanding of where it was heading. In 1968, Texarkana was a city of contrast. A railroad line divided its neighborhoods with middle and upper class whites living on the north side, poor whites, and blacks living on the south. Schools were completely segregated, as they were in most southern towns at the time. The federal Model Cities program, which was to bring more than thirty million dollars in improvements to the city during the next five years, was just getting organized.

*As a city divided by two states, Texarkana has two separate city councils, community agencies, and other public offices. Unless otherwise stated, all references in this chapter deal with the Arkansas-side municipal entities.

Further out in the Red River bottoms of Miller County, the small town of Fouke maintained similar double standards with an even less sophisticated display of local sentiments. Volunteers recalled a sign visible from the road leading into Fouke that welcomed visitors to the "beautiful town" but cautioned others not to let the sun "shine on your black ass" within the city limits.

To Volunteer Jack Fleck, Texarkana and most of southwest Arkansas was a place where the Old South met the Wild West. It was a blend of rednecks, cowboys, and blacks. Aside from a shockingly high homicide rate, Texarkana could boast of having more rats per capita than any other American city, Fleck said. The area's main employer was a munitions plant that manufactured bombs destined for Viet Nam, he added.

Fleck's reference to the rat population was based on an August 15, 1969, article in Time magazine that reported Texarkana having approximately nine hundred thousand rats or thirty times the national average for a city its size. The problem, the article said, was aggravated by the city having had no public trash collections until a week earlier. While the article made no mention of Texarkana as either the most rat-plagued city in the nation or as an urban area with the nation's highest homicide rate, several Volunteers mentioned those dubious honors in their recollections.

Two additional factors undoubtedly had some influence on the Volunteers' impressions of the city. One was the movie *Easy Rider,* a landmark counter culture film that ends with its two protagonists murdered by shotgun blasts from Southerners in a pick up truck. To the northern Volunteers, several of whom saw the movie just prior to their Arkansas assignment, any Texarkana pick-up with a rifle rack in its rear window brought immediate associations of the movie's ending.

Most Volunteers opposed American involvement in Viet Nam, and several admitted to joining VISTA for the draft deferment it offered. The presence of Red River Army Depot and Lone Star Munitions, two major Texarkana employers directly supporting American military efforts, also colored Volunteers' views.

When Texarkana Volunteers came to the city, they formed immediate impressions of right and wrong. They assessed the situation and tried to act on their feelings. Volunteer Al Karlin viewed the division within the city as representing the negative potential of his VISTA task.

> While State Line Boulevard divides the city, it is also a metaphor for union. The tradition of cowboy violence represented by Texas and the West joins the plantation racism of Arkansas and the South. Together, bound by a common Bible Belt Fundamentalism, they present a vital barrier to meaningful social change.

The Texarkana receptivity toward change, or more accurately, its determined effort to preserve the status quo, is the essential theme of the VISTA history there. Perhaps more than in any other Arkansas community, an aggressive and vocal resistance to change was displayed in Texarkana—change as represented by the VISTA presence, by the federal Model Cities program, and by civil rights advances in its schools, government, and churches.

Fleck recalled a lecture he received during VISTA training which forewarned him of the attitudes he would face in Texarkana.

> One of the best talks we got described the mind of the white South as anti-intellectual, religious (with emphasis on being saved from sin rather than on love and peace) and violent, racist, and shrewdly political. I was to see all of these traits in my year to come, hardly the image of "southern hospitality" I was taught in school.

The city's resistance to change is partly linked to a pose it adopted concerning its own history, according to Rev. David Stephens, minister of the Bethel United Presbyterian Church. Bethel Church was the city's first integrated house of worship, and Stephens, who became closely allied with VISTA efforts, had difficulty accepting what he saw as Texarkana's self-professed identity.

> I characterize Texarkana as very self conscious, having developed many things about the Old South. Yet the place started as a result of railroad interest and didn't even exist until after the Civil War. It was strange to see the city talking about southern manhood and womanhood.

Racism in Texarkana had an economic root, Stephens believed. He took the position that since the city economy was based on the railroad and military supply facilities, it did not have an established racial structure built up over decades, such as the one based on the plantation system in east Arkansas. Economic shifts and an influx of new workers created a lack of unity in the Texarkana racial structure. It was a community where change was possible, but resistance could be unpredictable.

Economics became the ultimate leverage in breaking the Texarkana status quo. To maintain quality public education, the city was dependent on federal assistance, funds that would not be available unless approved integration programs were in place. Racial views were not directly changed to accomplish that goal; they were simply set aside in a practical trade off.

A sense of compromise became the overriding strategy in achieving progress at Texarkana. Ardent segregationists such as Dr. Mitch Young, the local doctor who created Freedom, Inc., a group that supported freedom of choice school integration, were eventually recognized as holding views not in the community's best interest. Such was the case in a 1970 walkout of black students from the recently integrated Arkansas High School. Several weeks into the walkout, the school could no longer absorb losses of several thousand dollars in federal assistance, and the students were allowed to return.

Yet compromise was not always an acceptable alternative for the community or the Volunteers. During a political campaign, Volunteer Tom Utterback said he was asked to solicit black votes for a white candidate for the state senate. Utterback said the candidate's staff contacted him because they didn't want to jeopardize their white support by having the candidate openly campaign in black areas. Utterback said he refused the request.

Compromise was also accompanied by stalemate on several fronts. Within the Southwest Arkansas Development Council (SWADC), a seven-county agency that sponsored the Volunteers, county judges showed little interest in allowing VISTA to implement social change.

Volunteer Frank Fuller found the agency attitude reflected in an off-hand remark from a deputy director. While watching television news coverage of the 1968 Democratic Convention at Chicago, the man confided to him that the Pentagon had proof Martin Luther King was a registered Communist, Fuller said. The same deputy director later accused another Volunteer of being a Communist because he maintained a file recording alleged police abuse of local blacks.

Most of Texarkana's white power structure were more sophisticated in their confrontations with the Volunteers, and they avoided direct statement of their racial views. Yet the Volunteers saw through the facade and viewed Texarkana as a city with an oppressive atmosphere. For Karlin, it was a city ruled by small minded people. Despite having many individual blacks with high levels of pride and self identity, Texarkana had remained outside the civil rights movement, Karlin said.

> Maybe Dr. Young was right to be afraid. We symbolized alternative role models they didn't want to see. Blacks and whites were supposed to stay apart. We symbolized change in that.

The Volunteers came to Texarkana expecting to find clearly defined groups of people, but they found more divergent groups than they had anticipated. In addition to the conservatives who opposed change, the Volunteers found a group of middle class families interested in improving community conditions. This group, primarily the membership of Bethel Church, did not appear to be affected by color or economic barriers, Volunteer Bruce Neft said.

> These were nice, southern, middle class families motivated from within themselves to do what was right, not political people or community organizers who had something to gain. They were dedicated to what the church was about and the kind of program VISTA was interested in promoting.

In contrast to the conservative and distrustful people who didn't want them around, the group of supportive Texarkana families was a welcome and pleasant surprise that encouraged Volunteer commitment, Neft said. Arriving when they did, the Volunteers felt

Volunteer Bruce Neft and Model Cities community organizer Willie B. Berry

as if they had been thrown into the middle of a family feud with people lined up on either side of the issues, Neft added.

Much like being in a long standing feud where original points of conflict are difficult for newcomers to recognize, the Texarkana Volunteers had few opportunities to directly confront racial issues. Instead, they had to first deal with the social pose or curious logic that masked a more sinister and less obvious level of belief. A debate held at Texas High School in April 1970 illustrates this.

According to Fleck, a current events class invited one of the Volunteers to debate Col. John Warnock from Camden on the question of racism. Warnock, a retired officer from the US Army Judge

Advocates Corps, was an attorney representing at the time an Arkansas school district's opposition to forced integration. Warnock said he was contacted by Dr. Young to speak at the debate. Fleck said he prepared a thorough argument that revealed the fallacies of various racial stereotypes. The preparation did little good against Warnock's straightforward argument, Fleck said.

> Unfortunately for me, Warnock was very intelligent, articulate, and polished. . . . He said that Blacks were inferior. His theory was the old "lack of incentive in warm climates" line.
>
> As I watched all the white students listening intently to him about the superiority of white intelligence, I flashed on a recent meeting I had with some black supporters. We were conducting a lively discussion with give and take of ideas when Mrs. W., a SWADC social worker, arrived. I was amazed to see everyone go through a whole personality change. Suddenly everything was slower than molasses in January. Everyone seemed sick or practically immobilized. When she left, we resumed with everyone making faces of relief that she was gone.
>
> Mrs. W. must have left with the feeling that these people must be nearly incapable of taking care of themselves. She had no idea the whole thing was an act just to get rid of her so we could go on with our business. It hit me that white people must be incredibly stupid to think that Blacks are lazy when it's obvious they would be crazy to act in any other way under the circumstances. The image of Blacks as lazy was simply the product of slavery and slave-like social relations.
>
> This whole incident flashed through my mind as Colonel Warnock continued. I wish I could say I leveled the Colonel with a few well chosen words and won the debate hands down. But I was quite taken aback by his unabashed racism. He never questioned that Blacks have unequal schools, health care, housing, job opportunities, etc. He just justified the whole scheme by saying Blacks are inferior. I could only leave the debate frustrated at my inability to explain what I had only recently learned myself.

Fleck's degree in civil engineering was probably little help in that debate. A more polished presentation might have been given by attorney John Hoerster, generally considered the most articulate and resourceful of the Texarkana Volunteers. Karlin, a Yale graduate who has followed his VISTA service with a legal career, might have also fared better in the debate. But neither of them were available that day, leaving Fleck to do his best.

Karlin's recollections of Texarkana provide an additional assessment of the local power balance.

> As Volunteers, we had become somewhat suspicious of the good will of our Texarkana neighbors. Our suspicions, nurtured by months of public and private harassment, occasionally prompted defensive rejoinders from friendly local residents.
>
> "You VISTAS," a sympathetic young attorney once said, "have much in common with the American Indian. Like Indians, you judge all our citizens by the actions of the cavalry. Texarkana's cavalry has tried to get you, but there are plenty of decent folk around."
>
> "Yes," I hesitantly agreed. Months in Texarkana had introduced me to many fine people, but the sad lesson remained. In Texarkana, the cavalry rules.

Bethel Church and Rev. David Stephens

The best resource for any VISTA project is a community member who can act on the Volunteers' initiative and create an on-going, grass roots organization. Texarkana had several key figures, black and white, who served the community in this manner. The city also had a far more influential person whose style and convictions set the tone for the entire Volunteer effort.

Rev. David Stephens, a west Texas native ordained as a Methodist minister, arrived in Texarkana in 1964. Having been involved in early desegregation efforts at Dallas, he had shifted his allegiance to the United Church of Christ, finding it more suited to his progressive views. Accepting a ministry at Texarkana, Stephens soon provoked his local church council. The problem was his preaching one afternoon at a newly integrated Presbyterian church, Stephens said.

> My church council forbade me to do that again. They said if I preached there Sunday afternoon, some of the black folks might come to our church Sunday morning. I resigned and joined the socially active, issue oriented Bethel United Presbyterian Church.

Texarkana learned that Stephens would not quietly tolerate the accepted ways. He further astonished the community by doing a great deal more than just preaching about change. He was, as a Texarkana city manager and Model Cities director called him, a "motorcycle priest." His commitment meant taking a stand, doing the lord's work by being out with the people that needed help the most.

Bethel Church began in 1966 in an old house on the Texas side of town. By 1968, funds had been raised to build a new, modern church on the Arkansas side. The new church had a large, open room that served as a sanctuary and community meeting hall. The new church also continued the weekend coffee house Stephens had started in the old building. The coffee house was named "The Sign of Jonah," and its emblem was a whale with Jonah in its mouth.

To those who gathered there for conversation, games of chess, evenings of music and film, the coffee house was a rare cultural and social gathering place. In 1966, poet W. H. Auden responded to Stephen's invitation and gave a poetry reading at the coffee house following his lecture at the local community college. "The Sign of Jonah" also had a graffiti wall, a foyer covered with white paper on which visitors could scrawl what they pleased. Phrases such as "God is a five thousand-pound jelly bean" upset senior citizens who used the building during the day, but Stephens supported free expression.

Karlin remembered the coffee house attracting black and white teenagers with leanings toward then-considered "hippie" values. It was the only place in town where teenagers of all types could congregate. Much of Texarkana society could not accept the racial interaction there, and rumors began to spread.

> The coffee house is known as the "Sign of Jonah" to those who attend, and the "House of Jonah" to those who spread the rumors. If a visitor asks in the appropriate place, he can learn the "House of Jonah" is variously: a drug ring funded by the Mafia, a place where interracial sex is forced upon innocent people in secret bedrooms, and generally a vicious immoral habitat.

Fleck recalled leading a local Methodist minister on a tour of Bethel Church and the man showing great curiosity about the upstairs rooms, making sure to look in every one. The outlandish rumor of the church having an upstairs bedroom reserved solely for interracial sex was taken quite seriously.

The community's attitude about Bethel Church was one of our first racial encounters. The coffee house brought together a diverse mixture of blacks and whites, including a number of long haired, anti-war youths, for evenings of discussion and socializing. One community person expressed a fairly common view of Bethel Church when he said, "The coffee house would be okay if it weren't for all the niggers."

To the first Volunteers assigned at Texarkana in 1968, Bethel Church was a far more exciting and socially active center than their sponsoring agency, the Southwest Arkansas Development Council. Volunteer Bob DeMarco said he saw Stephens as the pulse of what was happening in Texarkana, and he began spending time at the coffee house. Frank Fuller, another 1968 Volunteer, said he suggested that Bethel Church be designated the sponsoring agency for Texarkana's next cycle of Volunteers.

Stephens had contact with a lot of different groups and was leading the fight against freedom of choice in schools. He seemed a good base to have Volunteers operate on a number of fronts without being locked into the community agency. I advocated to people in Austin that the church board of directors sponsor the Volunteers. So the next group that came in went to work at the church.

Stephens' sense of social activism and Bethel Church's status as an organization independent of local politics would have created an outstanding sponsor for Texarkana's second group of Volunteers. By the time the Volunteers arrived in November 1969, Stephens said he had helped organize community action and Model Cities programs on the Texas and Arkansas sides of town. He saw Model Cities addressing many of the area's physical needs. His plans for the Volunteers were more in organizing roles, keeping them out of the main line of confrontation.

We wouldn't get shot at just because we charged at some windmill. There were needed services in the community not being delivered. I saw the Volunteers as a source of energy and labor.

Denzer Burke, designated co-sponsor of the Volunteers at Bethel, recalled how Stephens overcame a segregation policy at the city swimming pool. Making no progress with the local Optimists who controlled the Boys Club and the pool, Stephens learned that the Red River Army Depot was the largest donor to the Community Chest, a major Boys Club sponsor. Convincing the army depot to withhold funding quickly brought a new policy to the swimming pool, and it has remained integrated to this day. Using Stephens' techniques on other occasions, Burke said he was the first black to win election to the Texas-side City Council under a new ward system of voting.

> Stephens was very savvy politically. I learned a lot from him on how to represent people. Stephens left the seed of ability to promote change, and he was the single person most responsible for change. He proved you had to live it 24 hours a day. You had to believe it to evolve the leverage to get the job done.

Neft spoke of Stephens as a social catalyst who operated with an informal spontaneity. As the Volunteers' guide and leader, Stephens had great plans but few details were ever put on paper.

> He wanted the Volunteers to go out into the community and be instigators and spark plugs for change. David is that aggravating kind of leader who would tell us where we were going but would not tell us how to get there. In reality, he didn't know how to get there either but hoped we could all figure it out together.

Stephens stayed on at Bethel Church until August 1972. By the end of the following year the church had disbanded. Some former members believe this was caused by disputes relating to a legal services project the church was sponsoring. Others claim the minister that replaced Stephens couldn't maintain the needed leadership. For Stephens, Bethel Church had reached its potential and the break up was a natural end. By that time, integration had been achieved in Texarkana churches and schools, and Bethel's main agenda had been achieved, Stephens said.

Dealing with racism was the glue that held it all together. By 1971, it was already apparent that people had other agendas about which they couldn't agree—Viet Nam, electoral politics, church direction. When I left, there was no one there to be the buffer, no reason for it to continue. The church had served its purpose in a good sense.

Stephens left Texarkana to assume his current position as director of Back Bay Mission, a community ministry of the United Church of Christ at Biloxi, Mississippi. Under Stephens' direction, Back Bay Mission maintains family health and women's centers, and provides counseling, advocacy, emergency assistance, a congregate feeding program, and other services.

The Model Cities Program

The federal Model Cities Program at Texarkana and VISTA were essentially directed at the same target—improving the local quality of life. Their techniques and resources, however, were dramatically different, Ron Copeland, a Model Cities director, said.

> Model Cities was an administrative staff of grantsmen whose forte was understanding and using federal funds through existing federal programs. VISTA was a hands-on program with a lot more direct relation to the people. The Volunteers were politically unpopular and very threatening, particularly if your style was to control and manipulate opinion.

In many ways, Model Cities and VISTA reflect opposite extremes in social programs. VISTA was assigned to community anti-poverty agencies. Model Cities was incorporated into city government and reported directly to elected officials. Volunteers attempted to organize the community around perceived needs through communal efforts. Model Cities had the same organization goals, but it had money to spend and lots of it.

Model Cities was a Housing & Urban Development program that in 1967 selected Texarkana and sixty-two other cities across the nation to receive grants as part of a five-year development plan.[1] By 1972, the Texarkana Model Cities program and related grants had added more than $30 million to the local economy.[2] Hundreds of substandard homes had been demolished and new ones had been built. Paved streets, curbs, and gutters had been installed in low income neighborhoods. The epidemic rat population had been significantly decreased.

In contrast, the Texarkana VISTA project had been discontinued for almost a year by 1972. Aside from few specific goals being achieved, the results of Volunteer efforts were almost impossible to identify. To this day, most locals have not fully comprehended how closely linked the intangible work of the Volunteers was to Model Cities efforts.

The Volunteers worked with Texarkana's four Model Neighborhoods, areas designated by the Model Cities program, and helped them organize. Lurleen Page, an older Volunteer from Mississippi, is credited with making great progress in the primarily white area of South Texarkana. In the remaining three black neighborhoods, other Volunteers gained support by bringing people to community meetings and helping them understand the issues.

In its early years, Model Cities received the same criticism Dr. Young was to level at the VISTA program. Young's opinions of federal programs had more influence on the Texas side than in Arkansas. In 1969, he called the Model Cities concept a "communist, socialist plot by which the federal bureaucracy in Washington hopes to gain complete control of a community in return for federal funds." Young also blamed the program for racial tensions in the city.[3]

Tom McRae, the first Texarkana Model Cities director, overcame resistance to the housing effort by incorporating critics into the program. It was one thing to oppose the program as a whole, but another to oppose specific projects with clear community benefit, McRae said. Stephens said he applied a similar strategy when directing Volunteer efforts at a special education kindergarten.

> A point of view I adopted was to tie social change with delivery of service that people needed. While consciousness raising activity was important . . . it was difficult to attack delivery of services to little retarded kids.

No official overlap of services existed between Model Cities and VISTA, yet several Volunteers worked out of the Model Cities office. Their contacts with neighborhood councils and community leaders increased those groups' awareness to the point where Texarkana city fathers believed action was required. A series of events in the spring of 1970 illustrates how the Model Cities program was used to get the situation back under control.

APRIL 22—The city board of directors ordered McRae to cease any association with the VISTA program. The order meant Volunteers would no longer be able to use the Model Cities building, work with its staff, or use its resources. The order was a response to Texarkana black neighborhood councils attempting to incorporate. Such a move would have given the councils control of many programs administered by the city through Model Cities.

Apparently uncomfortable with the new ideas being evidenced by the councils, the Texarkana City Board questioned the authorship of the articles of incorporation, intimating that Volunteers had engaged in political activity. The decision to ban official contact between Model Cities and VISTA was a control measure on the level of book burning. It attempted to restrict progressive ideas by shutting off the perceived source. As a city-sponsored agency, Model Cities had to play the political game, McRae offered a noncommittal "no comment" when questioned about his feelings on the order.[4]

MAY 20—The president of the South Texarkana Neighborhood Council complained to McRae that citizen participation had been "adversely affected" by a Volunteer's presence at a councl meeting. The incident marks "the beginning of the end of Model Cities if corrective action is not taken," the council president warned.[5]

The incident was actually no more than Al Karlin being given permission to speak in behalf of South Texarkana teenagers. The youths, dissatisfied with voting results at the meeting, raised their voices, Karlin said. The council president falsely assumed the youths had been agitated and given unrealistic expectations by the Volunteers.

The episode reveals that even minor power figures thought they could influence the Model Cities program to serve their own ends, namely ridding the community of the Volunteer influence. The incident is representative of an old community organizing maxim—"when little men cast big shadows, it means the sun is going down."

JUNE 17—The city council voted to incur no further expenses under the Model Cities program until a decision was reached on the form of Texarkana city government. The council was reacting to the efforts of a community group. Committee for Representative Government (CRG), to change election procedures from the at-large election of seven board members to a ward-based election for four of the board members.

The change would have allowed more direct representation of certain areas. All seven city board members lived in the same area of Texarkana, and none lived in the designated Model Neighborhoods where most Model Cities projects took place. To bring the issue to a vote, 650 petition signatures were required. Approximately six hundred had been gained when the council issued its thinly veiled threat—either the community supported the current administration or a multi-million dollar federal assistance program would be shut down.

N. H. Hilliard, director of CRG, described the board's decision as a form of blackmail proving Texarkana needed a more representative government.[6] Nevertheless, the petition effort was dropped and the Model Cities program continued unaltered. Within a few years, the ward-based election system was implemented in Texarkana, a change some community members attributed to Volunteer efforts during the original confrontation period.

Working behind the scenes, Volunteers helped Hilliard and other Neighborhood Council leaders organize their assault on the Texarkana city government. The Volunteers raised funds to purchase a mimeograph machine and helped write a community newsletter titled "CHANGE." They were also active but remained in the background of Hilliard's campaign for a school board position in March 1970. Hilliard, the first Texarkana Black to file for a school board seat, lost that election. The Texarkana City Board of Directors, seeing Hilliard three months later at the forefront of another community effort, may have believed it was time to play their strongest card—the Model Cities Program—in maintaining the status quo.

Model Cities, like many political programs, was subject to the manipulation of those who allowed it to function. In Texarkana, however, the program's outstanding success and obvious community benefits gave it the stability to survive a changing political temperament. The program also maintained the necessary level of diplomacy. VISTA, on the other hand, had no widespread community base, no immediately perceived financial benefit, and its level of community relations was far more confrontational than diplomatic.

Texarkana used the Model Cities program to fund projects it couldn't otherwise fund by itself, such as street paving. Despite the obvious value of paved streets to a neighborhood, the Volunteers saw such physical improvements as not causing significant long range change. They were more interested in the people that lived along the streets than in the conditions of the streets themselves.

For all their differences, the combined efforts of VISTA and Model Cities contributed to the overall improvement of Texarkana. The fulcrum of radical and conservative efforts was community progress. The balance achieved was the original goal of both programs.

The Texarkana Volunteers

The first group of Texarkana Volunteers included two Program Development Planners to help the agency establish a work plan for its seven-county service area. One of them was Bob DeMarco, who said he joined VISTA primarily to avoid the draft. DeMarco spent his initial months at a desk in the basement of the Miller County courthouse studying for a bar exam. The agency directors' only concern seemed to be that he cause no trouble, DeMarco said.

DeMarco recalled VISTA training lectures about locating worthy community people and linking them to government programs. Yet with program funding administered by local powers, VISTA would do little more than maintain the Texarkana status quo, DeMarco believed. Other than Lurleen Page, 1968 SWADC Volunteers in Texarkana and nearby towns of Ashdown and Hope did not accomplish much.

This was not uncommon with first wave Volunteers whose abrupt placement was often too much of a surprise for communities to muster any significant positive or negative reaction. According to Erma Pondexter, a SWADC staff member at the time, the concept of organized poverty communities taking advantage of available government assistance was still too new for the area. It was a radical change the people could not yet understand, she said.

> The Volunteers were already educated to make changes in the lives of people where injustice was inflicted on them. We weren't ready for them.

Volunteers Joann and Tom Utterback

Why would a sharecropper come off the farm and start voting? . . . But the Volunteers were energetic people who wouldn't let things continue. They were a springboard for the second group. They were the ground breakers.

The other PDP Volunteer assigned in 1968 was Frank Fuller, a Princeton graduate with an architecture degree. Fuller admitted he knew little about community organizing but was intrigued by the chance of trying it. Fuller recognized the need for Volunteers with planning skills to follow his group at Texarkana. Having submitted to OEO the proposal for a bi-state program to be sponsored by the Bethel Church, he was sent to the Dallas regional office to help select the next Volunteers.

Among the Volunteers assigned to Texarkana in November 1969 were three married couples and two single males, Fleck and Karlin. A third single Volunteer, David Jewett, joined the group in mid 1970. Married Volunteers were generally more stable than others, and the Texarkana situation would soon put their stability to the test. Among the married couples selected were John and Carol Hoerster. John Hoerster, already an attorney, was described by another Volunteer as "soft spoken and deadly, our ace in the hole." Required to be relicensed in the state to practice at Texarkana, Hoerster received the highest grade among more than 350 lawyers who passed the 1970 Arkansas Bar exam.

Carol Hoerster had a degree in speech therapy, and she worked in a special education day care center with retarded and learning disabled children. Of all the Volunteers, her efforts were the most well received by the Texarkana community, and she became a source of credibility for the whole group. Her work was so well accepted that during a city council meeting aimed at removing the Volunteers from town, one of the councilmen exclaimed "one good apple doesn't save a rotten barrel."

Volunteer Tom Utterback remained a Volunteer for only a short time following his assignment to Texarkana. Upon Stephens' advice, Utterback resigned from VISTA and was elected Miller County representative to the SWADC Board representing low income community interests. Once inside the power structure of SWADC, Utterback gained political finesse and was voted Secretary/Treasurer of the agency, he said.

> I went from a lowly VISTA Volunteer to one of the top three members of the agency board. I signed the checks. We had no trouble with the agency after that.

Utterback's single vote in SWADC decisions carried little weight against the unified opinions of county judges and executive board members who governed the agency. On the whole, the Texarkana Volunteers did not know how to deal with the level of resistance they received. Their training had prepared them to implement assistance to low income communities. It had not taught them how to

Texarkana Volunteers, September 1970. *Front row (left to right):* Bruce Neft, Al Karlin, Tom Utterback, John and Carol Hoerster. *Back row:* unknown, David Jewett, Joann Utterback, Jack Fleck, Vera MacAlister (community member), Gail Neft.

survive in an environment where the loudest voices shouted for their removal.

This type of confrontation probably created a more adamant philosophy among the Volunteers, reducing their willingness to compromise, Mrs. Pondexter said. Two extremes were the result—the Volunteers and those they educated on one side, the county officials who opposed them on the other.

The Volunteers had little interest in helping establish SWADC programs such as feeder pig projects or subsidized public transpor-

South Texarkana family assisted by VISTA

tation. Bruce Neft admitted there probably was long range value in the agency's concern about economic changes. But the Volunteers weren't interested in being workers in programs.

We were more interested in being a catalyst for change in the people themselves. We wanted to provide them with enough education and information to continue the work that must be done for long term change. We found the existing programs didn't address those needs. In many cases, they were designed to block those needs.

Jack Fleck recalled how he learned to play politics according to the local rules. At a community meeting seeking neighborhood endorsement of the VISTA program, Fleck said he was put on the defensive by a blatantly racist critic whose slow drawl and careful de-

Texarkana Model Cities sign at street improvement project

livery made him a difficult opponent. The man, learning Fleck had a degree in civil engineering, asked what kind of professional would work for the VISTA wage of $45 per week.

> I responded with a defense of my scholastic record, but I could have responded better by talking about VISTA goals and how working to eliminate poverty was more important than earning a big salary. . . . Thinking fast on my feet when I was put on the defensive was not something I was at all accustomed to doing. Bruch was right about Southerners being wily politicians.

Stephens mentioned the Volunteers' occasional flaunting of local values. At a private Halloween party, he said several Volunteers arrived in costumes made up of colored sheets and signs. Those in yellow sheets were labeled "Yellow Peril" and those in pink sheets displayed signs reading "Better Dead Than Red." Stephens dismissed the incident as harmless, adding that anytime people are perceived as change agents, they will be viewed as lacking political finesse.

Another Texarkana supporter of the Volunteers, Barbara Clayton, society editor of the *Texarkana Gazette* and a Bethel Church member, was more adamant in her defense of Volunteer behavior. The Texarkana situation did not allow a time for diplomacy, Mrs. Clayton insisted.

> Everything the Volunteers did was appropriate at the time. I don't know how they could have proceeded differently. Diplomacy would never have gotten you anywhere. That was determined as acquiescence to the status quo. The Volunteers organized the poor, told them their rights, the laws. There was no diplomatic way that could have been done.

Project Sponsorship

No other project in Arkansas VISTA history gave rise to more speculation, false assumption, and community polarization than the program at Texarkana. Even more remarkable, this aggravated response to the Volunteers' presence was not based on anything they had done. It related to local sponsorship of the VISTA program and pressures put on the SWADC to initially refuse and then accept the Volunteers.

The confusion resulting from these events spread from Texarkana to Little Rock, and state newspapers repeatedly published incorrect information about the events in Miller County. What was undeniably clear, however, was a potential community rejection of the Volunteers who arrived on November 5, 1969, Hoerster said.

> The Volunteers developed a plan about what we'd do, some controversial and not so controversial things. This was a balancing act to move things in a positive direction without getting kicked out of town in the process. Our energies got refocused into trying to save the program, and we put a lot of time on that. We became the issue.

The second group of Texarkana Volunteers were much different from those first assigned there in 1968. That earlier group was spread out through the counties, and the few Volunteers working in Texarkana raised little controversy. The activity didn't begin until Fuller and Stephens brought in eight Volunteers under the premise of a bi-state program sponsored by a non-OEO organization, Bethel Church.

The concept was ambitious, and Stephens may have underestimated the opposition. To further tip the scales against his plan, an incident in nearby Marshall, Texas effectively blocked any cooperation from that state. A VISTA project in Marshall had recently been removed after the town's confederate statue had been painted with black power slogans. The Texas governor had also banned VISTA projects in eastern parts of the state.

In an attempt to overcome that decision and win the support necessary for a bi-state program, Stephens and the newly-arrived Volunteers appeared before the Texas-side City Council to review project goals. They knew city government could request a state governor to veto a VISTA project. Support from the Texas City Council was crucial. At this meeting the Volunteers got their first dose of Dr. Young's criticism of the Model Cities program.

According to Karlin, Young made a presentation to the council based on the causal impact of Model Cities. He spoke of the Model Cities program at Washington, DC, and of that city's problems with crime, drugs, and social diseases, inferring that since Texarkana had a Model Cities program, those other urban attributes would soon follow. Young then read aloud the submitted VISTA project proposal, which included plans to help with art and drama in the schools, to set up coffee houses for cultural gatherings, to analyse welfare, special education, and other city services.

It is unclear if the Texas City Council voted to deny the VISTA project at the meeting or shortly afterwards. Stephens, having received a temporary thirty-day approval of the project from the Arkansas OEO, decided to delay pressuring the Texas side for approval.

But momentum against the project was beginning to build. An Arkansas OEO analysis of the Texarkana situation had recommended Governor Winthrop Rockefeller deny the Bethel Church project. On December 3, 1969, a rejection was issued by SWADC board members who said they thought such a program would not be supervised closely enough. The SWADC also refused to adopt the

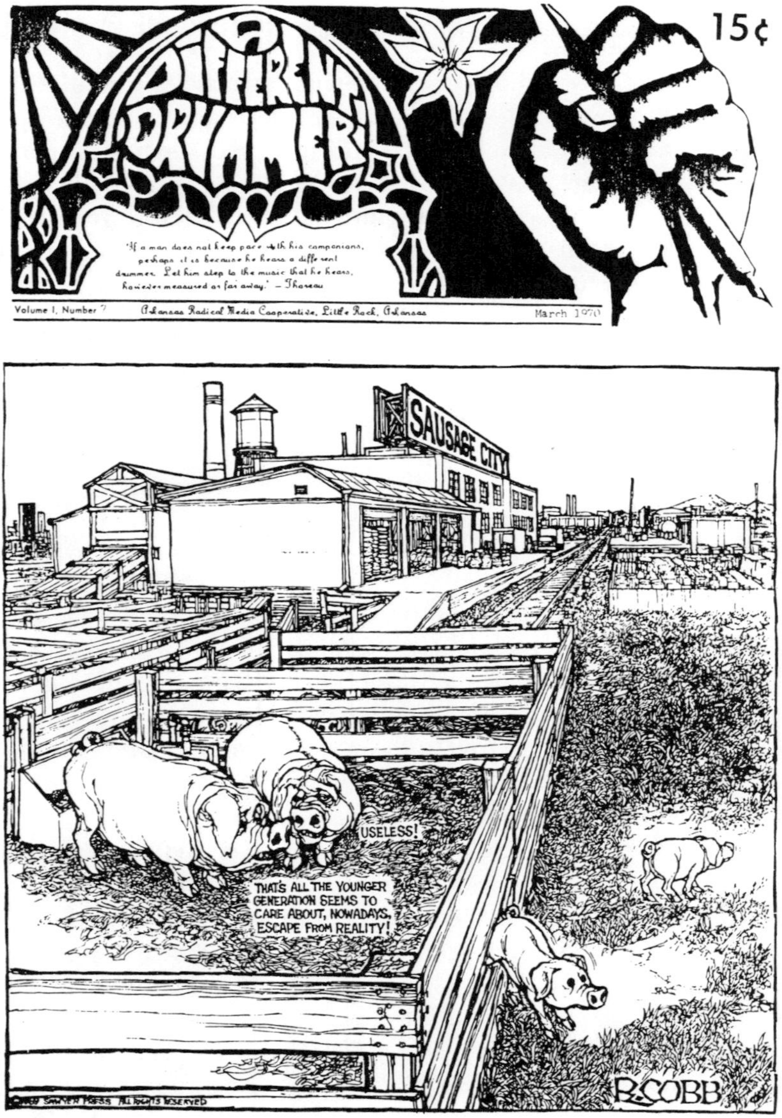

Cover from March 1970 issue of *A Different Drummer,* a Little Rock community newspaper

THE TEXARKANA VISTA HASSLE

Texarkana, Ark., Feb. 26 —
Dear people:

Sorry about the late reply, but for the moment anyway, the story has been closed. Southwest Arkansas Development Council (SWADC) has been forced to accept the VISTAs in Miller County due to pressure from SWADC's own Miller County Neighborhood Councils. The people really won this one.

Back to the beginning. Bethel United Church and its pastor, David Stephens, applied for a VISTA project late last year. An organization can be a VISTA sponsor simply by being concerned with the elimination of poverty and have office space and a telephone. Bethel United Church is the only integrated church in Texarkana, it also has books for sale of interest to open-minded people, and has a coffee house for chess, checkers and conversation on weekend evenings. Freedom Inc. and the police force have harrassed and slandered David and the church, for such things as "encouraging inter-racial mixing". The VISTA application was sent to both Governor Smith and Rockefeller so that the VISTA's could have worked on both sides of the stateline-divided city. David Stephens also has a good relationship with the black community, and with young people.

A response came from Sonny Walker in the Arkansas State Office of Economic Opportunity. He tried to hang the project up administrately by claiming all VISTA projects must be sponsored by OEO local offices. In this case, on the Arkansas side, it's Southwest Arkansas Development Council. So, David Stephens and the VISTA's began to seek a delegate sponsorship arrangement with SWADC. SWADC is a seven-county community action program. It is ruled by rural county judges. CAP agencies are supposed to be composed of 1/3 public officials, 1/3 private, concerned citizens, and 1/3 representing the poor. It doesn't work that way. All the representatives from the six rural counties are under the thumbs of the county judges. Miller County in which Texarkana and a sizeable poor-black-white population lie is different. The poor do control that segment of the agency, but the entire agency must pass on programs. Result of four years of operation; next to no anti-poverty work in Miller County.

While the project faced SWADC, it also ran into criticism from Mitchell Young and Freedom Inc. Calling the group subversive and other nasty things, he proceeded to begin a small telephone campaign to the Texarkana Arkansas City Board of directors. When the volunteers got wind of it, they tried to meet with the directors and the mayor to set them straight. The result was a "hearing" which, according to the mayor, was to be only between the VISTAs and the directors, with no comments from any community people. 50 to 75 community people showed up anyway on behalf of the VISTAs. The VISTAs were allowed to present their program for helping the poor of Texarkana. The Directors, however, chose not to question the program, but instead chose to bring before David Stephens all the ugly lies and slanders about him and his church that the racist section of the community had been spreading. The final motion which carried said something about them being good boys and girls, but they could not support the sponsor. A letter to that effect went to Winrock... Battle No. 1 - Mitchell Young 1, VISTA 0.

Next came the SWADC Governing Board. Even though the SWADC director refused to change the meeting from three in the afternoon, the community turned out more than 150 people to witness the fate of their Vista project. The meeting was an insult to democracy, the community wasn't even allowed to voice its opinion. Then in walks Hazel Hooper of Freedom Inc. She hands a letter to the councilmen (see box) and each reads it and passes it to the next. The delegate agency arrangement was rejected. Again the sponsor was rejected, not VISTA. Or so the motion said. Mitchell Young, 2; VISTA 0.

By this time, people in the poverty neighborhoods of Texarkana were beginning to realize what all this meant. They began to see that the VISTA project could benefit no one but them. They began to see that they were the ones that were losing. They began to see that they made up more than 1/3 of the population, but had absolutely no representation on the City Board of Directors, very little on the SWADC Governing Board, and none on other things such as school boards. The Miller County segment of SWADC finally revolted. They threatened to pull out of CAP unless the VISTA project was approved, and a list of other demands were met. The threat came in a Miller County Board meeting in which poor people, perhaps for the first time, told a county judge that he did not own them. The poor people told officials of the agency that the agency was for them, not the officials. They demanded action.

The SWADC needs Miller County because it has the largest population in its service area, an important factor in funding. So, the almighty dollar reigns supreme. SWADC broke to the pressure. The director was forced into convincing county judges to accept the VISTAS, but without David Stephens. As of the twenty-sixth of February the score stood at: The People - 1, VISTA - 1, David Stephens - 1/2, Mitchell Young - 0.

Peace and power,
name withheld

FREEDOM, INC.

Vista consists of political activists that have disrupted many communities. They have been run out of a number of cities in Texas. Texarkana, Texas wants no part of Vista. Vista works with OEO in many areas.

As you know the House of Jonah has been under surveillance for drugs, marijuana, etc. for some months. David Stephens who heads the House of Jonah and Denzer Burke who represents the NAACP are sponsors of VISTA. These individuals have caused nothing but trouble in this community. We also request that the House of Jonah be closed also (sic.)

Some other programs that VISTA hopes to participate in are the following:

1. They want to put on plays in the public schools, thus we may have our own production of <u>Hair</u>, <u>O Calcutta</u>, and <u>Fanny Hill</u>!

2. They want to advice (sic.) our school boards about additional needs for special education services in the school system.

3. Wants to set up model health programs.

4. They want to work to have criminals released on their own recognition instead of putting up bail. This creates more crime.

5. Supervise local youth centers.

5A. Open a Coffee House to encourage interracial mixing.

6. Investigate housing laws and codes.

7. They want to consult with law énforcement agencies on training program for employees. They want to decide what policemen are taught.

8. Analyze welfare system.

9. Want to set up an information center and handle all information to be released on Model Cities, CAP and OEO.

10. Work with Model Cities on Socialized legal care.

11. Set up a Rumor Control Center.

These are some of the plans VISTA hopes to get into in Texarkana. Freedom, Incorporated of Texarkana, Arkansas wants this city council to immediately ask the VISTA people to depart. We will bring more presure to bear on this City Council to get rid of this program if necessary.

—Mrs. Hazel Hooper
President, Freedom Incorporated
Texarkana, Arkansas

On February 21 Mitchell Young and Freedom Inc. sponsored a rally at the State Capitol to oppose busing of school children to achieve racial balance. Freedom Inc. favors freedom of choice school integration and its members maintain that it is not a racist organization.

The article in this edition of the Drummer which deals with the VISTA hassle in Texarkana includes a transcript of a letter passed around at a meeting. This letter resulted in the VISTAs being denied sponsorship in Texarkana. During the Saturday rally, Young stated repeatedly that he was opposed to forced segregation <u>or</u> integration and that he favored integration by freedom of choice. He stoutly maintained that he was not a racist and was not prejudiced against blacks and was only a freedom-loving citizen who wanted force out of education.

After the rally I asked Dr. Young how his statements at the rally tied in with #5A of the aforementioned letter which "accused" the VISTAs and David Stephens of encouraging interracial mixing at their coffee house. He said that Winrock had told him Stephens was unacceptable as a sponsor for the VISTAs because of his "reputation." He talked for several moments about the coffee house being under surveillance for drugs. I pressed him on the words "interracial mixing" and he replied, "David Stephens and the House of Jonah (the coffee house) have been encouraging white females to date Negro males and this just won't do."

Gary

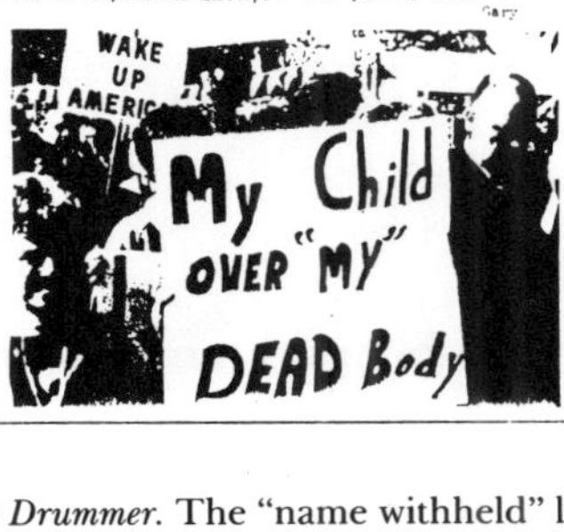

Page from March 1970 issue of *A Different Drummer*. The "name withheld" letter was written by Volunteer Bruce Neft. The Freedom, Inc. letter was submitted to the Texarkana City Council during their Jan. 23, 1970 review of the city's VISTA project.

church as a delegate agency and thereby indirectly approve the project. The delegate agency status was a compromise suggested by W. L. "Sonny" Walker who would become Arkansas OEO director on January 1, 1970. Two months later, Walker and others were instrumental in convincing the agency to directly sponsor the Volunteers. But in December, the outlook was bleak. County judges on the SWADC board were firmly against Volunteer presence, and agency director Thomas Hudman shared their feelings.

The feeling that the Volunteers were troublemakers created additional communication gaps between them and the agency directors, according to Erma Pondexter.

> When the Volunteers were first assigned to SWADC, there were some energetic ideas. As they began to do things, a force began to squash their efforts. That brought the energy outside and into the church. The church became a haven for the Volunteers, a means of shelter for them.

By January 1970, the Volunteers had received another extension from Governor Rockefeller, this one allowing them to stay until January 26. On January 14, they held a news conference at Bethel Church to explain their goals. Following the news conference, Hudman said SWADC itself would sponsor the VISTA project, but it would not accept Bethel Church as a delegate sponsor.

This brief upswing of VISTA support ended a few days later when the Texarkana City Council voted to reject the Volunteers and write Governor Rockefeller asking him to remove them from the city. The Volunteers responded with a request for a special meeting of the City Council. That meeting, held on January 23, was one of the most outrageous examples of parliamentary disorder in the entire project history.

The session began with Hoerster presenting to the board a briefing on VISTA history and the goals of the Texarkana program. Each Volunteer gave a presentation of his work assignment. The Volunteers brought approximately three hundred petition signatures in their favor from Texarkana residents and a number of respected local people to speak in their behalf.

The City Council seemed unimpressed by this showing of support. They insisted the Volunteer efforts would be a duplication of services already being provided by the Model Cities program. They refused to let presidents of the neighborhood councils speak and suggested these presidents did not really support the VISTA program. One of the presidents was told to be quiet when he tried to respond directly to the allegation.

Midway through the meeting, a woman entered the crowded city council chambers and pushed her way to the front of the room. Hazel Hooper, president of the Texarkana, Arkansas, chapter of Freedom, Inc., handed a sheet of paper to the board, and it was read in silence by each member. Hoerster's request for a copy and a public reading of the paper was denied.

A copy of the letter was later obtained by the Volunteers. It stated that VISTA had already been run out of Texas for disrupting communities and that Stephens and Burke "have caused nothing but trouble in this community." The paper also listed eleven VISTA project goals, and then gave the Freedom, Inc., version of what those goals meant—such as drama programs in the public schools leading to nude theater, a coffee house encouraging interracial mixing, and a bail bond program for the indigent creating more crime.

The city council meeting came to an abrupt end with a unanimous vote to write Governor Rockefeller that the city did not need a VISTA program. Though it denied endorsement of the VISTA program, the board voted to endorse the Volunteers as individuals. A council member called them "good boys and girls," Hoerster recalled. Dr. Young, speaking with the press following the meeting, was not so kind. He said the Volunteers were political activists who had "contributed to disruptive activities in the city."[7]

Utterback, learning of Young's remark, offered this challenge:

> If Dr. Mitchell Young would like to talk with me, I will meet him anywhere, anytime. Apparently, this man deals in fear, but I see no fire breathing out of his mouth.[8]

At a press conference held at Bethel Church the next morning, the Volunteers, Stephens, and several community supporters offered detailed examples of the uniqueness of VISTA service in Texarkana. They accused the city council of attempting to gain a "totalitarian control of all public and private programs," and they announced a campaign to send letters and petitions supporting VISTA to the governor's office.[9]

Nevertheless, the Volunteers were in a state of limbo. Their temporary extension expired and another thirty-day extension had been granted. But the fact was the city did not want them working there, Karlin said.

> So, we were asked to leave. No one, of course, said they didn't want to help black and poor people. They said instead that northern VISTAS, who don't understand the South and its need to move slowly, would cause agitation and discord. Coincidentally, such statements of dogma always originated with people who had nice homes, two cars, and a sincere desire to preserve the past. Poor people didn't talk about the need to move slowly.

The next defeat for the program came on January 29, 1970, when the SWADC, influenced by the City Council and Freedom, Inc., reversed its earlier position and voted to deny sponsorship. That same day an editorial in the Arkansas Gazette offered this assessment of the situation:

> . . . complaints expressed against VISTA by the notorious Freedom, Inc. offer evidence in themselves that a need exists for VISTA. The principal concern should not be with the feelings of freedom-of-choicers or the city fathers . . . but with the real needs of both races trapped on the lower rungs of the economic ladder.

Certain members of the SWADC board were unmoved by those remarks. Hoerster recalled at the agency meeting a number of black board members, those representing the low income community, rose to express their approval of the VISTA project. They were stared back down by the county judges and did not vote in the project's favor, Hoerster said.

The SWADC wrote to Gov. Rockefeller, requesting a phase-out of the project by February 26, 1970. Once again, Stephens and the Volunteers responded with a press conference condemning Texarkana elected officials as nonresponsive to the needs of poor people.

Bethel Church returned to its original position, asking the governor to establish it as independent VISTA sponsor.

Walker, having assumed leadership of the state OEO, had to follow the most judicious public policy. Based on what he said was a lack of community support, Walker recommended the governor deny the project and not grant it any additional extensions. Walker referred to the "climate of opposition" that had developed in Texarkana despite "meaningful, worthwhile efforts" of the Volunteers.[10]

As departure day for the Volunteers grew closer, a new level of activity began. Three neighborhood councils expressed their endorsement of the Volunteers and more than 1,200 petition signatures were collected. The Miller County Board, in defiance of its parent agency, the SWADC, issued a public statement supporting the VISTA project.

The SWADC, in a curious attempt to show support for the general concept of VISTA, requested thirty new Volunteers from the state OEO. Maintaining its refusal of the eight Volunteers on hand, the agency said the new Volunteers would be assigned throughout the seven-county area. Freedom, Inc., with victory just days away, held a rally and march down State Line Boulevard at Texarkana, then repeated the public display on Capitol Avenue at Little Rock on February 21.

A conclusion came suddenly and with great surprise to most all concerned. On February 24, Hudman announced that the eight Texarkana Volunteers were being accepted into the SWADC program. Dramatic reversals of this type, while not uncommon in the political process, do not occur without significant pressure being applied. Yet each group that influenced the SWADC claimed its efforts caused the change.

The Volunteer influence may have remained in Texarkana even if the agency refused them. The Volunteers said they would continue their community service through Bethel Church and direct local support. Local support of the Volunteers had already been evidenced in the endorsement of three neighborhood councils. This support, further heightened by community dissatisfaction with the SWADC, was channeled into a new proposal that Miller County withdraw from the agency and create an alternative OEO organization in Texarkana.

This last threat was the least probable, yet the Volunteers, having gained an education in the political game, delivered their bluff with a casual air of confidence. Fleck recalled the message was something like "you can either work with us or against us, it's your choice." Basically, the Volunteers told the agency if it didn't sponsor them, they would shut it down, Fleck said.

On other levels, certain SWADC staff members who supported the Volunteers were trying to sway opinions. Tom Lockhart, then deputy director, said he and others influenced Hudman's change of mind. Representing Texarkana's liberal community, Floyd Sexton said he was making frequent trips to Little Rock to communicate with the state OEO and governor's office. Finally, Walker said his agency was also involved in encouraging Hudman and the SWADC to accept the VISTA project.

The combined efforts of these groups brought about the VISTA approval. With little knowledge of what the others were doing, each one presumed its efforts were responsible for the end result. For the Volunteers, the decision was an overdue admission of the value of their work, Fleck said.

> So we won the battle. The regional OEO office said we had pulled off a minor miracle. We were jubilant but had to shake our heads at the absurdity of it all. Winning the approval had taken about four months. It was now the end of February. We began the work of being normal Volunteers.

VISTA architects Stanley Kozinsky (center), Gilbert Bullaksen (right), and Bill Peters (left) work on the new door of the College Station Firehouse in 1972. *Photo courtesy of ACTION*

VISTA Activities

Not all Volunteer activities in Texarkana were held in limbo until the project sponsorship issue was resolved. Under Stephens' leadership, the Volunteers worked at projects despite the threat of expulsion, and their accomplishments gained the community support that helped bring about their ultimate acceptance.

Earliest of these activities was a drive to influence a local television station to provide more programing time to Texarkana community issues. The station, KTAL, was originally licensed in Texarkana, but it had established its main office and was doing most of its business in Shreveport. According to Tom Utterback, they had done so without approval or knowledge of the Federal Communications Commission.

The Volunteers were instrumental in gaining affidavits from Texarkana residents attesting to the station's lack of local interest programing. The station, in danger of losing its license, agreed to remain in Texarkana and signed a contract to cover community affairs. In an article in the New York Times, the agreement was described as "perhaps the first of its kind in the communications industry," and it stipulated that renewal of the station's license was conditional on meeting the community demands.[11]

Denzer Burke was allowed to host a weekly thirty-minute magazine type show, a program he said he continued for about five years, and the station agreed to broadcast "Sesame Street," a children's program usually shown only on public television stations, in one-hour commercial free periods. The station also agreed to hire two full-time black reporters and provide a toll-free telephone number so community members could convey news or suggestions.

Utterback and other Volunteers called the KTAL encounter an easy victory, but it also involved lobbying efforts at the FCC in Washington, DC, and major assistance from the communications staff of the Church of Christ. The combination of these efforts was so successful, Burke said, similar campaigns achieved equal results at two television stations in Shreveport.

The most noncontroversial project involving a Texarkana Volunteer was the special education school and kindergarten, a program begun a few years before the Volunteers arrived. Carol Hoerster, whose college degree in speech therapy made her an ideal resource for that school, spent her year of VISTA service helping retarded children overcome speech problems. In her second year at Texarkana, Hoerster worked on the school staff.

With no speech therapy program in the Texarkana public schools at that time and no funds at the special education kindergarten to hire one, Hoerster's work provided an immediate and obvious benefit to the community.

Children enrolled at the school came from outlying communities in Texas and Arkansas, and the Volunteers would drive out into the country to pick them up. One child in particular was remembered by several Volunteers. Joann Utterback said a black youth named Henry, at first thought to be retarded, was later discovered to be blind and afflicted with a hearing problem.

> We found Henry and his family in an old country shack. They were living like a bunch of animals, kids wallowing in urine-soaked burlap sacks, one sister so retarded she couldn't sit up. The family was so retarded and uneducated they had no idea what their own name was. They just took their name from what was on the mailbox when they moved in.

Henry was tutored by the Volunteers and passed a test for enrollment at the Texas School for the Blind. Before their efforts, there was little chance for him to escape the squalor and ignorance that dominated the life of his family.

Joann Utterback also made personal contact with Texarkana youth through what she called her "charm school" classes. These were personal improvement classes for adolescent and teenage girls, teaching them such things as hygiene, grooming, and how to apply for a job. In response to her request, Utterback said one cosmetics company sent cases of fragrant soap, which became a special treat for some of the girls whose poverty had denied them the use of a toothbrush or a bar of soap of any type. The enthusiasm shown at her classes, however, did not lighten the criticism from some white parents who objected to Volunteer-provided transportation in which their daughters rode in the same vehicle with black girls, Utterback said.

The Volunteers' personal influence extended into many Texarkana homes, such as the deteriorating residence of Lilly Mae Gossett. According to Bruce Neft, Mrs. Gossett was a "poor white from whom we learned that to be poor and white in the South is not much different than being poor and black." The Volunteers helped her apply for a new government subsidized house and enroll in a nurses-aid program. Based on Mrs. Gossett's spirit and willingness to change her condition, Neft called her "one of our shining victories."

Locating the right community person to carry out VISTA plans is perhaps the most important contact a Volunteer can make. Such was the case at Garland, a small Miller County town on the Red River with an urgent need for a new water system. Jack Fleck, the civil engineer Volunteer, assumed the project was ideal for him, but he rapidly found out it was more a political problem than an engineering one.

Garland had been run by the same core group of white families, owners of rich farmland and businesses, for close to a century. The city council hadn't been opposed in election since the 1940s. They simply appointed each other to positions each year. City boundaries excluded the majority black population from voting. Basic poverty kept them from drilling sufficiently deep wells to avoid contamination from regular flooding of the Red River.

Fleck realized the only way to get the city a water supply system was to elect a new city council or force the existing council to apply for it by ballot incentive. The situation dramatically changed, however, when Martha Franklin announced her candidacy for mayor. Franklin, a white woman who served as the town mail carrier for close to forty years, a mother of six children and a former president of the PTA, said the Volunteers first contacted her when they learned she was running for mayor.

> If it hadn't been for the Volunteers to help me at that time, I couldn't have proceeded. I know how rich people think and poor people feel, but it was too far to go in that short time and too much to do. The Volunteers were experts in their fields. I knew local politics but couldn't do the work.

Advised by the Volunteers, who also rallied black voters, Mrs. Franklin was elected mayor of Garland in 1970. More than fifteen years later, Mayor Franklin still holds that office, and Garland has gained distinct improvements as a result. Water and sewage systems have been installed through low interest federal loans. Grants have been received for rehabilitation and construction of close to ninety homes. Most significantly, a much higher level of voter participation has been achieved, due in no small part to Mrs. Franklin's annexation of new areas in the city limits.

Volunteer influence brought measurable improvement in Garland and Texarkana, but the community organizing efforts that helped initiate those gains are intangible at best. How does one credit the Volunteer effort to raise money to purchase a mimeograph machine and the time spent writing, editing, and printing copies of *CHANGE,* the newsletter of the Committee for Representative Government? How much recognition is due the Volunteers who consulted N. H. Hilliard in his near-successful campaign for a Texarkana school board position?

Bob Douglas, who was serving as a state senator at the time, defeated Hilliard in that school board election, but Volunteers' legal expertise eventually brought about his resignation from the board. Arkansas statutes indicated that individuals could not hold more than one elected office at any time. On behalf of the black community, Hoerster filed a suit that went all the way to the state Supreme Court before Douglas agreed to step down.

VISTA community organizing efforts conformed to a basic policy taught them in training, a procedure one Volunteer described as "meet the people, play the game, be a hustler, stay in the background." At Texarkana, the Volunteers recognized an important part of their job was to prepare the community to impact the political process, to show them how decisions were made. In effect, teach a course in practical civics. Erma Pondexter recalled how effective that preparation was.

> Once at the Model Cities office, the Volunteers and neighborhood council presidents went through a review of how federal money would be used. The Volunteers had a whole flow chart of where the money would go. I thought the locals would never be able to digest all that and use it. To my surprise, they met again and developed their own format to present it to the neighborhoods. At the meeting, the voting went the right way, which was a shock to Model Cities and the city council. Of course, the blame was put on the Volunteers.

In the freewheeling atmosphere of community organizing, Volunteers took whatever steps were appropriate. Vera MacAlister, a member of the progressive black community and close friend to the Volunteers, recalled Tom Utterback, whom she said had a distinct talent in mimicing people, dressing up one night in overalls and an old shirt and attending a Texarkana Ku Klux Klan meeting in that "redneck" disguise. Utterback came out of the meeting with a full membership list that helped the black community better understand who their real opponents were.

Successful community organizing requires a flair for dramatics, a sense of theater to create situations that force one's enemy into making errors. Street theater is an offensive strategy more concerned with bringing problems to a larger attention than proposing long term solutions. The risk behind such actions is the further polarization of opposing forces, but ridicule has always been a powerful weapon.

Barbara Clayton recalled one such occasion when Stephens and the Volunteers held a mock funeral to gain attention for Texas education. The funeral was held during the time when school integration was being contested. The idea behind it was that without integration, federal funds to schools would be cut and education would be dead.

> They had a coffin and mule-drawn wagon, and a procession was planned to go from Texas High School to a nearby park where a ceremony of some kind would be held. The school shut down at noon that day to keep the children from joining in, but they stayed around and joined the march. At the park were fire engines, helicopters overhead, and every policeman and patrol car in Texarkana. The city must have expected a mass riot, but nothing at all happened.

Other than a good sense of timing and bravado, no specialized skills are necessary for a display of this type. Yet the Texarkana Volunteers, and John Hoerster in particular, were a highly skilled group. Several Texarkana residents credit the existence of the current East Texas Legal Services as a result of early efforts by Hoerster to establish a public interest law firm in the community.

But Hoerster's major work in creating a community service law firm took place during his second year in Texarkana, when he was no longer a Volunteer but had been chosen to receive a Robert Kennedy Fellowship. Similarly, Tom Utterback's most important contributions to the Texarkana community came after he had resigned from VISTA and was serving as a board member of the Southwest Arkansas Development Council.

VISTA brought together the forces that allowed these developments to occur. From a community organizing sense, it matters little who pays your salary or to what organization you must officially report. More importantly, the beneficial results of such actions may not be perceived until years after the principal players have departed.

Long Range Results

The VISTA legacy in Texarkana is a matter of subjective appraisal. Like many Volunteers in other Arkansas projects, the Texarkana group does not consider a positive long range influence on the city to have resulted from its service.

These negative feelings must be understood in light of the Volunteers' present distance from Texarkana and the essential community organizing work that takes years, or even generations, to show results. When the Volunteers left Texarkana in November 1970, there was little specific progress they could claim. Their feelings were further colored by the time lost fighting for their existence.

Stephens recognized the level of dissatisfaction such an experience can produce, saying that one of the most difficult things is that after a day's work, you don't see the furrows you've plowed. Yet Stephens also sees VISTA as experiential education, a program designed more to eduate young American leaders than produce good works or instill real change. That belief is confirmed in these remarks by Al Karlin made shortly after his service year.

> Those who wonder why the young berate the establishment should consider Texarkana an example of irresponsible, but quite established power. The men who opposed us were not uneducated demagogues; they were respectable businessmen, lawyers, and doctors. In opposing our mere presence and simultaneously denying the reasonable petition of the black and poor white communities, they provided a caricature of the arrogant power which, in more subtle forms, infects America.

Karlin called his Texarkana experience a "personal catechism in the radical faith." Like four of his Volunteer peers, Karlin has pursued a career as an attorney. Yet the education he received in Texarkana would not have been achieved without his originally going into the community believing change was possible, Stephens said. No matter how naive that conception, it could provide gain to both the Volunteers and the community, Stephens added.

> The crucial point is getting people to believe that change is possible. Replacing apathy with a sense of hope. These young people coming into the community were part of that creation of hope.

With hope comes the ability to transform defeat into victory. Karlin recalled an incident where four elderly black ladies filed for a fair hearing after receiving notice their welfare rights were being cut off. Just the feeling that they could go in, look the welfare director in the eye, and say "I protest" was a form of victory not affected by their ultimately losing the appeal.

Denzer Burke mentioned more tangible social advancements at Texarkana following the VISTA project. A black man was elected to the Texas school board, the city's long-segregated housing projects were integrated, and the special education kindergarten expanded its services to include housing, transportation, and elderly care. These gains were achieved in spite of an attempt to frighten the black community into its former, submissive role. One evening after the Volunteers had left Texarkana, three black churches were burned on the Texas side and a brick was thrown through Burke's window.

To Vera MacAlister, the Volunteers' most substantial contribution was in making the community more sensitive to human values. Current programs in education, health, and other government services are part of the permanent legacy of VISTA, a legacy that remains intact because of the Volunteers' influence on local leaders.

> Those community leaders are still here and still active. You can see it in the legal services office standing up for the poor person. That inspiration came from the Volunteers. I don't think we could have thought such things

were possible. That is a mind set laid to rest. We give the Volunteers credit for that. They had the genius to find good in all things.

Erma Pondexter agreed on this point and defined the Volunteers' most effective contribution as educating the people to be good politicians in their own areas. Mrs. Pondexter recalled one Volunteer telling a group that they were their own worst enemies by refusing to think for themselves. The Volunteer advised them to learn from the county judges and mayor how to attack the issues.

But Mrs. Pondexter strongly differed from Mrs. McAlister in her assessment of the contemporary situation in Texarkana. The VISTA lesson, once forceful, has not endured; in recent years there has been a loss of momentum, Mrs. Pondexter said.

We ran out of gas and lost sight of the real issues before us. The Volunteers were successful during their time. When they turned us loose, we had homes and cars. But we became complacent and forgot about where we started. We're now back to that level, and our children have not realized the battles fought.

Taking advantage of the current complacency, the power structure makes only token gestures, giving a few good jobs to blacks to keep the entire group pacified and avoid bringing about the disenchantment of the Volunteers' time, she said. But a lot of people don't realize this; "we get into our holes and stay there," she added.

Notes

1. *Arkansas Gazette,* July 1, 1969.

2. *Arkansas Gazette,* January 1, 1972.

3. *Arkansas Gazette,* October 22, 1969.

4. *CHANGE, Newsletter for the Committee for Representative Government,* Vol. 1, No. 1, April 30, 1970.

5. Letter from Vince Glorioso, president of South Texarkana Neighborhood Council, to Tom McRae, director of Model Cities Program, May 20, 1970.

6. *Arkansas Gazette,* June 21, 1970.

7. *Arkansas Gazette,* January 24, 1970.

8. *Texarkana Gazette,* January 24, 1970.

9. *Texarkana Gazette,* January 25, 1970.

10. *Arkansas Gazette,* January 30, 1970.

11. *The New York Times,* June 11, 1969.

A CONVERSATION
WITH BOBBY MORGAN

Fayetteville is a prosperous hill town surrounded by the rough beauty of the Ozarks. From its higher elevations, the view in all directions offers a hawk-like perspective, a panorama of mountains and valleys. In town, the highest peaks are dominated by prestigious neighborhoods and distinguished public structures such as the large banks and hotels on the revitalized town square. The Washington County Courthouse, its pointed clock tower a landmark restoration project for the city center, has stood for more than a hundred years on its hilltop location.

The slope behind the courthouse drops rapidly down, and the gleaming downtown steel and glass is quickly replaced by the ragged growth of scrub trees and bushes, a hillside spotted with discarded trash, and rusted, junked cars. The land levels off for a short distance but soon begins another rise. In the late afternoon, shadows of the courthouse climb that opposite incline where low-income housing projects establish the black neighborhood character of East Fayetteville.

Sherman's Tavern, a small building on the level ground between the two hills, is another Fayetteville landmark. Near the former site of an unofficial town dump still known as Tin Cup, the bar has been a community gathering place for decades. Its owner, Sherman Morgan, has long been recognized as a leading member of the black community in its continuing struggle for progress.

Bobby Morgan, a former VISTA trainer, consultant, and an outspoken activist in many state and local projects, shares much of his father's social commitment, so the tavern seemed a fitting site for a discussion of the younger Morgan's past activities.

On the Friday afternoon of a Thanksgiving weekend, warm sunlight shone brightly on the dirt parking lot of the tavern, on the old sign post with its tattered remains of a plastic name plate, and on the weathered building. A few black men were sitting on benches in the sunlight along the tavern's front wall, their inertia easily mistaken for a seasonal good will. The blaring sound of soul music spilled out through screened wooden doors.

Inside the bar, afternoon light filtered through dusty windows, giving the room a soft yellow glow. Kids scrambled around a quarter-a-game pool table, drinking soda from bottles they had pulled from an old Coke machine. The patrons of the bar, a fair mixture of white faces among them, sat comfortably in the dim room, the smoke from their cigarettes filling the air.

Morgan walked in and sat down at the table. A semi-mountain of a man, his enormous chest and belly filled out the gray sweatshirt he wore beneath a light jacket. His round face seemed an expressive black moon with a scraggly gray goatee, as the wrinkles around his eyes hinted at the depth of emotion he would soon reveal. With his "Coors Light" cap pulled low on his brow, he held out a large, fleshy hand to shake; then he lowered himself into the opposite seat of the booth with a heavy grace, and the power of a man whose body has carried burdens beyond our knowing.

"Twenty years later, I'm still not satisfied," he said, referring back to his VISTA days. "The parents are better off and a generation of kids got it better, but no one wants to get involved."

Gesturing to the kids by the pool table, he spoke of their present opportunities and the complacency it seemed to breed, of the clothes, the cars, the homes with running water they so readily took for granted.

"They think that's part of America, the way things are, yet the attitudes of poverty and dependence are still there," he said.

Bobby Morgan, VISTA trainer and Summer Associate program administrator

"They'll want to go to school to get the jobs, but they won't get the loans, so they'll settle to just get by. The whole thing will be starting over. No hope. Nothing out there for them."

In the years following his VISTA experiences, Morgan said he still searched for something. A fellowship at the Ford Foundation's Leadership Development Program in Atlanta helped him gain some organizing skills. His contacts in various black communities gave him access to militant groups such as the Black Panthers and the Weathermen. He was in Greensboro, North Carolina, following the civil rights violence there in the early 1970s and in Chapel Hill to learn from that city's first black mayor.

"Back then they thought the problem was education, but I found education wasn't worth a damn unless you got common sense to go with it," Morgan said. "Cats get education and they just become middle class."

Education for Morgan began as it still does for many fortunate blacks, with an athletic scholarship. His "job" at a Hot Springs high school was to play football and run track, but it separated him from his family in Fayetteville. After graduation and a year at a small college in Texas, he rejoined his family for a move to California. The athletic Morgan began working out in a public park where he gained the attention of professional football player Tommy Mason.

The meeting led to an invitation to the Los Angeles Rams training camp, and Morgan made the team. After two years on the Rams' special defense squad, followed by another two years in the Marines, Morgan returned to Fayetteville a married man with a thirty-two dollars per week income from unemployment checks. When he finally got a well-paying job at a local manufacturing plant, he found the change brought with it more than just material improvement.

"I was the only black man working there, and that got me out of touch with my regular folks," Morgan said. "That had to change if I was to bring up my kids in this community. I thought EOA was the thing for all black folks, so I set out to do something about it."

His activism began with community interest, fixing up homes, singing in the church choir, he said. When nine black youths were facing ten-year convictions for breaking into a local meat store, Morgan said he went to court with them, got them a lawyer, and "started into a public defender thing." By 1965, he was writing grant applications and took leave of his job to become center director of the East Fayetteville EOA.

Grant money began to come in, and local political struggles began. The white power structure in Fayetteville—its mayor, sheriff, and judges—showed interest in the Tin Cup agency. A $480,000 grant to finance a mobile clinic for Washington County was somehow dispersed on other projects. Internal problems developed and community participation lagged. Morgan resigned from the EOA to help train staff at community action agencies across the state through the Rural Training Center, a national OEO program with an office in Little Rock.

By 1968, Morgan had begun counseling work for VISTA and had met Jim Ranchino, the Ouachita Baptist University professor who was organizing the first Arkansas VISTA Summer Associate Program. When Ranchino asked him to lead a voter registration facet of the program, Morgan agreed providing he could do it his own way, using his contacts in the major southern and eastern poverty counties.

"I liked Ranchino for the freedom he gave us and for the worlds of information he had you couldn't find out anywhere," Morgan said. "He would say 'if anyone could change it, you can' and he gave us the freedom to turn over a lot of rocks."

That freedom allowed Morgan and his group contact with a wide variety of Arkansans, people that eventually "ripped us off, put us in jail" and eventually destroyed the group's motivating strength, he said.

"We became non-productive citizens," Morgan said. "That's what happens if you don't continue. That's what happens when you go out and start turning over rocks."

The discouragement in Morgan's voice shifted to a positive tone as he recalled the early efforts of his Summer Associate Volunteers and their ten-week assignments across the state.

"We got two students, one black and one white, from each college in Arkansas, and we trained them for voter education instead of voter registration, things like who the elected officials were, their views and their voting records," Morgan said. "That was a no-no in most places, and the first place we got run out of was Ashley County."

The project was rejected at several other locations before finally establishing its offices in the Phillips County Courthouse at West Helena, a location Morgan accepted even though he learned from sympathetic sources that his office phone was tapped. His Associate Volunteers penetrated communities with information about elected officials, more concerned with doing their jobs well than establishing relationships with local power structures.

"Folks raised hell, but the Volunteers went on," Morgan said. "The Volunteers weren't too neat or looking good back then. They were supposed to be rebels."

Community reactions soon became apparent. Volunteers were accused of shoplifting in Camden and Forrest City. In Monticello, two volunteers who rode horses to their rural meetings were forced off the road by locals in a pickup truck. State police initially suspected Volunteers of the robbery of guns from a store in Crockett, and group efforts were periodically interrupted by police demands for identification, Morgan said.

> Something started to change from our training of folks on the neighborhood level. Community folks got hip or felt they weren't doing any good. We raised the basic humanity type of thing. We went into the dirt-floor houses of east Arkansas. No poor folks closed doors in our faces. We listened to their problems.

Under Morgan's supervision, the VISTA Associates studied county voter registrations and determined exactly how many votes would be needed to carry any particular race for office. Those figures were then used as goals in voter registration drives. A different approach was used in Madison County where two white Volunteers compared county voting records with the names on tombstones in local cemeteries.

"We knocked the top off the Faubus thing of votes from dead people," Morgan said.

Another situation that required creative problem solving was an attempt to integrate a public swimming pool in Camden. Emotions ran high in that city following the drowning in a river of a black youth. Morgan's Volunteers weren't making progress until he brought them a supply of Black Panther literature and had them secretly spread it around town at night.

"We started a fear of invasion and got the pool integrated by the end of the summer," he said, laughing.

Morgan recalled training his Volunteers with techniques of nonverbal communication, such as a daily exercise of forming two circles, one inside the other with the Volunteers facing each other.

> We moved the circles around and started a rapport. Smiles, laughs, kisses, you know. They became honest with each other so they would be honest out in the field. Nonverbal communication, just like poor folk who won't tell you something until they are ready, and then it might be just by a touch or the blink of an eye. The Volunteers really learned how to talk with the poor folks."

The VISTA Associates developed a knowledge of social welfare they could not have achieved in college classrooms, Morgan said. He expressed the belief that VISTA should be restructured as an educational program that would benefit from the student Volunteers' youthful energy while it aided in community affairs.

VISTA could be organized to pay a student's tuition for two years provided he returned some work on the community level, such as voter registration or education, Morgan suggested. Involving the student in politics would help by showing people how to get things done, while involving him on the human level would increase the student's personal growth, he added.

"You have to have some of that young energy and persistence to get into someone's house or heart to make a change," he said. "Once you have that energy, the knowledge will come."

Morgan looked over the bar again, his gaze lingering on the

youngsters who strutted around the pool table, and a weary expression came across his face. He spoke of his own sons, now grown and independent, of his continuing need to be involved and the inability to do things he used to.

He mentioned a breakfast program for black school children which he established in his house in the early 1970s, only to have the county health department order him to relocate the program. The county EOA had the funds and location to maintain the program, but it never happened, he said, adding that the substantial budget of the Washington County EOA has not significantly changed conditions of poverty in east Fayetteville, a problem which continued from one generation to the next simply because no one wanted to deal with it.

"The kids don't have a place to acquire the knowledge to be wholesome, so they pick up what they can," he continued. "Now there is a lot of gay activity in the black community, incest in the young generations. It's going wrong, and I don't know what to do about it."

Morgan believes that a sense of black history is a thing of the past, with little cultural identity surviving from which the young can be taught, and with a scarcity of educated teachers, who have really lived in the world and not just learned of it in school.

Morgan said his lowest personal moment came in the early 1970s when he served as president of the local Human Relations Council. Trying to organize a memorial march for Martin Luther King, he was denied permission by two black churches to have the march originate from their front steps.

"The system has a way of turning around your ideals and making you seem the trouble maker," he said. "What's to come of all our work? Who are you going to select to develop leadership?"

In recent years, Morgan's confrontations with established authority have decreased but not totally disappeared. In 1981 he opened an east Fayetteville beer store, but his low prices rapidly drew criticism and "suggestions" for change from other distributors, he said. Refusing to comply, he was arrested and convicted for what he considered totally fabricated charges, selling beer to a minor and possession of a controlled substance.

"I done the whole route for these folks. I know how the power structure works, so they try to get me out of the way without raising hell," Morgan said. "Now I'm just off probation. I'm 47, my boys are grown, and all I can do is enjoy."

There was a hollow ring to his voice when Morgan used the word "enjoy." He had the air of a man in forced retirement, a man whose sense of enjoyment was so closely linked to struggle and achievement that the two concepts could not be separated. He spoke of some voter registration work he had recently done for the Jesse Jackson campaign, of a small shoe shine business he currently operated with his brother, and the cooking work he was doing at a fraternity house on the university campus.

"The fraternity pledged a black, and when he moved in, the white brothers all moved out of the house," Morgan said, shaking his head with a dark laughter. "These are the new leaders, that kind of mentality."

Morgan agreed to step outside for some photographs before the afternoon light was completely gone. He stood on the wooden porch of his father's tavern and looked up and down the street, east Fayetteville's black neighborhood on his left, the downtown city center with its banks and hotels on his right, and the Tin Cup district set directly between them.

"Make sure you get a shot of my Rainbow button," he said, displaying to the camera the white Rainbow Coalition button on his coat lapel.

NATIONAL VOLUNTEERS

VISTA Motivation

Volunteer Style

Volunteer Achievement

VISTA Motivation

Arkansas' nationally recruited Volunteers bore similarities to those who served in many other states. Few Volunteers came into the program with a commitment to the "Land of Opportunity." Most assigned to Arkansas either listed it as one of their least desirable choices or had no preference where they would work.

Arkansas' national Volunteers, much like others across the country, represented a core group of young people who came of age during the 1960s, a decade of civil rights confrontations, political assassinations, and the increasing American involvement in Viet Nam.

Older Volunteers made a distinct contribution to the Arkansas program; but for the most part national Volunteers were recruited from college campuses between 1965 and 1975. According to Joe Bruch, that awareness was a key motivation for VISTA participation.

> They knew something was wrong. They could see where the system broke down for parts of society. One way of getting at that might be VISTA. The most successful Volunteers were able to see their role in the balance of the situation. They understood bureaucracy and its nonsense and their own limitations. They still got up every day and went after it.

VISTA offered a degree of security. It included medical coverage, payment, and official government status. Yet the Volunteer choice made one no less radical than those who joined in confrontations on college campuses or city streets. The Volunteer choice was influenced by compassion and caring. It was an idealism directed at people, a human activism.

Volunteer John Boyle spoke of serving God by working with the poor. Volunteer Sandy Smegelsky said VISTA was her solution to the conflict faced by a self-proclaimed college radical and pre-med major whose personal hero was Tom Dooley, the American doctor in southeast Asia. Volunteer Joann Rose said she wanted to make deep political changes, right the wrongs so all would live happily ever after.

The naive idealism many Volunteers brought with them did not last long. For some, it was destroyed in confrontational training sessions where activists taunted and screamed at them. Others learned the same lesson in the field: One year of service, no matter what degree of dedication it carried, would not change the world. Volunteer Gene Richards commented on that realization.

> For a little time, VISTA was a wonderful naive excitement. You were doing tangible things. As time went on, people asked questions about the long range value. We asked those questions a lot.

Richards said he joined VISTA after burning his draft card. Public service as an alternative to jail brought many young men into the program after their college years ended. For those who seemed to know more what they couldn't do than what they could, VISTA presented a sanctioned escape, a one-year deferment from making a decision. To Volunteer Bill Peters, it was more a journey of adventure than one to make the world right.

> Idealism was part of my motivation, but mostly it was the realization I was not ready to go out and get a real, straight job. I had the experience of five years at Berkeley during the time of Cambodia, Viet Nam and People's Park protests. I had to get away from it all.

For Volunteer Loren Ivener, VISTA offered an escape from a far less dramatic reality. The Iowa native admitted no great idealism prompted his service. Instead, it was family pressure for him to join an uncle's farm implement business. VISTA offered six weeks of training in Florida. It was a cold winter in Iowa in 1965, and Ivener went south.

In contrast to an aimless impulse to do something new or simply visit new places, many Volunteers joined VISTA with a sense of purpose. Volunteer Harry Conard said public service was an important family tradition. His family traced its roots back to the Pilgrim era, when one ancestor gave two hundred gold sovereigns to help establish the town of Lynn, Massachusetts.

For Volunteer Anna Gottlieb, VISTA was both a personal fulfillment and her initial exposure to America. A child of Holocaust survivors from Poland who came to the U.S. in 1950, Gottlieb said her family didn't travel or participate much. She described herself as a strong person who thought she knew how bad the world could be.

Other Volunteers, particularly those with professional skills, joined the program with the simple expectation of doing the job for which their education had prepared them. For Dr. Robbie Wolf, VISTA service in Lee County had a clear objective.

> I expected to heal sick patients in what was viewed as one of the 10 poorest counties in the U.S. We accomplished this. Fifteen women alone were saved just by instituting routine pap smears on everyone coming to the clinic.

Architect Jim Mercado saw VISTA as a logical continuation of the community service work he had done in graduate school. Like Mercado, many specialists had no idea how dramatically VISTA would influence their professional careers.

Ollie Neal, the Lee County attorney who directed a medical clinic initiated by Volunteers, spoke of the national Volunteers as some of the most inspired people this country has produced.

> No question these folks were on the job. They did what had to be done with no expectation of compensation. If you hired them, you forced them into a different role. The Volunteers were motivated by a commitment to something they believed was righteous. They were bigger than anger. They figured out how to do things. They were committed to righting a wrong.

Volunteer Style

Some Volunteers adopted a personal style based on a refusal to compromise or pursue a diplomatic course of action, even to the point of rejecting administrative support. Gene Richards is attributed the saying that a Volunteer would cross the street just for the opportunity to meet an antagonist head on. In 1977, state program officer Wally Gursch commented on that attitude.

> VISTA at one time seemed to be mostly people who came galloping into Arkansas to show the people how to wear shoes and teach them you don't say "haint." They did right a lot of wrongs, but they also created a lot of ill will. They fought the local power structure instead of showing it how to change.[1]

According to Rev. Murrine Williams, this forthrightness was the result of a northern upbringing that encouraged young people to voice their opinions regardless of the consequences. The fact that Volunteers were doing things they believed to be of value added to the problem.

> The Volunteers came in to help, but they ran into opposition they knew nothing about. They saw it as a challenge, and with a youthful philosophy said they were going to do it anyhow.

Another catalyst to the Volunteers' confrontational style was the chance to test their skills in both threatening and non-threatening environments. Some felt an indebtedness to the poverty communities that accepted them. These factors put the Volunteers in situations where they could give their all regardless of the consequences.

While younger Volunteers pushed the situation to its limits, older and more mature Volunteers were willing to settle for reserved roles, seeking the long range results of their assimilation into the community. Most younger Volunteers, for better or worse, lacked that patience. Realizing there was little chance of winning long term acceptance from community power structures, some Volunteers sought the acceptance of the poverty community. One Volunteer, looking back fifteen years later, offered this explanation.

> The energy we had then is so amazing to me now. We were so full of life and ourselves, and I think all the sexual energy that most of us seemed to have then had somehow to do not just with our youth but also with comforting each other and making some life-affirming stand. It was action as a reaction to the ugliness and soul-crippling poverty.

An educated young person facing the isolation and frustration levels of early Arkansas VISTA service might attempt to elevate his situation through philosophical analysis. This was the approach of Volunteer Bob Kinderman, author of an extraordinary letter to a VISTA friend while Kinderman was stuck at a garage in Missouri because his GSA vehicle had broken down.

In the first part of the letter, Kinderman explains his predicament—how the vehicle's fan had broken loose and destroyed the radiator, how he tried to sleep out on the grass on an impromptu bed made of paper toweling, how he was awakened at 2:00 A.M. by a heavy rain storm, how he was forced to wait two days for a lost bus shipment supposedly bringing replacement parts.

Kinderman's letter, written on a four-foot length of brown paper toweling taken from the rest room of the service station where he was waiting, concludes with these paragraphs:

> All of this shit kind of gets to me. Now I can tolerate the boredom and general physical discomfort, but what does wear heavily on my mind is the feeling of total helplessness that all of this brings about. In the purest

existential sense, I am presently the sad victim of an amoral, absurd universe in which fans fly into radiators and bus shipments are lost at the most inopportune time. I can only sit here totally alone surrounded by people who can at best only pretend a mild concern for my plight. All I can do is sit and wait for the end of all this to come.

By now I suspect that you are seeing that this narrative isn't just about time spent in a gas station. In this instance, the gas station and waiting there is a rather neat, perhaps trite, microcosm of all human existence. A philosophical phrase maker has said that all of man's life is but a drop of spray splashed up from an eternal ocean to fly through the air as an individual droplet for a brief second and return forever to the sea. The point of this was that men should accept their fate, benignly accepting life as it comes, forgetting that they are anything but an indistinguishable nonentity in the finite universe.

I see the reality of this concept but reject the conclusion. This particular drop of spray is going to assert its uniqueness against the whole damn ocean as long as it is airborne. To borrow from another allegory: man is described as being belched forth by a mindless tiger onto an infinite desert. From the beginning of his existence, man is tirelessly pursued by the tiger. Man spends his entire life choosing which direction he will travel in his flight. He spends his days going from here to there until he can run no longer and is devoured by the tiger. So what are you going to do? You either run or you lay down and let the tiger take you.

But I see another choice. I choose to fight the tiger, to confront it totally, to flaunt my individuality in its very face. Life may very well be a terminal illness, but I am going to assert my health even though it kills me (I am not sure what that means myself).

So what's my problem? Well, sitting here in this gas station, the tiger seems to have overwhelmingly gotten the upper hand. The hardest part about fighting the tiger is that you apparently have to do it alone. I found however that there is support in genuinely acknowledging the existence of others. By knowing that you exist, this writing becomes more than just ink marks on paper toweling. I feel a little less alone and a little more able to defy the absurdity of the universe. Thanks for existing.

Bob K.

Volunteer Achievement

In addition to their idealism and dedication, the national Volunteers shared another important quality—a willingness to listen. Volunteers were good listeners, but selective. What many lacked in listening to their sponsoring agency, they made up for in the attention they paid to their assigned communities and to each other.

Jim Mercado explained this trait as an extension of Volunteer interest in solving problems.

> You get a bunch of Volunteers together and we'll always talk about how so and so resolved a problem. No matter what it was, poverty or bureaucracy. That's our hobby, trading war stories or project stories. How we stole tires or siphoned gas from our sponsoring agencies so we could travel to the projects.

Listening well was more often a skill the Volunteers learned through their service than one they brought into the program. Many Volunteers confused community reaction with substantive change. In retrospect, they recognize that part of their job was to listen to people and follow suggestions. At the time, however, it was far easier to get people to shout at them than to work with them.

For some Volunteers, even a negative community reaction was better than nothing. Those who challenged the power structure with little concern for tradition and established social order sometimes did bring about change. In some cases, it was necessary to disrupt the status quo in order to change it. Volunteer Bob Frank commented on those who showed little understanding of bureaucratic limitations.

> Don't underestimate the value of naïvete. If you don't know what can't be done, you just might end up doing it. The neat thing about VISTA was nothing was consistent. You couldn't plan on it, and that made things happen. It was run by personalities, by people. That is the essence of VISTA.

A tolerance for different personality types was both a VISTA strength and a program weakness. Detracting from the Volunteers' capacity to deal with human issues was their inability to deal with the social forces that kept people in a dependent condition.

Elijah Coleman, director of the Arkansas Council of Human Relations, an agency that sponsored a VISTA summer associate program, believes that Volunteers were not discouraged by human conditions but by the justice system itself, the local government or power base that would let such situations exist.

A VISTA trainer and farm manager of an east Arkansas agricultural co-op, saw the Volunteers' limited experience as the basis of frustrations. In a 1970 letter, he described the real world that greeted two recently arrived Volunteers.

> We just got two national VISTAS, a married couple, one a nurse and the other a BA generalist, to describe them in official language. In my own language, they are both very unexposed to life. They are good Christian members of the Assembly of God Church (don't drink, smoke or say "fuck"). They have seen a few black people before, but they were all educated school types rather than the field nigger so dominant around these parts.
>
> They got thrown out of the house they were renting. The woman they were renting from found out they would be associating with blacks. Not that she had anything against "nigras." The Bible more or less says integration is sinful, etc., etc. I guess they have had a good case of culture shock since they arrived.

VISTA frustration grew out of many things. For some, it came from listening passively to supervisors instead of challenging them.

For others, it resulted from assignments to office tasks or paperwork. As one resigning Volunteer wrote, "I prefer banging nails to writing proposals."

While they may have lacked exposure to the world of poverty and local power groups, national Volunteers generally had a liberal education and the ability to laugh at themselves. Self mockery is mixed with strong program insight and social observations in the final report of Aviv Goldsmith, a national Volunteer assigned to Jonesboro with Community Energy Futures, a 1980 project to increase community awareness of solar energy and other low cost systems. In a section of that report, Goldsmith wrote:

> As a naive, young college type, I thought, sure, this can work. All it needs is some dynamic people to stay on top of things. Everybody should be concerned by the energy crisis. Reality slowly impinged upon my notions. The most obvious flaw was that the community did not apply for our assistance . . . One bead of sweat on a local builder's forehead in a solar greenhouse is worth a lot more than one hour of a community energy council meeting. How many faces have we seen light up after feeling the hot water coming from a solar heater?
>
> I've learned that social change takes more than just one bright guy from New York. It takes time, time, time, and it takes attacks at problems from every possible tack. I learned about bureaucracy, about Southern life, about Baptists, about grits and hushpuppies. It is not a college town. There aren't always bagels and funky bars. It is rural America. It's Ronnie Reagan and Frank White and my election day ballot cast for every losing ticket.
>
> It was a year in which the energy consumed by eight Vistoids in their state-wide travels exceeded any aggregate energy savings they might impart to their communities. I met and learned to love my Vistoid brothers and sisters. I got beans and beads and crabs in New Orleans. I set a new personal record for celibacy. I drank a lot of alcohol and slept a lot. I took a lot of pictures and sent a lot of letters. Hopefully, the experience will be more than a hemmorroid in the annals of history. Nothing ventured, nothing gained/lost.

Most national Volunteers, pressed to make a personal assessment of their VISTA time, admit to failures and victories. Community figures who knew the Volunteers well also generally offer a balanced appraisal. Yet, for the most part, it is their positive work that is remembered.

Robert Johnson, who worked closely with two female Volunteers at a Mississippi County farming co-op, said that the women never let the community down. The Volunteer presence and the lessons they taught are vivid in his VISTA memories.

> They did something that had never been done before. They taught us to be self-sustaining, that you go and make a living and don't wait for someone to do for you. When they took a chopping hoe and went out into the fields or stood over a hot stove and canned, that was the contact. Others would send us out but not go with us. The Volunteers kept themselves below the people looking up, not above looking down. They taught us that all people were created equal.

Notes

1. *Arkansas Gazette,* September 22, 1977

EAST ARKANSAS

POVERTY AND CIVIL RIGHTS

Social Perspective

Racial Perspective

Health Advocate Program

Sandy Smegelsky

Gene Richards

Respect, Inc.

Jerry Hornsby and the GE Office at West Memphis

Margo English and the Abson Wynne Co-op

The United People's Co-op

Lee County Co-operative Medical Clinic

Ollie Neal

Long Range VISTA Impact

Social Perspective

The VISTA experience in east Arkansas is a story stripped bare of social pretense and the mask of cooperation used by many communities to disguise a mistrust of the Volunteers and their projects. In east Arkansas, the Volunteers encountered primal forces that matched the open landscape and the seemingly endless fields of dusty cotton and soybean rows. Frances Woods recalled these physical impressions:

> I remember the stark beauty of the Delta, especially the sunsets, the rich black earth, the flat horizons, magnolias that evoke feelings in me no other place can. It seemed so earthy. Cold rainy winters, mud everywhere. Springs so full of promise and sweetness.

For the young Volunteer of the late 60s, particularly one from an urban background, the Delta landscape could reaffirm his life values. Gene Richards spoke of the Delta as:

> . . . a kind of place without traditional beauty, but I had a real sense of being alive there, close to the elements of heat and cold. My feelings of the Delta are so positive. I still love the place.

Others saw the landscape and the life styles it imposed with a more cynical eye, a view that mixed impressions of the physical surroundings with the motivational values that originally brought them there. Christel Brellochs recalled:

Homes and outhouses in the Black neighborhood at Osceola. *Photo by Gene Richards*

. . . cars are lined up for miles behind the full, waddling cotton trailers, the compressors roar with regularity and a yellow haze reminiscent of Los Angeles comes from the fields . . . People won't be able to work by the end of the month. Back to the plantation version of Bank Americard. Interest, though, is higher.

East Arkansas is a land where cotton was king, and society was shaped by the plantation system. The poor of east Arkansas are victims of that system. Plantation system economics remained long after the implementation of minimum wage laws and mechanized farming turned the simple agrarian iniquities of sharecropping into the starvation and degradation of labor displacement.

The Delta poverty conditions that greeted the first wave of Volunteers in the late 1960s were staggering. More than half the area families earned less than three thousand dollars per year, the poverty level at that time, and 80 percent of the area housing was substandard. Yet it was not statistics that greeted the volunteers, but the appalling effect of an impoverished life on the human body and spirit.

PROBLEM SOLVING CASE #1

Mamie Reeves, 34, lives with 10 children in a two room shack without indoor plumbing. Wood is burned for heat in a very small pot belly stove. The top of the stove holds one pan for cooking. Water is hauled a quarter mile for washing and cooking. Rats frequent the dwelling. Mamie applied for welfare assistance for her children two years ago. She was refused without explanation.

Her only income is part time farm work, and she purchases food stamps for $3 to obtain $96 worth of stamps. During the months she has no income, she borrows money to buy the stamps. Without welfare assistance she cannot afford aspirin. She has "adjusted" to bouts of cold and flu. She cannot afford soap and sundries, so the children are dirty and live in unsanitary conditions which lead to medical expenses that cannot be afforded. Without adequate clothing, the children of school age are reluctant to attend. Apathy is apparent as their life continues its cycle.

You are a VISTA. Break the cycle of Mrs. Reeves' life for the better.

(From a 1969 General Electric training manual for east Arkansas Volunteers)

Jerry Hornsby, VISTA project coordinator in West Memphis, said the attitude at that time in county welfare departments and food stamp offices was to keep people off benefits rather than to extend benefits to those eligible. He spoke of an elderly black man with a chronically bad back that made him unable to stand erect. The man was denied welfare disability payments, Hornsby said, because the county office thought it acceptable for him to pick cotton on his knees.

Hornsby also recalled a member of the white community far more direct in expressing his degree of human concern.

Some of the volunteers would go to the Mississippi River and collect driftwood to distribute to poor families for fuel. The driftwood piled up in enormous quantities and was there for the taking. We would cram it into our VISTA vehicles and deliver it door to door. This infuriated Mr. R . . . , a prominent white businessman who owned a hardware store near our office.

"I wouldn't haul wood to any niggers," he once said. "If they run out of wood, let them rip up their floors."

Agriculture had always been the primary source of revenue for the Delta. By the late 1960s, federal subsidies to farms were supporting major plantations in a six-county area with approximately $25.4 million per year. At the same time, government support of the area's food programs for the poor totaled just over two million dollars per year.[1]

Hornsby brought this situation to the attention of a Congressional committee debating a twenty-thousand dollar ceiling for farm subsidy payments. Congressman Silvio Conte of Massachusetts read into the *Congressional Record* these remarks from a letter Hornsby wrote him.

Our company, under a contract with the Office of Economic Opportunity, is training and supporting the VISTA Volunteers in six counties in eastern Arkansas. These counties are among America's poorest. The volunteers here, while working on the whole spectrum of poverty problems, are concerned particularly with the health and hunger problems of the families with whom they work.

Daily we see the paradox of people going hungry and malnourished while large tracts of productive farm land are permitted to lie idle; the paradox of people being underfed while Congress frets about farm surpluses that would hurt the pocketbooks of plantation owners; the paradox of mothers not having enough money to buy food and milk for their babies, while wealthy farmers receive large payments not to produce crops; . . . the paradox of malnourished babies suffering irreversible brain damage in their first 18 months of life, while rich farm people, beef gravy dribbling from their lips, deride the mental capacities of the tenants who shovel the barnyard manure and hand gather the last remnants of cotton left by the picking machine.

. . . And how's this for paradox . . . at Hughes, a tenant farmer recently collected 23 cents for two weeks' work. The man labored 63.5 hours at $1.30 an hour for gross earning of $82.55. The plantation owner deducted $3.96 for Social Security and $78.36 for the plantation store account, leaving the laborer a net of 23 cents. This same plantation owner received $80,110 in subsidy payments last year.[2]

Hornsby's letter went on to suggest that the farmer might be paid to grow food for the poor on his idle land. Such an idea was an idealistic fantasy for the Arkansas Delta in the late 1960s. Community attitudes would not tolerate any notion of a federal subsidy for the poor beyond the limited assistance provided by county offices.

Grass roots efforts to organize poor farmers into cooperative farms and buying clubs met a similar resistance. Lucille Warren, board chairman of the United People's Co-op, a 1969 VISTA project spread out over three locations in Mississippi County, commented on that opposition.

After we started the buying clubs, the grocers began complaining. When the Volunteers started to help the poor with food, money, and housing, all hell broke loose. The landlords didn't want tenants to know how poorly they were being treated. Newspapers came in and started spreading stories of a Communist invasion. Then the big stores in Osceola began fighting us. Since the people got together, there's always been opposition trying to keep the small man down.

A 1968 study identified Lee County as one of the six poorest in the nation, a place where tuberculosis, parasites, and malnutrition were widespread, where the black infant mortality rate was more than twice the national average, where the school dropout rate was nearly seventy-two percent, and almost half the adult population were functionally illiterate.

Based partly on that report, Governor Winthrop Rockefeller agreed to a large VISTA undertaking, a multi-county project whose volunteers would be called Health Advocates. Among the early members of that group was Dr. Dan Blumenthal, the first VISTA physician in the nation, and one of the Volunteers who assisted in establishing the Lee County Co-operative Clinic at Marianna.

We viewed a scene archetypical of rural poverty in the cotton South. Outside of town there were scattered plantation houses owned by white gentlemen farmers. Down the road was, typically, a collection of tumbledown wooden shacks inhabited by black field hands. Living in similar shacks were elderly blacks and poor whites too old to farm and too unschooled to do anything else, who lived on social security checks or on food stamps, or on seemingly nothing at all. Typically, their houses were located on dirt roads that became impassable when it rained.[3]

The Arkansas Gazette called the VISTA project "A Test At Marianna," and reviewed initial local resistance to Volunteer work in a 1969 editorial. The "paternalistic society of East Arkansas' rich farming empire" would be given a chance to display its attitudes, the Gazette editors wrote, and the situation at Marianna offered "an opportunity to show that Lee County is more committed to the proposition that the poor need VISTA's services than it is to . . . putting down the Negro."[4]

The response from outspoken Lee County white citizens was immediate. T. H. Barker, president of the Lee County Farm Bureau, sent these remarks to the Little Rock newspaper:

> Lee County did not acquire this poverty status until a group of bureaucrats decided we should wear this label . . . an untrue stigma placed on our people by such as you . . . I hope the VISTAS have been frustrated by the "farming empire" . . . for we have been frustrated by many bureaucratic mandates . . . that you and your kind have administered on an unsuspecting community . . . The fact that the Arkansas Gazette is sympathetic to their cause is enough evidence to run VISTA out of town.[5]

Echoing the regional dissatisfaction with VISTA and state policy, Milton Davis of Marianna also made his feelings known in a published letter.

> I know of no town that VISTA has been in that has not had racial strife and turmoil. When the good citizens get fed up and run these trouble makers out of town, they run straight to Little Rock to a man from New York who has bought out the Statehouse, and he puts them on the OEO payroll at a ridiculous salary so they can expand their trouble making . . . To me this is

Young girl in east Arkansas—*Photo by Gene Richards*

nothing but socialized anarchy. It is about time we all . . . demanded that our government put these funds to better use.[6]

Into this environment, the first wave of VISTA Volunteers came, bringing with them their personal motivations, their ideals, their hopes for social change. Despite the physical conditions of poverty and the prevailing negative attitudes, many of them found what they were hoping for, found it in the indomitable spirit of the area's most destitute people.

For a Forrest City black woman, VISTA became an extension of a personal commitment to human service. Mrs. Delcinia Robinson, who became one of the area's outstanding locally recruited VISTA Volunteers, told of a life in poverty that could symbolize the world of many east Arkansas blacks.

Back then we just had a wood heater and all six of us would stay in that room. It was terrible. I didn't like living in two rooms, with an outside faucet that would freeze up. We felt separated from others. Ashamed of being in this condition.

Every day I'd pray, "Lord, help me to get out of this situation to help others." My feelings started with my neighbors. We had nothing, but some of them didn't even have that. My kids would walk to school in winter in tennis shoes, but some kids didn't go to school in the winter because they didn't have shoes.

That was my motivation, to get myself out so I could get others out. I am glad I am poor, because if I weren't, I might not know how to treat people and understand their problems. Maybe I wouldn't have this feeling to help.

Racial Perspective

The origins of poverty in East Arkansas were undoubtedly rooted in the slow demise of its agricultural system, the decades required for the fall of a cotton empire, and the gradual dissolution of the meager sustenance on which field hands and tenant farmers depended.

While a state of poverty may begin with a single historical turning point, it can grow into a complex network of accepted values and, breeding on itself, create a life standard which establishes itself as the encompassing attitudes of an area.

In Forrest City, a town named for the Confederate General who founded the Ku Klux Klan, those values were well articulated by Robert Shelton, Imperial Wizard of that same malevolent cult, who spoke at a 1970 rally in the municipal auditorium.

> You who are God fearing, above those despicable "isms," Communism and Judaism, I have come to help you in your decisions . . . Are you going to be brainwashed by television into accepting the idea of peaceful coexistence, the downfall of morals in schools? . . . Black children make fences with their bodies and rape our children. News of these rapes and beatings are being suppressed . . .
>
> And take my word, to get the Jewish vote, Nixon will withdraw troops from Vietnam . . . The survival of the Christ nation is at stake . . . Christ was not a Jew. Christ was conceived by an act of God, by the Holy Ghost, was conceived in a virgin, not an act of man. Christ was not a Jew . . .

[On the welfare program] The first illegitimate child receives $30, then Susie Q lives in low rental housing paid for by you taxpayers. Up drives the boyfriend in a black Cadillac paid for by the Small Business Adminstration. They drive to the day care center, leave the $30 baby, then realize its commodities day—they slip in for surplus food and sweet susie wine, then to bed to start work for a salary increase . . . after nine months it materializes.[7]

The civil rights struggle in the Delta lagged far behind that of most other areas of the country. There were strivings, but in Hornsby's view, much of the area's black leadership were from the "old school," the school of patience founded on a fear of causing too many ripples and a reluctance to confront the established order head on.

A level of militancy had not been reached. You had only white VISTAS agitating for improvement. The anger in East Arkansas had not yet become focused, the organizing not yet developed, the leadership not yet emerged. The Delta of 1969–70 was a kettle that had just begun warming. It still had a way to go before boiling over.

For the Volunteers, some personal adjustments were necessary to deal with the area's outwardly expressed and accepted racism. Separate drinking fountains and facilities, columns in the newspapers for "Colored News," communities with token black police officers not allowed to arrest whites, and the local white citizens councils—all this took some getting used to. Blumenthal said even the local medical community had some lessons to teach the Volunteers

Dr. Dwight Gray taught me what Lee County was all about. He leveled with me as a fellow southern doctor, one of the clan, and said he had segregated waiting rooms because that's what the colored folks wanted, and he winked.[8]

Any initial confidence by the white community in the Volunteers quickly gave way to anger and harassment when it became clear where their sympathies lay and what actions they were planning.

Due to their association with black people and their efforts for improvement, the Volunteers were viewed with the same blind hatred reserved for other pariahs of the established white community.

In a 1971 letter that was one of many attempts to remove VISTA from the Delta, the Lee County Citizens Council called on its own to rally support of the ideals they believed in jeopardy.

> Most of you are aware of what happened in Forrest City just two summers ago. Some of you may even know the riots and civil disorders were a direct result of the NAACP (NATIONAL ASSOCIATION for the AGITATION of COLORED PEOPLE), OEO, VISTA (VIPERS in SUBVERSION to AMERICA), and other trouble making organizations. These same Communist organizations are the cause of the population ratio in Marianna to change from approximately 50% white–50% colored in 1968 to 40% white–60% colored in 1971.
>
> . . . There is only one question left to answer. Are YOU going to join with others NOW OR AFTER they burn your business or home or assault your wife or daughter? . . .[9]

Those Volunteers who closely associated themselves with the black community ran the highest risk of harassment. Gene Richards, never one to shy away from a confrontation, recalled wrestling with a Wynne cafe owner to keep him from using a shotgun on two black girls. Richards recounted two other troubling incidents:

> After an auto accident with a drunk man driving on the wrong side of the road, I learned he was anti-VISTA. I had found this dog and took it in. It had mange when I found it but I brought it to health. Then it disappeared. I later learned the dog used to be his. He took it back and shot it. Kind of makes you want to stop being a pacifist.
>
> The most obvious, ugliest police harassment came when the West Memphis police rounded up a half dozen neighborhood stray dogs, brought them to our yard, and shot them. I don't know what prompted it. A demonstration that we were not terribly welcome.

For all the outward manifestations of Delta violence, the most damaging attack on a VISTA Volunteer was inflicted on two visitors to the area who happened to be in the wrong place at the wrong time. In June 1969, a VISTA Summer Associate and his friend were

VISTA nurse Corrine Cass teaches use of an oxygen machine at the Lee County Co-operative Medical Clinic. *Photo courtesy of ACTION*

in a Hughes cafe when, mistaken by locals for Gene Richards and another Health Advocate, they were brutally attacked without cause and severely beaten with coffee cups and other items.

One of the youths emerged from the beating with a severed artery, a "spurter," according to Joe Bruch. Bruch credits Corrine Cass, a Volunteer nurse in Lee County with saving the boy's life after he was refused treatment by a local doctor.

Bruch said he also learned the local police were "polite but uninterested" in the beating and that state police refused to assist the boys until they got themselves across the county line. Bruch's investigation of the beating brought him to the conclusion that the "wheels of justice have ground to a halt," that the "system" had failed them completely.

Only after repeated attempts to pursue a judicial follow-up, after threatening federal prosecutors with Time/Life exposure if they did not get involved, did Bruch manage to get some results. In February 1970, an indictment against the two attackers was returned by a federal grand jury in Little Rock.

Such was the environment of East Arkansas at the end of the 1960s, a time when the flower decade was withering on the California coast, when Viet Nam raged and Nixon raised his arms in twin victory signs, when close to forty Health Advocate Volunteers were being trained or were on site at their east Arkansas assignments.

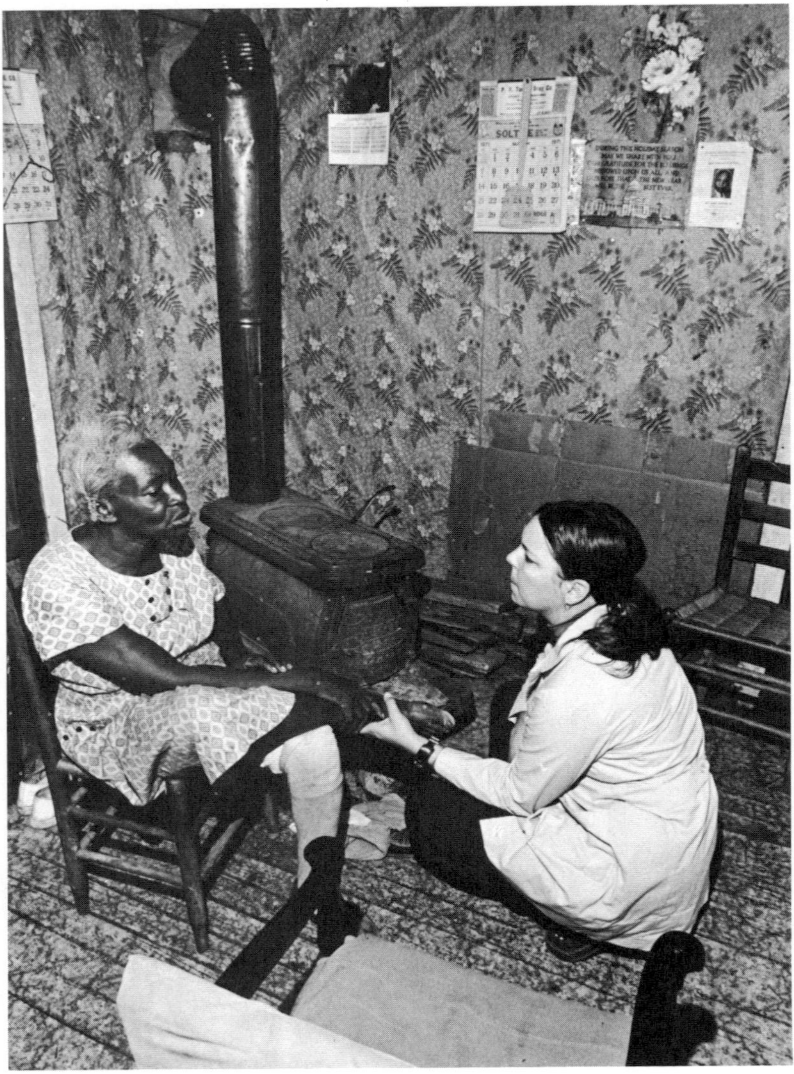

Joan Smith, a Volunteer nurse with the Lee County Clinic in 1971, makes a home visit. *Photo courtesy of ACTION*

Health Advocate Program

The Health Advocate Program, designed as a pioneering effort, was the most ambitious VISTA project undertaken in Arkansas. Six East Arkansas counties (Cross, Crittenden, St. Francis, Lee, Woodruff, Mississippi) were to receive up to fifty specially trained national volunteers for a one-year experimental program.

It was to be a VISTA program of massive proportions, and its successes and failures proved in time to be equally enormous. It brought to Arkansas a group of people who found themselves in a "sink or swim" situation. Those who survived were able to establish their independence, a feat few Volunteers in later projects were able to match.

The Health Advocate Program attempted to enlarge the scope of health services by coordinating medical professionals—national and community Volunteers—in areas of health and nutrition, housing, sanitation, economic development, and programs and laws. The Volunteers were expected to channel information back into a newly created Arkansas Health Planning Commission for development of a comprehensive health program for the Delta.

On a larger scale, the program was also to create a national health planning curriculum. The original training contract was awarded by the Emergency Food and Medical Services of OEO to the Westinghouse Learning Corp. The contract was taken over in the spring of 1969 by the General Electric Corporation who established the Austin training cycle and opened the project support office in West Memphis. The GE staff was to document the overall program and its many subsidiary projects, then report to OEO on how a similar program could be implemented nationally.

In concept, the Health Advocate program was like all VISTA projects in that it attempted to create an on-going social mechanism that would eventually stand on its own and improve the nature of life. Conceived as more than "Band-aid" assistance, the program would not be limited to providing needed medical attention, according to Dr. Clyde Hart, then state OEO director.

> We'll never do much for the poverty problem if we concentrate only on getting someone to a hospital. If we are going to make progress, we must deal with a problem before it happens.[10]

The failure of many Health Advocate projects may have been that its designers did not realize the human dimensions or the depth of problems that existed in East Arkansas—details such as a community's ingrained racism, a national corporation's concern for its public image, or the capacity of a Volunteer to subjugate personal service for the collective good.

Hornsby commented on the Volunteers' inability to turn off their human concern in support of objective policy.

> VISTAS cannot be passive observers. They must play the advocate's role. The Volunteer soon learns that people's day-to-day survival can not be put off or take second place behind the noble cause of organizing. There are times when direct service and organizing flow hand in hand. But when a nine-year old boy walks two miles on a freezing day to tell you his family has nothing to eat, there is your priority. And there are 20 more just like him lined up.

Brellochs expressed the same concept with the Volunteers' characteristic candor:

> The project was so designed to solve hunger and malnutrition problems. Our conclusion was that people needed more and better food. That or just more money.

Brellochs' conclusion does not identify the steps necessary to reach that obvious goal. To prepare her and other Health Advocate Volunteers for their work, GE trainers created a detailed curriculum that gave each Volunteer a wide exposure to his specific area of service.

Programs and Laws specialists took a crash course in Arkansas civics—three weeks of meetings with state government officials and community representatives, including shifts in a police patrol car, sessions at juvenile court, hospital emergency rooms, and more.

Economic Development specialists learned co-op principles by visiting buying clubs, credit unions, farmers' co-ops, and agricultural marketing associations in other southern states. They picked vegetables and were sent to bookkeeping classes.

Housing and Sanitation Volunteers visited Alabama and Mississippi cooperatives where communities made the bricks, roofing trusses, and other materials they would later use to build their own houses.

Health and Nutrition Volunteers visited the Tufts University-Delta Health Center at Mound Bayou, Mississippi (as did most of the other Health Advocates) for a first hand look at how a successful community medical clinic operated.

The training was more intense and longer than for most Volunteers at that time, and it was superior because of the specific orientation presented. During training, the Volunteers were also visited by John Clark, then director of the East Central Arkansas Equal Opportunities Council, the agency that, along with the Mississippi County EOC, would sponsor them.

> I was invited to tell them what East Arkansas life was like. I told them and tried not to pull any punches. I told them you could come up missing if you upset the power structure.

Clark also had to convince his local board members to ignore the negative image they had picked up from news accounts of Volunteers as troublemakers. His strongest selling point to the board was the specialty training the VISTAs had received and their ability to do things that no one else in the area could do. He finally overcame their hesitancy to approve the program by reminding them they could always have the Volunteers removed.

When the Health Advocate Volunteers arrived, Clark and Ted Wilson, the agency supervisor let them identify problems in their assigned communities and work on them as they saw fit. The lack of initial project structure and guidance contributed to the failure of some Volunteers, but Wilson believed it was the only way the overall program could be run at the time.

> For those for whom it did not work out, it was my hope they did not leave feeling a failure. It was less they had failed personally as this was simply not an environment for which everyone was made, no matter how much they wanted to believe they were able to function in it.

As a group, the Volunteers relied more on each other for their planning and evaluation than they did agency personnel. According to Brellochs, some of them believed the agency was an integral part of the problem they were trying to solve.

> We treated the local sponsors as obstacles and didn't see them as people we could co-op into the process. [And we made] an attempt to keep them out of our way. I think we thought we were hot shits, and we treated people who gave us advice accordingly. Their job was to get us the car and resources. The group of Health Advocates saw ourselves as a unit, had regular meetings. Joe Bruch was a positive force, took care of us, kept our egos massaged.

Sandy Smegelsky

Sandy Smegelsky was a twenty-two-year old Health Advocate Volunteer trained in Programs and Laws. The Syracuse, New York native recalled her first weeks in the Delta when she and another volunteer received their on-the-job training at some unidentified country location in the home of an elderly, retarded woman.

> That first day, I kept looking for facilities. No outhouse either. Finally went out into the field at night. That was when I first met a cow. I literally bumped into it. I screamed and Monica came running out.

Smegelsky spoke of the heat, the bedbugs, the isolation of that rural existence, and the empathy it created in her for persons deprived of motivation. When the training period ended and she was placed in West Memphis, she remembered being told to do good and stay out of trouble, but she could not recall being given any specific assignment.

Smegelsky began acting as an advocate in employment and welfare hearings, and was soon making frequent trips in her GSA car to Little Rock and Memphis in support of applicants' cases. Hornsby remembered her as tireless in that role.

> Sandy was a revolution all by herself. She could tackle the toughest case where an applicant had been denied welfare, food stamps, or social security benefits, and through her skill, perseverence, and superior knowledge of the regulations, get the applicant approved more often than not.

Volunteer Sandy Smegelsky

Sandy taught us many things. I have the memory of her on an icy day when the roads were impassable. Sandy came in needing a car to get people to their appointments. She would not accept the icy streets as an excuse. Somehow she borrowed a car and kept the appointments without accident. It was a feat of the highest bravery.

The actions that impress others are not always the same ones an individual considers significant. Smegelsky laughed when she recalled a mail-order minister's card she used to take advantage of the Southern respect for religion and gain access to the West Memphis jail. When the police discovered she was using it to visit and counsel black prisoners, she said she was roughly escorted out and told never to come back.

Respect for authority was not always a humorous matter in the Delta, particularly when the authority was an enigmatic stranger with a shotgun in his arms who stopped your vehicle on a dark country road and inquired about your destination.

Smegelsky recalled such an encounter when she and three other Volunteers were driving out to visit a little black church one winter night. There had been a lot of Klan activity and the man whose truck blocked the road came up to their vehicle with his weapon in his arms and asked them if they knew anything about "Commies" around the area.

Informed of their destination, the man said. "That's a black church. I don't think you should go there." The volunteers turned around and returned to town. Smegelsky recalled her emotions at the time.

> We were scared. We had a sense of being overpowered, but we were guilty as hell. It was a combination of anger and frustration, the feeling that there was nothing we could do. I had heard of the three civil rights workers killed in Mississippi. It was terrifying for me. Other times, I was more angry. It was all you could do to keep from being angry, but anger was not effective in problem solving.

Smegelsky remained in West Memphis following her VISTA service, completed law school, and spent several years as director of East Central Arkansas Legal Services. She currently lives in Memphis and works out of St. Patrick's Church for Habitat for Humanity, a community development organization.

Gene Richards

A sense of confrontation accompanied by the desire to challenge perceived wrongs can be found in many VISTAs. In east Arkansas, the Volunteers lacked no opportunity to exercise that particular tendency and no Health Advocate seemed to make a more deliberate attempt at it than Gene Richards. Richards was a twenty-five-year-old from a Massachusetts working class family, who had burned his draft card, then chose a stint in VISTA in preference to a term in jail. In 1969, he was assigned to Augusta (Woodruff County) to develop a youth recreation program and assess community health and housing needs. He didn't last long there.

Richards immediately violated social rules by cultivating friendships with black youths and hiring black assistants. Rumors spread of his liaisons with black females. He was warned that bringing black children to the local movie theater was inappropriate, and the local police broke up a swimming party he arranged for black youths at a White River segregated swimming area.

In VISTA, I was alone for the first time in my life, and my pride in being able to function alone was mixed with a great deal of loneliness. The only people who understand are those in your group, but like friendships that depends on situations, when the conditions broke, the friendships broke. It became a private thing you didn't want to give up. Reminds me of dreams, so vital, change you so much.

Volunteer and Respect member Gene Richards

Richards was transferred from Augusta, but the confrontation at the Wynne cafe soon followed. Within six months of service, Richards resigned from VISTA and began a two-year involvement with Respect, Inc., a private anti-poverty organization he founded with other ex-Volunteers in West Memphis. Richards received several beatings during his East Arkansas years, and he was attacked and slashed with a razor by a man in West Memphis. He was hospitalized for a short time and subject to periods of amnesia.

Serving as a reporter and photographer for *Many Voices,* the newspaper published by Respect, Richards began taking the photographs of East Arkansas and black poverty scenes that would later be published in the book, *Few Comforts or Surprises: The Arkansas Delta.* In an unpublished introduction Frances Woods describes Richards' delta photography.

Some will criticize it as belonging to that class of work which titillates the liberal bleeding heart, feeds a neurotic guilt, and produces no human change. Some will object that the impressions are one sided. Where is the joy? Why does it all seem so stark and terrifying . . .

This book is not a documentary account of people's lives, it is not documentary photography . . . I view this work as an intensely personal one . . .

Richards is currently a New York-based photojournalist with several published books.

"The pride of the Delta people is not to lay their grief on you. As a guest, they don't want to upset you. Improper to burden a guest. Biggest disturbance was the amount of ill education and retardation. That was the biggest shock. And the fact that I couldn't do anything about it."—1984 interview with Gene Richards. *Photo by Gene Richards.*

GENE RICHARDS

"When you first come into a community, you meet the most vocal at first. The shocks come later. You meet folks with cataracts or missing limbs, loads of retardation. Their pride keeps those problems out of sight at first. The children tell you of their dysfunctions. Initially, it looks bad. Later you find out it's much worse." —1984 interview with Gene Richards. *Photo by Gene Richards.*

"People in the Black community put me through the wringer. I was just beginning to make photos. People didn't want to be shown as poor. They made me eat chitterlings and spend the night before I could take a photo. The best work comes from sharing a lifestyle."—1984 interview with Gene Richards. *Photo by Gene Richards.*

"I spend most hours on the south side of town where the people, for all their woes, are at least much alive, communicating with each other, not internally frozen." —1970 letter, Gene Richards to Frances Woods. *Photo by Gene Richards.*

Respect, Inc.

The VISTA program in East Arkansas could continue only as long as the sponsoring agencies agreed to keep it there. This meant Volunteers could not attack the social issues that most directly affected poverty without disturbing a complacent system and jeopardizing their own placement.

Inadequate consumer protection laws, ineffective welfare administration, and substandard education were some of these issues. As a result of his attempts to confront them, Gene Richards was transferred from Augusta. Another Health Advocate, Charles Imhoff was advised to cut his long hair if he wanted local cooperation, and he too was transferred out. Both resigned from VISTA soon afterwards.

Richards was replaced by Earl and Cheri Anthes, an Iowa couple considered more socially acceptable because of their marriage. Earl was trained in Programs and Laws, while Cheri, a nurse, was assigned health related duties. They recalled the county sheriff's reaction to their placement, "just glad they didn't send us any more of those perverts." The Anthes also resigned from VISTA within a few months for reasons similar to his own, Richards said.

> VISTA never had the goals we wanted it to. The role of VISTA was not to enforce laws or comment on existing situations. It was to bring help. How do you do that without admitting a problem? We had to get out.

Volunteers and Respect members Cheri and Earl Anthes.

The ex-Volunteers regrouped in West Memphis and formed Respect, Inc., a private, anti-poverty organization that undertook direct services to the poor. Its first efforts involved a food distribution program supplied by contributions from Massachusetts and Minnesota with a trucking company providing free transport of the goods.

Respect received a VISTA grant to inform residents of their welfare rights and a contract from the federal Human Rights Commission for voter registration work. It also provided transportation for rural applicants to county welfare offices. Despite the grants, the group's primary support came from Cheri Anthes, whose salary as a county health nurse was their only real income.

The most visible work performed by Respect, however, was the publication of the newspaper *Many Voices,* an attempt to give the

Charlie Imhoff, Dorothea Lynch, and Gene Richards outside the West Memphis office of Respect, Inc., 1970.

black populace of East Arkansas its own vehicle of expression and establish a balanced reporting of events. Common practice in area newspapers at that time was to give racial identification of black criminal suspects and state racial requirements in classified employment ads.

EXCERPTS FROM *Many Voices*

8/70—PRIVATE SCHOOLS WILL EXCLUDE BLACKS—"Not Anti-Negro"—Travis Case, pastor of Tabernacle Baptist Church of West Memphis—". . . if any blacks show up at Tabernacle Baptist Academy they will be turned away. It has nothing to do with race. We are not anti-negro."

Rev. Bob Alston of the West Memphis Central Baptist Church and school called his facility a "Christian school" . . . however, only white Christians will be allowed to get in. Alston cited the Bible as absolute and irrefutable proof that God intended for the races to be separate . . .

11/70—BLACKS PLAN FOR CIVIL ACTION . . . 700 ATTEND LEE COUNTY RALLY . . . SCHOOL LUNCH LAW: DOES YOUR SCHOOL MEASURE UP? . . . LAW 'N ORDER IN EARLE—Black students staged a school walkout protesting segregated classrooms . . . 29 arrested. VIOLENCE ERUPTS—students and adults march through Earle streets to protest . . . gunfire and shotgun wielding whites dispersed the group . . . Mrs. Jessie Maples shot in the stomach . . . Mrs. Ezra Greer, a candidate for mayor, and her husband, a civil rights activist, were severely beaten and arrested.

11/70—MADISON ELECTS FULL BLACK SLATE . . . BLACK ALDERMEN ELECTED IN GILMORE AND TURRELL . . . LIVES DEPEND ON ENFORCING HOUSING CODE—Caution: Your House May Be Hazardous To Your Health.

5/71—FORREST CITY TEACHERS FILE SUIT— . . . class action suit against school district on behalf of all black teachers, charges district paying different salaries for black and white teachers, race distinction used in promotions . . .

Many Voices also featured articles advising readers on welfare and voting rights, and it provided a community sounding board for issues and activities.

In a letter written at the time, Richards said working on the paper was "usually fun, much more work than I've done in a long, long time." He predicted the journal would soon be community run and said it had received letters of support praising it for its "superior blackness and black enterprise."

The white community was expectedly less supportive. Lon Mann, a wealthy white farmer and school board president from Marianna, called the paper a "hate sheet that dwells on envy and hatred as vote-getters for the black power group."[11]

Many Voices never achieved its goal of creating the black community support needed to keep it going. It stopped publication when Respect was disbanded. That occurred soon after funds from a sizable grant disappeared under questionable circumstances linked to a local black man hired as director of the organization. Anthes, however, believes the newspaper made a valuable contribution.

Many Voices accomplished its purpose of raising consciousness. Its value was to link the organizations in small towns around the Delta and show others in the same struggle. The ball was rolling, the political pot boiling. I don't think *Many Voices* could have done more had it the time or money. It was a powerful tool in its day.

Following Respect, Earl Anthes joined with Jerry Cronin, an ex-volunteer from south Arkansas, to form Independent Community Consultants, a private training and consulting firm that has provided assistance to many Arkansas VISTA projects as well as national and international nonprofit organizations. Cheri continued her work with area health agencies. The Anthes are the only original Health Advocate Volunteers who continue to live in East Arkansas.

Jerry Hornsby
And the GE Office at West Memphis

Major national corporations became involved in the poverty program by bidding to OEO for the training and support contracts. General Electric Corporation was awarded the contract for the Health Advocates project, and in late 1968, all seemed full of promise. By the spring of 1970, GE's involvement in the project had been withdrawn and the support staff had been fired, as the company narrowly averted a consumer product boycott that would have undoubtedly created a major public relations scandal.

These events were engendered largely by the efforts and idealism of one man, Jerry Hornsby, the project coordinator hired by GE to oversee its involvement in East Arkansas. According to Ted Wilson, GE could not have made a worse hiring choice in terms of achieving the project's corporate goals.

> Jerry Hornsby was a man possessed. There was a determination in him to bring change and empowerment to poor people that was messianic in its dimensions. He was so unrelenting in his pursuit, there was bound to be conflict. He refused to play any kind of politics or even discuss politics or his own standards of conduct and behavior.

GE hired Hornsby, who had recently resigned as an editorial writer at a Birmingham, Alabama newspaper, to develop funding proposals to OEO and the Department of Labor. Assigned to the newly created socio-economic section at Bay St. Louis, Mississippi, Hornsby said he rapidly learned from section executives that the company's real motivation was to win favors in the government and gain lucrative space and defense contracts.

Hornsby's disillusionment with GE was strengthened by what he called the "slap it together" approach taken in creating budget and text proposals for poverty projects. Hornsby also contends that GE somehow learned competitive bids in certain projects and deliberately lowered their figures to win contracts.

The price of "buying in" would be recovered by revising the budget later on to require additional government financial support. Hornsby claims he witnessed several of these maneuvers, but took no action at the time to expose them.

In December 1968, Hornsby received an invitation from OEO to bid on a program to train VISTA Volunteers for placement in five southwestern states. Though the deadline was just two weeks away, the proposal was written, submitted in time, and, with a proposed budget of $500,000 being the lowest submitted, the contract was tentatively awarded.

GE sent Hornsby and three executives to Washington, DC, to defend the proposal before an OEO-VISTA panel. According to Hornsby, the men admitted to him on the plane they hadn't even read the proposal but assured him they would have a brain storming session on it that night. Following a large dinner, Hornsby said this episode occurred.

> One of the three men was a renowned farter, a maestro of farting. He could deliver different farts with each step. He could deliver certain sounding farts on request. He could virtually play a tune. Once a year he would play a joke at the Bay St. Louis office by farting in the building's air ducts. That night was a farting party at the motel, with the three men trying to outdo each other. There was no discussion of the proposal.

The GE team stumbled through the hearing the next day and somehow won the contract. With that auspicious beginning,

Hornsby was sent to Austin, Texas to help coordinate the Volunteer training at St. Edward's University. Soon afterwards, he learned he would be coordinator of a pilot project that would place up to fifty Health Advocate volunteers in the Arkansas Delta.

The GE office at West Memphis opened in July 1969 with Hornsby in charge. An initial conflict with GE developed when the company sent in a writer to report on the Delta project and develop the major parts of a VISTA training program for Health Advocates nationwide.

Hornsby decided not to submit the report to GE. He faulted the report's research and lack of real contact with the community and the Volunteers. He refused to produce a "pretty pamphlet for GE to strut before OEO" and, with the Volunteers' help, planned to produce a more substantial document.

That plan got pushed rapidly to the rear as daily emergency needs became more clear. The center soon became less a place where VISTA activity was coordinated and more a service center to which people turned for assistance, Hornsby said.

> It was in West Memphis that VISTAs became Robin Hoods. They were able to put thousands of dollars into the hands of poor people to meet emergency needs. Band Aid assistance, to be sure, but terribly important when an empty pantry or eviction notice were the alternatives. It was grand larceny of the highest moral and ethical order.

Operation Robin Hood, as the scheme was sometimes called, had the Volunteers giving cash payments directly to individuals they considered in need. Payments averaged two or three dollars each, and a few went as high as twenty-five dollars. The listing of entries included funds given for food, rent, clothing, utility bills, bus fare, wheels for a wagon, hospital bills, to prevent eviction, for a man who walked in needing money, school lunches, and dozens of other daily needs. Approximately $3,500 was given away in this manner.

To cover up this giveaway program, the Volunteers created a fictional recipient who was credited as receiving the funds, a character they identified by the initials FJR, Hornsby said.

There was an OEO bureaucrat in Washington at this time, Jack Ramsey, to whom we took a particular dislike. The JR stood for his name. The F stood for whatever we wanted it to.

Money was not the only thing given away through the West Memphis office. Donated clothing, drugs, building insulation, and other useful supplies passed through its doors. While these items had clear benefits to the area poverty community, the concept of direct assistance was totally foreign to OEO, VISTA philosophy, and the GE contract.

These activities attracted the attention of certain governing agencies. The office phone was tapped, or so it seemed to the Volunteers. Once after a phone call in which critical remarks were made about the county welfare director, the county prosecutor burst into the office and demanded an immediate halt to the attacks on that public servant.

On another occasion, a meeting for all the Volunteers was held at the office, and though no journalists were present, a few days later an area paper published a full and accurate account of the meeting, quoting some dialogue verbatim. It was never learned if a recorder had been smuggled in or if the office itself was bugged.

The FBI was also interested in the activities of the Volunteers at the West Memphis office. Some years later, Hornsby obtained a copy of his FBI file, available as a result of Freedom of Information laws. The file is marked with large, black censor blocks that hide the names of all information sources.

Curiously, the FBI file left one name uncovered, an individual identified as a confidential source, a "ghetto informant" at Earle. Such an obvious oversight in a file so deliberately marked with censor blocks is puzzling. The identity of that individual, made known to local black militants, could certainly have endangered him.

Yet Hornsby's FBI file is made up for the most part of official observations, descriptions almost comical in their detail. One refers to a GSA truck with "VISTA Funmobile" and a large apple painted on the door, the vehicle covered with flowers. Describing the GE office, the file states:

> . . . there was painted on a wall in the office a symbol designating "Ban The Bomb." The symbol is a circle with a line cut in the center of the circle and it has two lines coming out from the center line near the bottom. . . . a confidential source advised that there was displayed a poster reflecting "Live Like a Dog. Test President Nixon's Welfare Plan.". . . . One of the white females, name unknown, was in the office wearing a medallion around her neck, which was identical to the symbol painted on the wall.[12]

The file also makes several references to "Sweet Willie Wine," Prime Minister of the Invaders of Memphis, a black activist group. Wine, whose real name was Lance Watson, was a Memphis freedom fighter, a magnetic speaker, and widely recognized propagandist. The GE office, through Operation Robin Hood, was able to send Sweet Willie to crash Nixon's White House Conference on Hunger in December 1969. The FBI somehow learned of this secret funding, and it was noted in the file.

Wine later undertook a protest march for poor people in Arkansas. Walking with a few of his disciples from West Memphis to Little Rock, he said he would call off the march if he woke the next morning and found all poverty had been abolished in Arkansas. Some small towns along the route virtually shut down that day. Some residents took up arms in anticipation of the worst. Wine's march got as far as Forrest City, where he was attacked and received a broken arm.

As time went on, certain elements in West Memphis became more vocal in their opposition to the Volunteers and the office. Hornsby believes they resented VISTA's informing people of their rights and helping poor and black people obtain the benefits to which they were entitled. The county welfare director also complained about the Volunteer's aggressiveness in helping persons qualify for welfare. The complaints were picked up by a state representative from the area who passed them on to the GE corporate office in New York. In addition, West Memphis GE dealers were being told by white community members that a product boycott was planned unless the VISTA office was closed.

Hornsby said he was then contacted by GE officials who suggested he "slow things down" and not cause any more friction with county officials and other powers. Hornsby's letter of reply clearly indicated that was not his plan.

> We are too concerned about hurting the company's image, and thereby selling fewer light bulbs in Kokomo, than we are in helping correct social injustices . . . I say damn the community relations and let's get concerned about poor and oppressed people. Either that or let's remove ourselves from our so-called involvement in socio-economics.
>
> It is a sham and a betrayal of poor people if our company is involved in the anti-poverty program but is squirming around like bacon in hot grease every time one of us dares take on the established order of things . . .

Corporate retribution came swiftly. Hornsby was fired and the West Memphis office quickly shut down. GE drafted a summary report and submitted it to OEO. The VISTA program continued under the sponsorship of local CAP agencies, but GE's role was over.

Hornsby stayed in West Memphis and, with his friends at Respect, attempted to bring public awareness to the issues. National appeals were made to the NAACP and all Volunteers to join in a boycott of GE products and to protest the awarding of poverty project contracts to large, profit-motivated companies. No significant results came from those efforts, and Hornsby finally left West Memphis in the fall of 1970. He currently lives near Nashville, Tennessee, where he works as a newspaper editor.

In a final assessment, the actions and ideals of any one person may have little influence, but Hornsby's story would not be complete without some mention of the support and sacrifice his family made during this period.

Because the West Memphis school system was strictly segregated at that time, the family decided their children would attend the all-black Wonder schools in the city, the first whites to do so. The Hornsby children were made to feel welcome in those schools, but a price was paid.

For its stand on racial issues, the family was ostracized by its white neighbors in West Memphis and pointedly told by relatives in

Bumper sticker created by Respect, Inc. after General Electric Corp. closed the West Memphis VISTA office following local opposition to Volunteer work.

Alabama that they were not welcome at a family gathering there. A year of harassment with hate-filled and threatening phone calls was the Arkansas response to the Hornsby family's attempt to live out its values.

Margo English
And the Abson Wynne Co-op

Though a Volunteer might organize a co-op, a buying club, a store, some vehicle through which achievement and pride could be gained, the Volunteer often relied on his own energy and effort to get such a project going, hoping it would catch on and achieve the momentum to continue. Projects of this type rarely succeeded.

Such was the case of Margo English, a Michigan native who organized a food co-op in the middle of a cotton field near Crawfordsville (Crittenden County). Ted Wilson recalled her energy and commitment.

> Margo was a human dynamo who never took no for an answer. I don't think the community served by the co-op saw the project as being as important as she did.

Wilson recalled the co-op as little more than a shack surrounded by a cotton field, both chilling and inspiring in its isolation. The co-op failed soon after Margo's departure. An event during her time in east Arkansas was a stark reminder of the primal forces that characterize the area. A local Volunteer and mother who quietly supported the co-op, died unexpectedly. Jerry Hornsby recalled the funeral of Julia Sherod, the few white VISTA faces among the otherwise all-black crowd, and Margo English standing and delivering a moving eulogy for her friend, saying it was the hardest day of her life.

Wilson was also at the funeral that day; he recalled the grave freshly dug beside the plain, country church and the burying of the coffin after the service. It was a situation for which no training could have prepared the Volunteers, but it was not English's only encounter with a poverty-related death.

Because patients of Dan Blumenthal, the VISTA doctor at Marianna, were not allowed admission to the local hospital, it came about that English was driving a mother and ill infant to a Little Rock hospital in her GSA vehicle. The baby died in route. At a meeting later, one of the Volunteers said his reaction to the tragedy, had he a gun, would have been to hunt down and kill the local white doctors, kill them all. Hornsby said those feelings were shared by many.

> I actually think that at that moment, we were all capable of doing just that. And thus another day in the Delta left its indelible mark on our souls.

The United People's Co-op

In June 1969, community groups from three small Mississippi County towns—Birdsong, Burdette, and Osceola—joined together to form the United People's Co-operative. Their goal was to attack their problems—food, clothes, underemployment, housing—using their large numbers, the most obvious strength of poor people in Mississippi County.

That ambitious first step was the result of almost a year of VISTA presence. The actual organizing was a result of efforts by Frances Woods and Christel Brellochs, Health Advocate Volunteers trained to work with food and medical problems.

We developed the idea of the co-op from training in Austin, and we went to East Arkansas and started one. The whole thing was so naive. My objective was to stimulate poor people who had never before been organized to solve some of their problems collectively. The goal was to enable them to acquire the skills and confidence necessary to accomplish what they desired.—*Frances Woods.*

We didn't do anything to analyse the system and figure out what we could do to change it. We just went off and created this little alternative—*Christel Brellochs.*

Despite the naiveté that contributed to the start of the co-op, the "little alternative" set into motion by the Volunteers and the poverty communities of Mississippi County lasted almost five years.

Cover photograph of booklet published by United People's Co-operative

During that time, buying clubs and co-op stores were created, donated land and rented acres were cultivated for vegetable planting, major government funding was acquired, and farm equipment was purchased and put to use in profitable ventures that brought food and employment to many area residents.

More significantly, the United People's Co-op achieved what VISTA had been created to do—develop a sense of accomplishment in poor people by creating a mechanism that would change their lives for the better. Though the co-op itself did not survive to become a permanent fixture in the Arkansas Delta, it created a lasting impression among the people who worked in it, a community pride Woods said she was not totally aware of.

I always had doubts about what we had done there, about raising hopes and not following through. I'd always known that most of the good was for ourselves. Yet I talked with Robert Johnson recently, and he said it taught the people they could work together to accomplish something. Now Birdsong is incorporated and has a water tower. He feels like the co-op was the beginning of something important.

Robert Johnson said he left a job in Memphis to work with the co-op at less than half the wages he had been earning. He did it, he said, because he could foresee the county as a whole being motivated by the efforts of Woods and Brellochs. At that time, the two Volunteers were organizing and working in community gardens and introducing people to the co-op concept.

Their efforts resulted in an initial group of seventy-five families banding together in a cooperative effort, a number that rose to more than 240 families at its prime. With fifty-three thousand dollars received from federal grants, the co-op rented seventy-five acres, purchased agricultural equipment, and hired its first employees. Johnson remembered those early days with great satisfaction.

That first season was a good one. We bought two metal bath tubs and washed and sold about $10,000 worth of greens. We were looking real good. We rented another 75 acres alongside and another 100 acres up at Birdsong

While the initial efforts of the co-op seemed to have been successful, forces were present both internally and in the community at large that would soon overwhelm the fledgling organization. According to George Ivory, VISTA supervisor for Mississippi County Volunteers, the local press was not supportive of the poverty program. Articles appeared in print referring to the co-op as a socialist program, Ivory said.

The resistance was from store owners, merchants who felt the established forms of order being threatened. They felt somehow that government

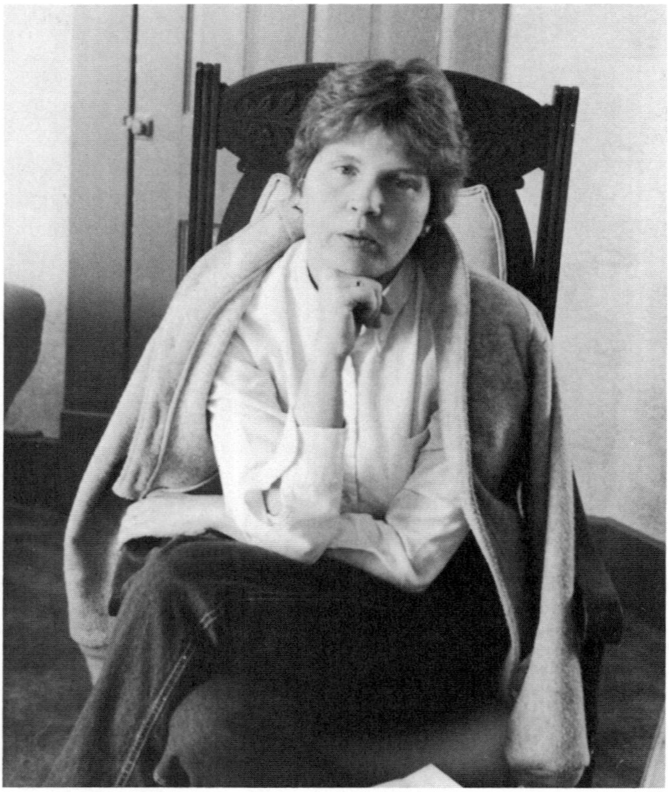

Volunteer Frances Woods

money was being used to teach people to resist them. It was a fear of competition and the government support of a business that would compete with them.

Ivory recalled that the CAP agency itself also felt threatened by the Volunteers, who seemed to get more done with less money than the agency ever had. The distance between the CAP agency board and Woods and Brelloch was increased by the Volunteers' stated distrust of the agency and anyone who was associated with it, Ivory said.

> When I first got there, the agency gave me a list of problems, began telling me things that made it clear some people didn't have any perception of why the Volunteers were there. To some, the program was the most ridiculous thing they had ever heard of.

He describes Woods and Brellochs as protective of the co-op, not allowing Ivory any contact with the organization for his first six months on the job. It is a tribute to the Volunteers' ability to dedicate themselves to a cause, that two white women, complete strangers to the culture and community, could so strongly win the hearts and minds of the black locals, even to the degree where the Volunteers could create a sense of distrust in the people toward Ivory, a black man supposedly there to help the people.

Unfortunately, it is also a testament to the Volunteers' inability to deal with the full aspect of the problem, a situation that could not be significantly changed by the limited resources and time-restraints applied to it.

Ivory perceived the problem as rooted in the poverty community itself and the co-op board members who had neither the experience nor training to maintain the organization. As an example, he told the story of a co-op employee who once asked him for a ride to a Blytheville grocery store.

> The man, in his late 20s, was for the first time in his life being paid in cash and allowed to shop where he pleased. I remember how new it all was to him, that there was more than one brand of beans or coffee.

The community's difficult transition from a plantation wage system with its credit at the farm store to a free enterprise system was one of the larger problems faced by the co-op board. For them, it was almost an instant confrontation with decisions regulating their own destiny, a forced acceptance of the concept of self-assertion in a world which had always kept them dependent. This was another level of human relations faced in her daily assistance to the co-op board, Woods said.

> The issue we struggled with a lot was to treat people independently when they needed basic skills. The woman who was co-op bookkeeper needed

Volunteer Christel Brellochs

basic math training. How do you do that without making her feel like a child and you the teacher?

Ivory suggested the Volunteers could have made some attempt to bring blacks with some business skills into the co-op. There were people on the peripheries of poverty, he said, who could have gotten involved and given the co-op a better chance to succeed. He questioned the logic of the Volunteers who may have only wanted the "purest" of the poverty community. He also conceded there may have been some relationship problems within the black community itself, a fear of those more sophisticated than others, and a desire to maintain control of the co-op.

Whatever the reasons, after the Volunteers completed their assignment and departed, the co-op began its inevitable collapse. Disagreement among board members soon led to faulty decisions, and money was lost. Robert Johnson resigned as farm manager in 1973, returned at the board's request a year later, but left again after one planting season. The problem, as he saw it, was that the co-op board members had become middle-class, were no longer poor people, and they made decisions only to benefit themselves. By 1975, the United People's Co-op had ended.

Ivory, who went on to work for the Arkansas state government in a branch of community services, is currently an attorney in Little Rock. Volunteer Frances Woods returned to school, obtained a Ph.D. in psychology, and currently has a private practice in Fayetteville.

After her VISTA service, Christel Brellochs received a masters degree in Public Health, and she has held several community development and policy analyst positions. In 1985, she completed a project that initiated medical clinics in south Bronx poverty neighborhoods.

Robert Johnson went on to become the mayor of Birdsong. Under his leadership, the community was approved for a locally recruited Volunteer in 1985 to help in a project for a sewage system.

Lee County Co-operative Medical Clinic

The most dramatic events in the East Arkansas VISTA story and in the total history of anti-poverty efforts in Arkansas occurred in the quiet, Lee County town of Marianna. Quiet does not always mean peaceful, and the status quo which Marianna had always maintained rapidly disintegrated soon after the first Health Advocate Volunteers arrived there in 1969.

The suppressed emotions of black and white communities in that distinctly segregated culture soon lost all restraint, and in outbursts of wild and oftimes destructive expression, the two sides began a stand-off whose intensity did not diminish for close to four years.

Firebombings of homes and businesses, a student protest rally dispersed by firehoses on a chill January day, an economic boycott that nearly bankrupt the downtown business district, racist hate mail and phone calls, shots fired at certain public figures—these were some of the daily events that brought Marianna a national notoriety in the early 1970s.

Yet it was during that violent and emotionally charged period that a VISTA project was initiated, took root, and grew to become one of the most successful in the nation, a project which continues to this day as a vehicle of community service and a rallying point for black and white community pride. In many ways, the Lee County Co-operative Medical Clinic has been an ideal VISTA project, and its on-going success has visibly improved lives and attitudes in the area.

To understand the complex history of the Lee County Clinic and the role VISTA Volunteers played in its early years, one must recall the abysmal social and medical conditions which gained Lee County ranking as one of the ten poorest in the nation. Physical conditions in Lee County created a sense of apathy and despair among the poor. Yet for Alice Morgenfield, clinic administrator, pre-VISTA days in Lee County had brought blacks close to the breaking point.

> It was a time when blacks and poor whites were afraid. Then blacks became tired of being treated like they had been. You either had the money to see a doctor or you lived on a plantation where the white boss would tell the doctor to see you. You can only treat people so long like that. The VISTAs came at a time when people in Lee County were tired of being treated like children. What did you have to lose, your life? It wasn't much to begin with anyway.

Conceived primarily by Jan Wrede, a teacher, and Corrine Cass, a nurse, the first Health Advocate Volunteers who arrived in Lee County in early 1969, the idea for a central medical facility to serve the poor gained community support through the Neighborhood Action Committees. Organized by the Volunteers, the committees held meetings in Marianna and three rural locations across the county. Lee County had just been incorporated into the East Central Arkansas EOA at Forrest City, seventeen miles away, and approval for any VISTA project had to come from that agency's board. According to Wilson, the distance between the towns influenced key decisions.

> Lee County was so sleepy, so ignored, so backwaterish, that the clinic came to pass almost before anyone had a chance to mobilize any real opposition to it. It was easy for the EOA to support the clinic because it was not located in their county and not a real threat to them.

Wrede and Cass were joined in August 1969 by other Volunteers instrumental in turning the idea of a clinic into reality. Among them were Dr. Dan Blumenthal, the first VISTA physician in the nation, and his wife Jan, a child development specialist. In addition to a highly trained professional background, Blumenthal and the later

Recruiting poster for the Lee County Co-operative Medical Clinic. The figure in the photo is Dr. Dan Blumenthal. Blumenthal was the first VISTA physician in the nation; he served at Marianna, AR.

VISTA doctors who worked at the clinic possessed a motivation to serve very similar to that of any other Volunteer.

I wanted to get into something where I could really treat people and not just diseases. I just didn't want to treat that cardiac arrest patient in bed #2.[13]

Told that all facilities would be set up for him on arrival, Blumenthal found no GSA car, no medical office, no supplies, nor any equipment at his disposal in Marianna. So he began making house calls using his own vehicle, visiting eight homes a day, and dispensing medicines provided him as samples by drug companies. The need for a community medical clinic was recognized when Volunteers attended local meetings, Blumenthal said.

Discussions at the community meetings generally turned to health because the VISTA team was there to attack it. A leading problem was the lack of a place where poor people could go when sick. We heard many stories of people turned away from hospitals and doctors' offices because they had no money.[14]

The Lee County medical community resolutely denied that poor people had been denied medical treatment because of their inability to pay. Yet Dr. Blumenthal's application to the Lee County Medical Society was voted down by Marianna's five other doctors on the grounds that only doctors in private practice could join the local hospital staff.

The refusal meant Blumenthal's patients could not be treated at the city hospital and could only receive care at a Memphis charity hospital more than sixty miles away or at the state hospital in Little Rock, one hundred miles to the west.

Lee County physicians and pharmacists also urged Arkansas Senator John McClellan to block funding of a forty thousand dollar grant application submitted to OEO for the establishment of a clinic. Dr. Mac McLendon, one of the few doctors to speak on the issue, commented on Blumenthal's activities:

He's going to the churches and telling Negroes all they have to do to get what they want is rear up. That's enough for me.[15]

Only one Marianna doctor voted to allow Blumenthal into the County Medical Society, Dr. Elizabeth C. Fields, who defended her colleagues' decision with these remarks:

It's not the doctor they're fighting. They're fighting VISTA. The other doctors would welcome him with open arms if he would resign from VISTA and set up private practice. VISTA workers don't understand the psychology of the population. They're sometimes misled by good intentions.[16]

With the news of Blumenthal's rejection by the local medical society, an opportunity to place the clinic in a vacant Marianna building was suddenly lost. The town railroad depot, owned but no longer used by the Missouri Pacific Railroad, had quickly been rented to another party in the midst of the Volunteers' negotiations to gain its use.

Sleepy Marianna started to wake up rapidly when a CBS television crew came to town. In a program titled "Don't Get Sick In America" and broadcast nationally on December 13, 1969, journalist Daniel Schorr gave this description of Marianna's doctors:

One is 80 years old and semi-retired. One is sixty and relatively inactive. One is a middle aged woman who says that "the exchange of money is necessary to establish the proper relationship between doctor and patient." The youngest, in his early forties, has a "Wallace For President" button on his desk, segregated waiting rooms, and says "these people" spend their money on whiskey and cigarettes.[17]

Blumenthal was also interviewed on the program, giving this assessment of the medical and psychological conditions he had witnessed.

The health care, or lack of health care, the people receive in an area such as this leads to early death. Perhaps its more than an early death. It's an early death following a lifetime of frustration and hopelessness . . . People suspect, I'm sure, that they're dying younger than they need to . . It's a hopeless feeling.[18]

Other events took place at this time which reflected the emotions that would later surface with such intensity. Members of the predominantly black United Auto Workers Union local voted their support of the Volunteers and donated a mobile health trailer which became a satellite clinic in the community of Haynes.

In January 1970, the First Baptist Church of Marianna held a special service honoring the town's doctors, a service to which Dr. Blumenthal was not invited. Rev. Lewis Clarke, perhaps confused at his own intentions, first told reporters from the Memphis *Commercial Appeal* the service was a response to the critical report shown on CBS. He later told *Arkansas Gazette* reporters the program had nothing to do with the controversy over Blumenthal, and the VISTA doctor wasn't invited simply because he hadn't been in the county long enough. Rev. Clarke said Lee County doctors were "color blind" and treated all patients equally.

That same month the grant application to OEO was approved, and the still-homeless Lee County Clinic suddenly found itself with forty thousand dollars to cover operations until August of 1970. Another $2,500 had been raised at the NAC meetings. Soon, a Marianna house owned by Lacey Kennedy, a prominent black man who operated a funeral home, was made available. After extensive renovation and repair, the Clinic officially opened its doors on March 5, 1970. The original five-room house had severe space restrictions, but Blumenthal believed it was proper to begin on that level.

> We wanted to start small, to begin with a facility that could be effectively governed by a board of unsophisticated country people. Preferable for the community to govern fully a small facility and for the clinic to grow as the board and community grew in sophistication.[19]

With the Volunteer efforts in nutrition, housing, child care, pharmacy, and nursing, with community workers assisting in many ways and being trained in new areas of expertise, the clinic began to serve a wide area of need. Ted Wilson recalled the immediate potential the Clinic projected.

> Visits to the clinic were a highlight for me. It was a natural fit of Volunteers and community people working together. Impressive to see community people being trained to take on roles within the clinic, learning to be health

professionals and paraprofessionals under the tutelage of the Volunteers who had the skills.

> The Clinic provided the Volunteers the kind of structure and system in which they were best able to function . . . an environment that reflected their values and provided a unifying tool around their efforts.

The intentions of the clinic were stated from the outset to be beyond the necessary but limited scope of medical services. It was hoped that if the community saw it could work together to control one aspect of its life, it could take collective action in other areas as well.

Volunteers Wrede and Cass recognized they would need a local figure to help implement those concepts. The person they found for the job and who became Clinic director through its turbulent early years was Ollie Neal. A Marianna native, Neal, more than any other figure, influenced the destiny of the clinic through his determination for its success, his articulation, and his steadfast refusal to be intimidated by any person or group that stood in his way.

Neal was living in Memphis and working with a community food distribution program when he was contacted by Wrede and Cass. He was asked to help the clinic get started, he said.

> When Dan came on, it influenced some specific medical notions, but Jan and Corrine delivered to me some of the best concepts about how people ought to be involved. They were putting that together but having difficulty implementing the concepts. They needed to find someone with contacts in Lee County to help organize these things beyond the neighborhood councils. My role was to implement those concepts.

College educated, well-traveled, and possessing a fearlessness that distinguished him among local blacks, Neal was to emerge within a short time as the dominant spokesman for the clinic and the black community. As events began to pick up pace, it became clear a strong spokesman was needed.

A suit against the Lee County Memorial Hospital was filed in May 1970 in federal court by Dr. Blumenthal, his newly recruited VISTA replacement Dr. Robbie Wolf, and four local blacks. The suit charged the hospital, which continued to refuse service to Blumenthal's patients, with violating the rights of VISTA doctors and the equal protection clause of the Fourteenth Amendment. This denial of rights was one of the first clear errors made by those in power.

In an *Arkansas Gazette* editorial titled "The Closed Hospital," the newspaper stated the hospital was built and operated with federal funds yet denied its facilities to physicians sponsored by the government. The newspaper called it an "outrageous situation" and said "the wrong here is obvious."[20]

Joe Bruch, in a June 1970 OEO memo, wrote, "I will not back off from calling any and all of the so-called establishment of Lee County involved in this matter racists of the worst order." In August, Bruch received a phone call from a leading member of that establishment, Dr. Dwight Gray, then president of Lee County Medical Association.

In another memo, Bruch wrote that Gray's phone call was an inquiry into how the VISTA program might be removed from Lee County. According to the memo, Gray stated the program "served no purpose whatsoever," the project would cause the closing of the local hospital, and that he spoke for ninety percent of the people in Lee County. Bruch closed his memo with the prediction of a major petition coming from Lee County requesting the governor remove the Volunteers there. Bruch's foresight proved to be keen.

As tensions mounted in the area, the opposing sides took more forceful measures to secure their positions. The black community, assisted by Republican efforts to reelect Gov. Winthrop Rockefeller in the 1970 elections, sponsored seventeen black candidates for Marianna and Lee County offices.

This move was directly in line with the long range plan of the Clinic to empower the people, but it was far too premature. Only four of the positions were won, and those were for relatively limited roles as Justice of the Peace. The election also saw the incumbent Rockefeller defeated by the Democrat Dale Bumpers.

What setbacks the black community might have felt from defeat at their first political test were probably forgotten with the gains they made that fall. In September 1970, the Clinic's operating budget was increased by OEO to $131,000 for the coming year. Its first annual meeting was attended by close to five hundred citizens, with four hundred of them becoming charter members of the institution.

The white community at this time continued to misjudge the situation and increased its resistance to the VISTA presence. What it failed to realize was that the Volunteers, while still providing a crucial teaching and service role through the clinic, were already being left far behind in the larger social issues developing. The Volunteers were a catalyst to which an unstoppable reaction had already begun, Neal said.

> This clinic exists because the black community supported it . . . The clinic had to grow from grass roots. They know this is their clinic because they made it. That's what gets you a change in self attitude in the black community and a change in the white community attitude toward the black. The white community doesn't want to believe its eyes, so it talks on and on about outsiders.[21]

Organizations such as the Arkansas Farm Bureau, the Association of County Judges, and the Association of Citizens Councils of Arkansas adopted resolutions to discontinue VISTA in the state based on the Lee County situation. According to Haskell Adams, Lee County Judge at the time:

> VISTA workers are unclean, morally, physically, and mentally. My prime objective is to remove VISTA from Lee County.[22]

Just prior to Adams' comments, the *Arkansas Gazette* referred to the Association of Citizens Councils as "that celebrated citadel of racism" and said its attacks were proof that VISTA had not lost its effectiveness. Other editorials spoke of the "farm plantation mentality" evidenced by the white power structure and suggested VISTA work ought to rub some power structures a little raw.[23]

In mid-1971, the pace of events quickened. The suit against Lee County Memorial Hospital was decided in favor of the VISTA doctors, giving the clinic the medical backup it lacked. Then, like tinder setting off a blaze, an incident at a local pizza restaurant resulted in the economic boycott that paralyzed downtown Marianna businesses.

In other times, the rude treatment of a black patron by a white employee at the restaurant might have been overlooked, but Marianna blacks would not tolerate another humiliation. Like the denial of medical rights, arresting a black woman for refusing to purchase a pizza she didn't order was a foolish mistake on the part of the white power structure.

The boycott, a stand off that lasted from June 1971 until July 1972, led to eleven business bankruptcies with at least five structures lost to fire. The boycott was organized and led by the Concerned Citizens of Lee County, a black group that developed from the original political support office established by Rockefeller.

The Volunteers had no role in the boycott. Though eleven of them were in Lee County at this time, they were all assigned to the Clinic, and they continued to work and train community aides there. The Clinic was gaining in strength all the while. With a $525,000 budget request submitted for the coming year, the Clinic was able to hire its first staff physician, Dr. Irwin Redlener.

It was Redlener who contacted folksinger Joan Baez, and at his request, Baez visited Marianna, the clinic, and several poverty families in the area. In March 1972, Baez held a benefit concert in Memphis that raised $6,800 for the clinic. The concert also brought more national attention to the planned budget request of $1.2 million for the construction of a new and far larger facility.

In addition to these events, a walkout by black students at the newly integrated Lee County High School began January thirteenth and lasted through the end of the school term. Initiating with a sit-in to protest the school board's refusal to allow a memorial program for Martin Luther King, a protest rally ensued and 117 black students were arrested after firehoses were used to disperse them.

Judge Adams, a volunteer fireman who observed the mélée, remarked, "We had no choice. It was too windy to use tear gas."[24] In a separate incident, Adams was fined for assault and weapon possession during the economic boycott after he was accused of trying to run down in his truck two blacks distributing handbills and later threatening them with a pistol.

In retrospect, it seems difficult to understand the views of white moderates in the community, such as Lon Mann, former school board president and wealthy farmer, who still believes an attitude of cooperation could have been worked out on both sides.

> My frustration with VISTA—there was a real need for it, but I couldn't understand why it couldn't be done without animosity. Always easier to stir up people to hate and vote to hate. The VISTAS were a catalyst to community stress.

Mann believed that progress toward social justice was being made in Marianna, but a greater sense of patience was required. More than a decade after the event, one can ask if the same progress might have been made if blacks were less insistent on change. In the early 1970s, however, neither side showed a willingness to wait.

In the midst of and following the economic and school boycotts, Ollie Neal became more aggressive and outspoken in his leadership role. He was featured in state and national newspaper interviews. It was a time when he and other black staff at the Clinic kept guns in their desks, and the thought of a violent attack on the Clinic or on Neal was a daily reality.

The white community increased its pressure on the governor and federal government to restrict the VISTA program, and the black community countered with their own public displays. Petitions were signed and federal suits filed, but those affairs were beyond the immediate environment of the Volunteers.

The $1.2 million grant was approved, and the current Clinic building was constructed in 1973. More medical staff were brought in and the reliance on Volunteers was slowly phased out. In the process Marianna itself evidenced a change, Morgenfield said.

> For several years we were dependent on the VISTAS for any medical staff. Then we didn't need them out front as spearhead of anything . . . We've

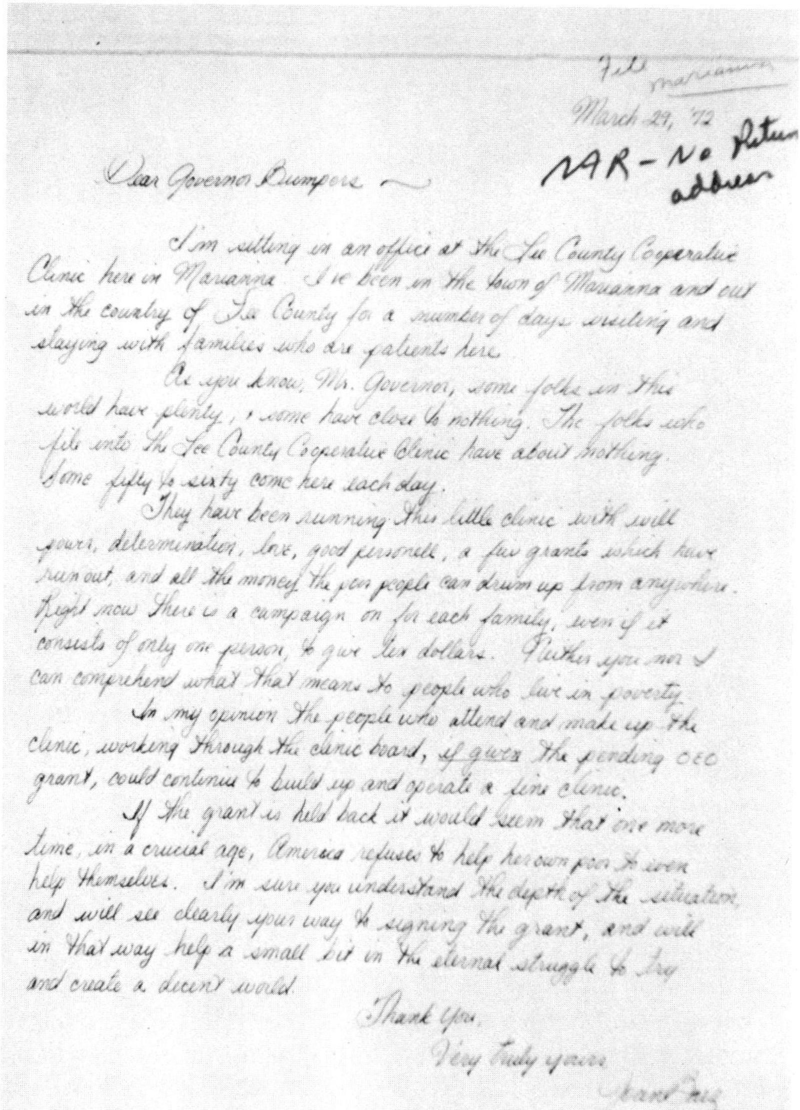

File Marianna

March 29, '72

NAR – No Return address

Dear Governor Bumpers –

I'm sitting in an office at the Lee County Cooperative Clinic here in Marianna. I've been in the town of Marianna and out in the country of Lee County for a number of days visiting and staying with families who are patients here.

As you know, Mr. Governor, some folks in this world have plenty, & some have close to nothing. The folks who file into the Lee County Cooperative Clinic have about nothing. Some fifty to sixty come here each day.

They have been running this little clinic with will power, determination, love, good personell, a few grants which have run out, and all the money the poor people can drum up from anywhere. Right now there is a campaign on for each family, even if it consists of only one person, to give ten dollars. Neither you nor I can comprehend what that means to people who live in poverty.

In my opinion the people who attend and make up the clinic, working through the clinic board, if given the pending OEO grant, could continue to build up and operate a fine clinic.

If the grant is held back it would seem that one more time, in a crucial age, America refuses to help her own poor to even help themselves. I'm sure you understand the depth of the situation, and will see clearly your way to signing the grant, and will in that way help a small bit in the eternal struggle to try and create a decent world.

Thank you,

Very truly yours

Joan Baez

Letter to Arkansas Gov. Dale Bumpers from Joan Baez during her 1972 visit to Marianna.

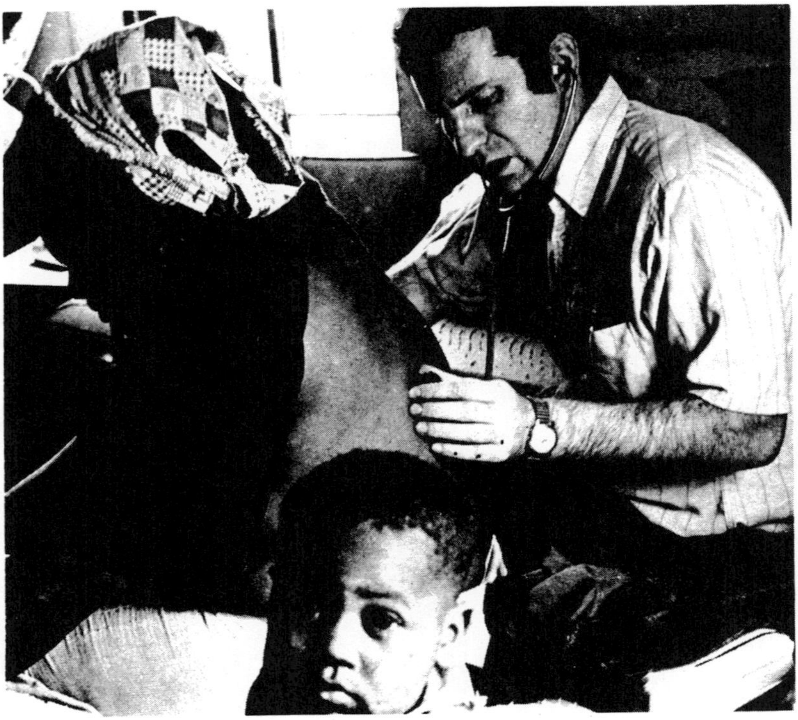

Dr. Blumenthal examining a Lee County patient. The photo is from a booklet published by the Lee County Clinic Co-operative Medical Clinic.

had several black doctors and dentists come through the clinic and settle here . . . These kind of people making homes here let black kids have role models other than teacher or preacher. It took white people a while to realize we weren't against them. We just wanted our share of the American dream. We realize now that change is not bad.

By 1975, the Clinic staff of about seventy people included no Volunteers. Of the original Health Advocate group, only two were still on hand: Corrine Cass, at that time a member of the Clinic nursing staff, and Harry Conard, who, with Ollie Neal, left the Clinic to lead the National Demonstration Water Project, a federally financed project to provide rural water and sewage service to the Delta.

Dr. Blumenthal making house calls in Lee County. Many of the area's dirt roads could not support automobile traffic in wet weather. The photo is from the cover of a booklet published by the Lee County Clinic.

The Clinic has now become a member of the Marianna Chamber of Commerce and is well supported by local, state, and federal sources. Offering its membership fees on a sliding scale relevant to a family's income, the Clinic has earned the respect and admiration of all levels of Lee County society, and even the most outspoken former critics refer to it as "our clinic" and boast of its continuing achievement.

Having achieved a dramatic turnaround in the area's infant mortality rate, malnutrition levels, and basic health practices, the Clinic remains to this day one of the state's outstanding symbols of success in its attack on community problems. Blumenthal, who has made several return visits to Marianna since his year of VISTA service, commented on the clinic's role in local history.

> The end of racial problems in Lee County and the end of threats to the Clinic's existence did not mean an end to the problem of the county's poor.

Illustrations by Ron Meyer, the *Benton Courier,* 1971

I'M GONNA CHOKE THE
LIFE OUTTA YA!
MARIANNA

Viewed from a distance, it is clear now that a community controlled clinic in one county cannot lead to the elimination of health problems or poverty. But the clinic helped create a new psychology in the county, a change in the collective consciousness of the black and poor who acquired power to make changes and gained the respect of the establishment and gained self respect.

I returned for the first annual meeting in 1971 and again at the sixth meeting in 1976. The first meeting drew five hundred plus, yet the '76 meeting had less than 100. The sparse attendance might have signaled a loss of support or interest, but the Clinic had by then become an established part of the county and a visible show of support was no longer needed.

The clinic had served out its role as a focal point for change. It was still more than just a health care facility for the community it served, but it was no longer an institution of social upheaval. The 1960s were finally over. Lee County, with the rest of the country, might or might not move further ahead in the 1970s, but it could never go back.[25]

Ollie Neal

Ollie Neal wore bib overalls the morning he agreed to an interview at his Marianna law offices. He said he had some farm work to do and couldn't spare much time. A large man with a deep resonant voice that added to his image of physical power, Neal spoke rapidly and gestured broadly as he spoke. Three hours into the interview, he was still going strong.

In detailing his role as former director of the Lee County Clinic, Neal touched on many subjects, treating all with a disarming candor and an unflinching self confidence. From the power in his voice and the imposing physical presence he created, he truly seemed larger than life, a man who shaped local history and knew it, a man who had more important things to do than dwell on past events.

Looking back to the Clinic's origins, Neal did not hesitate to admit that more than any other single person, it was Volunteer Jan Wrede who established the institution's original and lasting direction.

Probably the biggest contribution Jan made was conceptualizing and putting it together. She recognized that if the clinic was to be a permanent community activity, it could not depend on Jan Wrede for long term operations. Her position was that once she had ingrained a number of people with this philosophy, commitment, and direction, it was time for her to go.

Ollie Neal, initial director of the Lee County Co-operative Clinic

Some of the Volunteers really did take leadership roles. That's a normal thing. You deliver a baby, you ought to say, "Hey, I delivered this sucker." But Jan was perhaps the most profound person in staying in the background. There was never an attempt in Marianna to say that the folks who brought forth these ideas are the ones to make them go forward. It was always, "here it is, do what you will with it."

That was part of the reason why the clinic, once it got past its political opposition in the early 70s, became one of the best in the country with less threats to its financial state. It was always run by Marianna, the folks who modified the concepts were here. I have to give Jan credit for that.

Neal also credited Wrede and Corrine Cass with giving him the chance to learn his new role and create the persona he used to carry it off for the coming years. The bravado which characterized him in all his public encounters successfully concealed a less self-assured interior.

As long as Jan was here, I relied heavily, and this will shock a lot of people, on her to help me figure out who I needed to communicate with to make things happen. For the first three months I was here, all the letters with my signature probably came from Jan and Corrine. It was a situation where they said, here's the way you can do this, so the next time I didn't have to ask them.

When Jan left, that gave me full responsibility as primary executive. My position was that even the folk we described as Uncle Toms, that there was some explanation for that you had to deal with to be effective. You couldn't just say "Here's a Tom, to hell with him" and ignore him. If he was a Tom, as we perceived the word, there was some basis for that related to the whole black experience, to all of us.

I know many times in the early 1970s when I was talking strong, raising hell, my palms were sweating and my heart was about to jump out of my chest. I was scared as hell, too. I knew what the Tom felt.

So when Jan left, it meant I had to deal with these folks, folks not ready to stand up to white people who were doing things to harm black folks. Most folks would never admit it, but there was this fear. When Jan departed and Corrine became active in the delivery of health care, I had to go to the Clinic board for my support.

Having gained the board's support, Neal said he did whatever was required to create an atmosphere of strength. In many cases this required some extravagant creativity, such as the "performances" he said he staged at the East Central Arkansas EOA, the clinic's sponsor, to maintain its support.

Neal said that when he and Sterling King, another leader of the Marianna black community, made presentations to the EOA board, he would make a wild, emotional appeal, shouting and stomping about the room, seemingly almost out of control in his desperate plea for help, until King would jump up and take the microphone from him, apologizing for Neal's emotional commitment. Then King would continue the pitch in a controlled, articulate style.

Keeping EOA director John Clark in support of the Clinic also took some doing. When positive events occurred, Neal said he gave credit to Clark to make him look good, and when something bad happened, he would say Clark didn't really know about it, that "we kind of slipped that one by him."

According to Ted Wilson, Clark was rarely fooled, but it was easier for him to be convinced and supportive of efforts if the style of delivery offended as few people as possible. Neal was a master at this, but both men were aware of the game being played, Wilson said.

In other situations, Neal said he did a "lot of running," such as the time he had to fly to Washington, DC, and used the identification and travel expenses of a Mississippi County Volunteer.

> I went to the airport with a ticket that said Christel Brellochs. I couldn't even spell Christel Brellochs. And like a fool, I got there late. I really had to assert myself with the guy at the gate, because if he asked me for identification, I didn't have anything with her name on it.

The cause of that hasty flight was a surprise visit to the Clinic by an OEO inspector sent there by Senator McClellan who had been influenced by the Delta white community to investigate Clinic operations. Neal said he was in his attic office in the old Clinic building when he received a call from the downstairs receptionist that the inspector was on hand.

Slipping unnoticed down the back stairs and out the back door, Neal was on the first plane to Washington where he met with friends at the OEO who told him exactly what the inspector was looking for. Prepared for the interview, Neal flew back and met with the man the next morning. As a result, a reasonably good report was written, he said.

Neal's bravado had its influence on others, as shown during a 1972 meeting between Governor Dale Bumpers and Clinic board members. At this time, the major grant to construct the new clinic had been submitted and Bumpers had already met with representatives of the opposing white community. Neal said his contacts at the OEO had informed him the grant application could probably get an override if the Governor vetoed it, but that was confidential information he couldn't even tell the Clinic board.

Bumpers had been jockeying with the idea we ought to make the board half black and half white. I took that as completely out of the question. I never really did know what my board felt. At the meeting, an old lady on the Board said something that shocked me. She said "Governor, you want to make us tie up our corporation and act like it ain't nothing. That ain't right. The corporation is supposed to do like it's supposed to do every year. These things take time."

That was very profound, I thought. Then she said, "Another thing, these folks you want us to put on the board have been trying to destroy and tear us up for the last three years. We need your money, but we can't do what you want us to do. And if that's what you want us to do, we'll just have to give your money back."

I think that was really heavy. I know her palms were sweating. I know mine were. That was very profound for all. Bumpers later told me that he had always thought what I was bringing him was in Ollie Neal's head. That woman suggested that a substantial part of the community was of that view. And he subsequently approved the grant.

The long range success of the clinic can be attributed to many factors, but in the early days few left a stronger impression on critics than Neal's attitude of violence to be returned with violence. In a 1974 interview with Richard First, a University of Arkansas professor, Neal admitted that he used to be into "the nonviolent bag" and that in the early 1960s a test of one's manhood was "whether you could take whatever somebody put on you."

In his years at the clinic, however, Neal created an attitude of mutual respect in controlling potential violence toward the clinic. Neal told First there was a clear reason why a bombing never occurred at the clinic.

> The reason there hasn't been a bomb is that someone would have to throw the damn thing. I talked a lot about this publicly. I promised that if someone messed around—and was slow about it—I would get him with my shotgun. If he was fast, I would tear him up with the 30-0-6. I meant that.

Neal left the clinic in 1975 to direct a major water and sewage project in the area. By that time, the institution had in many ways outgrown him and required someone with more background in medical administration. Neal later received a law degree and opened a private practice. He currently works in a building on Marianna's town square overlooking the area where the economic boycott once raged.

Those days of conflict long past, Neal's interest in the advancement of black people in the Arkansas delta hasn't changed. He's just working at it differently, now with an emphasis on civil cases and political involvement.

In retrospect, he sees the clinic and its resulting conflicts as having caused the white community to change, to do some growing and become reasonable in its dealings with blacks. The economic boycott made it clear "we could be a force to be reckoned with," Neal said. "It happened because they realized this is in my best interest to work with these crazies," Neal said. "We all have some need to protect ourselves."

Long Range VISTA Impact

On July 16, 1970, while affairs in Lee County were beginning to gain attention, the following editorial appeared in the *Wynne Progress,* the newspaper for the largest town in Cross County.

THANKS TO VISTA

The VISTA program in Arkansas has met with varied response, ranging from outright antagonism to heartfelt gratitude. In general, we believe Cross County is grateful to these volunteers who have lived among us and tried to help.

One of the things we've learned from Mrs. Litta Robinson and Mr. and Mrs. Charles DeRousie is that poverty is not merely a lack of money. It is also a lack of the education that money provides, lack of communication with the more affluent society and with the governing agencies, lack of knowledge needed to get out of the poverty situation, and if poverty has been a family way of life for many years, there is not even the desire to escape.

The VISTA workers have attacked the problems as a whole. They have counseled families in procedures to take advantage of governmental help, such as food stamps, medical care, even welfare assistance. Many simply did not know these programs existed or how to get the aid.

Mr. DeRousie has given legal advice to the poor and "advised them of their rights." In some cases, this has brought criticism from good citizens who wouldn't think of oppressing anybody by force, but don't hesitate to allow them to be denied their rights through their own lack of information. We didn't fully realize the extent of this oppression until shown by the VISTA program.

The editorial went on to describe other activities of DeRousie and the public health work of Mrs. DeRousie, a registered nurse. It concluded with a mention of their leaving and DeRousie's plan to enter law school at the University of Michigan.

We are humbly grateful to this young couple who have given us a year of their lives. We know our community is better for their service. We hope their lives were enriched to a like degree.

A newspaper article is a temporal thing, but the concepts it communicates can have more lasting effects. Though the Health Advocates are gone from eastern Arkansas, their spirit remains in the changed attitudes they left behind.

VISTA achieved another lasting influence on community life in the Delta. It provided an opportunity for outstanding people to channel their energy into a functioning system. It helped them achieve the results for which they were already struggling. Mrs. Delcinia Robinson of Forrest City is probably the best example of this, Wilson said.

For Delcinia, VISTA was just another vehicle for her community giving. She so totally understands the needs of the people and can interpret them for others that she was a teacher while being a volunteer. I knew that whatever investment we made in her, we would reap the benefit ten fold. I also knew she would do the work of a volunteer whether she was paid or not. And I don't doubt to this day she continues to do it.

In Mrs. Robinson's small and well kept home, the living room had recently been cleared of the boxes of clothes and household supplies which she regularly receives and distributes among needy area residents. Though she hasn't been in VISTA since 1979, Mrs. Robinson continues to receive large shipments from friends in Wisconsin she met while a Volunteer.

Through VISTA, I made a trip to Prescott, Wisconsin for Operation HOPE. A lady up there invited me to her home. Such a beautiful experience to go to her house, to sleep in the guest room and not be treated like you're black. I spoke at schools and on the radio. They played my radio talk on Thanksgiving Day and the calls started coming in, people asking "What can we do?"

We started the clothing project. Got VanLines of Memphis to bring the clothes here free. They sent 32,000 pounds of clothing and appliances that first year. The program is still going on, but now sent by mail.

Through Operation HOPE we got a whole new change of life here. Some people didn't have curtains on their windows or two plates alike. People started fixing up their shacks. It made them feel better.

The daughter of a Baptist preacher, Mrs. Robinson raised her four children in a two room shack with no facilities. Her volunteer history, however, proves that personal achievement has little to do with physical or financial advantages.

She has served as a community volunteer in two VISTA projects relating to social services and nutrition. She has worked for organizations that challenged utility rate increases, worked to remove sales tax from medicines purchased by the elderly, and educated food stamps recipients in techniques used to discriminate against them.

Mrs. Robinson has also served as an advocate for nursing home residents and has been involved with Arkansas Women for Justice, an organization that assists battered women and abused children. She was the only Arkansan on the National Advisory Committee on Child Nutrition, and as a Volunteer, she has traveled the country and has met three presidents.

My family knew there was no stopping Momma. So they just joined me. They pitched in and helped. They love to.

Not always having possessed the determination that she now so clearly displays, Mrs. Robinson said there was a time when she was afraid to speak out what she felt. After fifteen years of working as a domestic for a Forrest City white family, bringing in a household income that supplemented her disabled husband's part-time earnings, Mrs. Robinson met VISTA supervisor Ted Wilson and opened up what must have been a long-dormant side of her personality.

Ted Wilson gave me confidence, made me feel I was somebody. Ted wanted people to stand on their own two feet and speak with their own mouths. I try to do that for others. Ted would tell me not to do things for people, to get them to do for themselves. Yet sometimes folks are so lost, you just had to do for them.

Recalling an old, crippled lady who lived far out in the country, Mrs. Robinson said she brought a judge from the state Social Security office at Little Rock to see for himself the conditions which the woman endured. The judge was shocked by the ramshackle house, by the old rug which served as her bed mattress, by the butane heater on which she cooked her meager meals. It was the first time the man had ever seen people living that way, Mrs. Robinson said, and he subsequently approved her application for adequate benefits.

VISTA opened up a whole new world for people in St. Francis and Lee Counties. The director of the EOA after John Clark said he would get rid of VISTA because we brought in too many problems. To him it was fine if people came to the agency with their problems. But we went out into the fields. People were ashamed or whatever, so we brought them in. They needed medicine, food stamps, transportation. We brought in sick folks and stranded families. That's why VISTA was pushed out. Even now, people will call here and ask me to call the agency for them.

Mrs. Robinson does not seem bitter or disillusioned by the phasing out of VISTA programs in her county. To her, Volunteer service was an effective means of getting things done in that time. After meeting and speaking with her, one has the distinct impression she is more than capable of finding successful ways to do necessary work in this or any other time.

Notes

1. *Congressional Record,* December 20, 1969, Pg. E10927.

2. *Congressional Record,* December 20, 1969, Pg. E10927.

3. Dan Blumenthal, "Building A Base For Reform," *Southern Exposure,* VI:2, 1978.

4. *Arkansas Gazette,* November 19, 1969.

5. *Arkansas Gazette,* November 29, 1969.

6. *Arkansas Gazette,* February 2, 1970.

7. *Many Voices,* November 11, 1970.

8. Blumenthal (see note 3 above).

9. Eldon Wright, Field Representative, Lee County Citizens Council, letter April 20, 1970.

10. *Memphis Commercial Appeal,* October 1, 1969.

11. Lon Mann, "One Mann's Opinion," unpublished paper, March 1972.

12. FBI correspondence, March 25, 1970.

13. *Memphis Commercial Appeal,* October 1, 1969. *Arkansas Gazette,* November 16, 1969.

14. Blumenthal (see note 3 above).

15. *Arkansas Gazette,* November 16, 1969.

16. See note 15 above.

17. Daniel Schorr, "Don't Get Sick In America," Aurora Publishers Incorporated, Nashville, TN, 1970, Pg. 34.

18. Schorr, Pg. 37.

19. Blumenthal (see note 3 above).

20. *Arkansas Gazette,* June 10, 1970.

21. Mal Schechter, *Hospital Practice,* March 1972.

22. *Arkansas Gazette,* December 2, 1971.

23. *Arkansas Gazette* November 27 & December 31, 1971.

24. Schechter (see note 21 above).

25. Blumenthal (see note 3 above).

LAUGHING AT TROUBLE

JERRY CRONIN IN SOUTH ARKANSAS

Pine forests crowd the road leading into Hampton (Calhoun County) with few towns to break the pattern. This is prime harvest land for the large timber companies that support the economy of most south Arkansas counties. Small signs on roadside trees declare each local hunting club's domain within the vast tracts of pine woods.

In south Arkansas, many of the social roles established years ago have been retained. You can work at a paper mill or on a farm, or you can drive to the closest city and try to find a factory job. Social codes, as well, linger. High school yearbooks in many towns still identify graduates with familiar titles—"Most Popular," "Most Likely to Succeed"—but each title is displayed for two students, one black, one white.

In 1969 the town's two new VISTA Volunteers made their home in the black part of Hampton, renting a room in an old house whose wallpaper flapped in the drafts on windy nights. "Builds character," Jerry Cronin remembers his roommate Art Hoffman saying as the two pulled blankets over their heads and tried to sleep.

Today, Cronin lives in a house directly across the street from that aging house. His current home is far better insulated than his original residence, but nothing about the green frame house distinguishes it from other homes in Hampton's black neighborhood. This is the neighborhood where Cronin made a place for himself, and where he has chosen to live ever since.

Volunteer Jerry Cronin with Jesse Ware of Hampton

That choice seems all the more remarkable when one learns of the challenges he faced on Hampton's quiet streets in those early days: a four hundred dollar bounty offered for his "removal"; several physical encounters with certain residents who resisted what he stood for; and Cronin's own understanding that his presence in Hampton would never be anything more than a beachhead, a symbol of the VISTA commitment to bring about social change.

Yet the frazzle-haired man who recalls those days, who breaks into a grin with most recollections, seems far from troubled. Cronin's grin is disarming, and you quickly get the impression it is one of his most effective tools.

"I come from a whole family of do-gooders, nuns, priests, all with a real Irish Catholic sense of right and wrong. The concept was 'This is right, so you do it.'"

Cronin warmed up and the stories began to flow. He prepared a pot of tea and set it to steep on the table where sunshine coming through the windows illuminated a bowl of oranges. Bunches of dried herbs hung from the open cupboard shelves. The room was especially bright and warm for a winter morning.

"College showed me how to apply my family ideals—that order was important, that you should never destroy things or be offensively confrontational. My father was totally opposed to any kind of violence. Not into passivism—he was into civility."

College was the University of Tennessee at Knoxville, a campus like many others in the late sixties caught up in the frantic activity of student rallies and protests. Cronin belonged to a campus group that based its identity on the university colors and was something like a consulting agency for student activists.

"We called ourselves the BODS—Big Oranges for a Democratic Society. We printed signs for your rally. We set up the bail bonds. We would handle your demonstration for you."

With a sure sense of the theatrics behind their activities, each BODS leader wore an elaborate costume when on assignment, appearing as a pirate, a Confederate colonel, or perhaps as a Shakespearean actor, with appropriate plastic swords, guns, or other props. The BODS' finest performance may have occured, Cronin believes, when its activities caused the University to reverse its position on a issue affecting minority students.

VISTA recruiters on campus were attracted by BODS' work and they allowed all members to sign up as Volunteers at the end of their junior years and to finish school before joining the program.

"When the time came to enter VISTA, I was offered transportation from Knoxville to the Austin training site. I chose to ride the bus, figuring I'd see some of the country in the southwest region where I was assigned."

That bus ride made an impression. When Cronin saw Hampton as one of the VISTA assignments at the training center, he listed it as his first choice. Offering Volunteers their choice of assignments wasn't standard VISTA procedure at that time, but Cronin said his group, about 250 from the Class of '69, refused to let their trainers decide where they would be placed.

"We organized a protest, carried placards demanding to know

where we would be going. The next day all the choices were posted on the walls of the room. I listed Hampton first, then Knoxville, Tennessee, then Dublin, Ireland."

Cronin paused in his recollections and poured the tea, making sure it was understood that his second and third choices were clearly impossible VISTA assignments. He continued, but the tone of his voice had changed.

"About 50 of us from that group were sent to Arkansas, some prepared for survival. I was an Irish Catholic optimist who thought everything will work out with a sense of timing and the ability to laugh at a dilemma. So I went from my father's influence to school to the opportunity of VISTA. I got sent to Hampton and found there wasn't a damn thing to laugh at."

Once in the Hampton low-income community, Cronin said he realized that people assumed he knew things, that he could provide them with advice to change their lives. The depth of their poverty brought Cronin to another essential understanding.

"Once I got the idea that the world was so bad for these people, how could I be so arrogant to think I could make it worse. I decided whatever I said would have to be upbeat. I clearly had no power to hurt anybody, so I didn't mind building up folks' hopes."

The infectious grin was back on his face as Cronin reached across the table and took three oranges from the bowl. He stood up and juggled them as he talked.

"Folks would come to me with their problems. I'd grab these oranges, say 'Hey, watch this,' just get them to relax and slow down. Telling them what they already know is low quality information. You got to say something, do something to counteract, not complement."

The oranges flew in a circular blur, then Cronin caught them and returned them to the bowl. He shifted mood again and continued.

"If the objective is changing the balance of power, you've got to help folks get the power and understand how to use it. If someone is blocking the people from using their civil rights, then you work on changing that delicate balance of power."

Cronin's VISTA techniques to change that power balance differed little from his college theatrics. Learning that the Hampton school district had very low participation in the state's free lunch program, he began meeting with high school boys and instructing them on how to complete the lunch application forms. Cronin wouldn't give the students his only copy of the federal regulations governing the program, but he created for them a mock folder: blank sheets of paper with one printed regulations page placed visibly on the top. He and the students used the prop in several evenings of role playing, alternating in the parts of applicant and official. When the time came, the students went on their own to the real meeting with the school superintendent, armed with what looked like a set of lunch-program regulations to back up their applications.

"A couple of months later we were among the leading schools in the state for free lunch. There were so many more kids in the lunch room, they had to hire more workers. So the kids got better nutrition and more people got jobs because there were these tenth graders with the rules, being civil. So everybody gets lunch."

The South Central Arkansas Community Action Agency had eleven Volunteers assigned to its three-county service area in the summer of 1969. Cronin said he and Art Hoffman, the Chicago native who was his VISTA partner, were considered lazy by the agency; it seemed all they did was sit around or walk the streets of Hampton. This was a deliberate pose, though, a chance for the community to get to know them and realize these two VISTAS would give advice but had no intention of doing things for the people. Cronin and Hoffman immediately got on the bad side of local white troublemakers, breaking the social code by living in a black family's home.

About three weeks into their assignment, the first overt signs of racism emerged when two black men, VISTA staff personnel, showed up for an evaluation visit. That hot summer day, the VISTA people walked to a local dariette for milkshakes. Disregarding the custom of blacks standing at the outside window or going around back to place their order, they went inside and sat down.

"Just by coincidence, Art and I, the two whites, ordered vanilla shakes, and the two black guys ordered chocolate. The poor waitress was totally flustered. Meanwhile, all the little rednecks were hanging around the pool tables in the back watching this. They told us that three brothers from Bearden, all just out of Cummins prison, were coming to town to kick our ass. As far I know, they never did show up."

By the end of their second month, Cronin and Hoffman heard rumors they were to be fired. Local whites were putting pressure on the county judge who pressured the agency director. The two were alleged to have failed to maintain proper contact with their sponsoring agency. Another effort to remove the Volunteers was based on the bizarre rumor that Cronin was running guns from Mexico to subvert the federal government.

While the agency could never use these or other complaints to justify removing Cronin and Hoffman from their positions, the attitude among many townspeople was far from tolerant. Frustrations with the Volunteers peaked one winter night in 1970 in the town square. Cronin and Hoffman had parked their government vehicle, a four-door pickup, on the square and gone with the county judge that night to a meeting in Camden.

"So the rednecks know our car, and they're hanging around by it waiting for us. When we show up, they start harassing us. Art turns to me and says, 'Wonderful rap sessions come out of occasions like this. This is a time when we can talk with them, reason with them and improve our relations.' I said 'Art, they're gonna kick our ass!'

"We walk up to the middle of them. Art starts giving them Sociology 101 at a mile a minute. There's maybe 12 of them and the two of us, and I am starting to get a little worried now. I figure all our humor is out the window.

"While Art is talking, another car drives up and this big ugly guy gets out, wearing just a T-shirt on a winter night. Art looks him over and says, 'Hey, I bet you're cold.' The big guy goes nuts and starts to push at us. He says, 'The state police say one of you guys knows karate and the other knows judo. We're gonna see which is which.'

"Then I reach for this little tear gas pen I thought was in my shirt pocket. But it's not there. I slap at my other pocket and fumble through my clothes until I find it. I finally say, 'Okay, make your move.'

"When they charged us, we jumped in the truck. I'm just about in the driver's seat when the big guy grabs hold of the door before I can pull my foot in. I can see him about to slam the door on my foot, so I pull out the pen and blow the tear gas in his face. It had an old style discharge capsule that made a loud bang when it went off.

"He falls back, screaming, 'I'm dead!' and all the others run over to him, thinking I had shot him. I slam the door and we take off. In a moment, they are in their cars and the chase begins. Now Art climbs over into the back seat, slides to the driver's side, then climbs into the front and takes the wheel. He's been a cab driver in Chicago and can drive like this. So we're driving and chasing each other all over town. Eventually we pull into the yard of one of our few white friends who comes out on his porch and gets the rednecks to back off. Soon the police arrive and it all settles down."

Cronin and Hoffman were charged with assault, possession of an illegal weapon, and disturbing the peace. Their trial, held in Hampton several months later, drew a packed house. Cronin meanwhile had been in Chicago and brought back assorted pins and posters from the celebrated trial of "The Chicago Eight." "Free the 8" and "Stop the Trial" were some slogans displayed by the Volunteer's friends. The town square boys had their own theatrics, appearing in court newly bandaged and willing to display the scars they said resulted from the encounter.

If there was any doubt as to the outcome of the trial, a turning point was most probably reached when the Volunteers' attorney was questioning one of the local men. An observer at the trial recalled that when the man was asked what his group would have done had they caught up with the two Volunteers, the fellow answered, "We would have stomped them." Sensing that his response might have been a little too direct, the man quickly amended his remark by saying, "We would have *tried* to stomp them," the trial observer said.

Cronin and Hoffman were acquitted, and their lawyer donated his government-paid fee to a day care center the defendants had been trying to set up in Camden. Cronin took that as a positive sign that other members of the white community might come to accept them. But the trial had so discouraged Hoffman that he resigned from VISTA.

Cronin said the departure caused him to re-evaluate his own reasons for staying. VISTA officials had told him that the central issue in Hampton was getting the town to allow whites to come in and help the blacks. A VISTA presence had to be established or else no one else could follow.

"The rednecks would harass me downtown. I just kept laughing at them. Ask one his name and tell him I had just been out helping his grandmother. He didn't know whether to thank me or kick my ass for making that public. It was just a bluff. Odds were that if you were a redneck here, your grandmother would qualify for VISTA help."

Cronin's front door opened, and a young black man came in to return a necktie he had borrowed for a date the evening before. He was a neighbor and an old friend, Cronin said, pulling out an old photo album that contained snapshots from 1969. The man pointed to himself in a photo where he was about seven years old, one of a group of Hampton children the two Volunteers had made early friends with back then.

The front door of the house opened again, and a boy, perhaps ten years old, came in. He wanted to borrow a hammer and some nails for a dog house he was building. Cronin lent him the few tools. Meanwhile, another neighbor knocked on the door and asked to use the telephone. Cronin waved his consent and went on with his story.

"So the little rednecks were mad because we had whipped them legally. One of them gets in his truck and drives back and forth in front of my house all night long. Now a friend had told me of the $400 bounty this guy was to collect, and I know he's got a gun in his truck. So when he finally pulls his truck into my yard, shines his headlights on my door and honks his horn, I stick my head out the door, shout 'Hey, good to see ya. C'mon in.' and quickly slam it shut.

"He comes up and knocks on the door. I open it a crack and quickly pull him in, then kick it shut, slap him on the back and say 'Good to see ya' and give him the best seat in the house. There he is supposed to shoot me and I'm treating him like an old friend. He doesn't know what to do, so he finally asks about getting some women."

"I tell him I don't mess around with any local women because I'm engaged to a woman in Shreveport. I wasn't engaged and didn't even know anybody in Shreveport, but it sounded like a good southern town. I tell him to go up to the local beer joint and see what he can find.

"When he leaves, a friend who had been listening to this whole encounter from the next room, runs out the back of the house and gets to the beer joint before this guy does. He tells the black folks there about the guy coming for their women, and they meet his truck with a barrage of beer bottles and bricks. He's now really pissed, and he drives up and down my street for the rest of the night."

The following day Cronin met briefly with the county judge and told him he planned to get a shotgun and shoot over the cab of the truck the next time it pulled into his yard. He then went to Little Rock, bought a shotgun, and showed it to the judge when he got back to Hampton. The message was apparently passed on, and it brought a temporary halt to the harassment.

"A couple of days later I'm driving out of town in the GSA Carry-All when some white folks drive up toward me from the opposite direction. They pull into my lane, stop when our bumpers are about a foot apart, and start cussing at me.

"Now this little devilment takes over me. I start smiling and waving back to them. I put the GSA truck into first gear and come forward. I tap the bumpers. They put their truck into reverse and we start to pick up speed. Soon I'm in 4th gear and we're weaving back and forth across both lines, me in foward and them in reverse.

"I know that on this two lane road there's no place to pull off and turn around for at least two miles. So while we're going, I casually pick up my gun and show it to them. Hold it up grinning. When we finally get to the turn off, they pull in and stop and don't chase after me."

These encounters are Cronin's examples of "not giving in," of disarming those who meant to do him harm. He remained a Volunteer in Hampton for two years on his own and eventually won the support of key members of the white community who recognized his potential benefit to the town as a whole.

One of Hampton's leading white citizens and an early friend to both Cronin and Hoffman suggested that the men had little choice as to whom they could help during their VISTA service. Their living with a black family so antagonized a large portion of the white population that the Volunteers were only able to help in the community that accepted them, he said. Even so handicapped, he said, the Volunteers helped effect the successful integration of Hampton's public schools. After Cronin's time in VISTA, the man said his service to the town continued in several ways, most notably in drawing up the plans for a successful rural health program called CABUN, named for its service area of Calhoun, Bradley, and Union Counties.

Hoffman, now living in New Mexico, recalled the animosity of certain Hampton whites, but he rejected the idea that their anger was based solely on his and Cronin's living with a black family.

"It was not so much where we lived, but who our employer was," Hoffman said. "Jerry's still living there and doing good work. We were the feds. That was the issue."

Cronin takes the middle ground in this debate, admitting that certain issues had greater priority than others on his VISTA agenda. Over the years he has had the benefit of learning from his neighbors on both sides of town and seeing issues that affect the whole community, Cronin said.

By staying on, Cronin has been able to do things in Hampton he couldn't do as a Volunteer. His continuing presence there is a statement that he is willing to help, a willingness he has demonstrated many times over the years. Cronin's VISTA years, however, were perceived by program administrators in Little Rock and Austin as one of high risk, he said.

"I would get calls from them, sometimes at 2 or 3 a.m., to check on me. They frequently brought me down to Austin to help with training sessons and get me out of town. That way I met hundreds of Volunteers and learned what they were about."

In the years since his direct VISTA service, Cronin has become a valuable resource to the program and other community efforts. With former Volunteer Earl Anthes, Cronin has established Independent Community Consultants, Inc., a nonprofit consulting and training firm that serves numerous Arkansas, national, and international clients.

Anthes and Cronin have known each other since that first Austin training session they attended in 1969. Like Cronin, Anthes remained in the area of his original VISTA service, West Memphis, and the two men successfully conduct ICC business from across the state.

Until the mid 1970s, ICC helped conduct a large number of Arkansas VISTA training projects. Since then, it has provided service to a variety of nonprofit organizations by designing programs and helping improve fundraising skills and long range planning. ICC also publishes several guides and instructional books for nonprofit organizations.

"I'm comfortable here in Hampton," Cronin said. "I like the people. I'm also not going to let some people think they can move me out. The power is shifting. Folks are becoming comfortable enough with themselves to know they can use some help. A VISTA trainer used to say the only thing a Volunteer needs to be is an information hog. Root it out and keep it. You need to know everything in case something comes up."

The streets of Hampton's black community were fairly busy when Cronin took a short stroll through the neighborhood that warm winter day. Groups of kids were out playing and older folks were working on their cars or yards. People exchanged greetings with Cronin in the casual style of small town friendships.

One man came up with a letter from the tax office and asked

Cronin to help him understand it. Cronin told the man to bring it by his house later, promising to help because of a favor that Cronin said the fellow had done him. A few steps down the street, Cronin explained the favor occurred a week earlier when a woman was being beaten by her boyfriend. Though no one had seemed able to break up the fight, the man with the tax form distracted the boyfriend and got him away from the woman. He did it, Cronin said, not by telling him to stop or threatening him. He just kept asking the boyfriend if he wanted to go off with him and do something else. It was a diversion technique similar to some Cronin might have used.

Before he circled the block and returned to his house, Cronin exchanged a few words with an old man who was also out walking. Cronin called him "Mr. Jesse," as they paused to joke about women, weather, longevity, and other matters. In that moment of exchange, an extraordinary resemblance emerged between the thirty-eight-year-old Cronin and Jesse Ware, the aged black man.

Both wore similar outfits—a soft cap pulled down low and a faded plaid shirt worn as a light outer jacket. Yet the similarities ran deeper. Both men engaged in the small talk with the same pleasant sense of banter. They joked about themselves and lightly complimented each other. There was a sense of mutual respect and enjoyment in the momentary encounter as though each man recognized in the other a clear likeness of himself.

It was the type of exchange no Volunteer could expect who had chosen to move on from his service role and cut the community ties that had begun to form in a one- or two-year service period. The moment becomes even more poignant in light of Ware's death a few weeks later. Yet at the time, it was for Cronin just a passing word in the community where he had made his home.

"As Art would say, 'This morning's good story is last night's pee down the leg.' It was creative and challenging, but also intense. If I had my choice I'd sit on the porch and rock and not face that challenge. I'd just laugh and keep on going."

LOCAL VOLUNTEERS

VISTA program designers did not immediately realize that community people could be as effective as recruited national Volunteers. Community leaders were considered a local resource, someone who could help the national Volunteer make the right contacts and communicate more effectively. This limited thinking was a result of modeling the program too closely on the Peace Corps, Joe Bruch said.

> VISTA came from a Peace Corps mentality, a national image of middle class America going out and doing things. Some people felt we couldn't recruit locally, so community Volunteers weren't considered for the program until after a few years.

Program administrators began to realize that people from low income communities, if properly trained, could also perform similar work as the national Volunteers. By the late 1960s, locally recruited or community Volunteers were becoming recognized for the distinct contributions they were making to the program. By the mid 1970s, they constituted the majority of VISTA workers. And by the 1980s, the use of national Volunteers had been almost totally phased out. In a larger sense, the ability of VISTA to utilize different types of Volunteers is a mark of its primary commitment to people.

The increasing use of community Volunteers was not a result of a declining national commitment. Quite the opposite, the

Volunteer Katherine Knight

value of local Volunteers was first recognized when national commitment was at its peak. According to state program officer Jim Crawford, VISTA administrators first recognized the effectiveness of using local Volunteers after nationals lost much time gaining community acceptance.

> The use of locally recruited Volunteers was absolutely the key policy change. They had the skills required for community development. It was difficult for national Volunteers to establish themselves, gain credibility, and understand local needs.

Local Volunteers had no adjustment period to limit their effectiveness. Nor could a charge of "outside agitators" stirring up the people be used against local Volunteers. Despite the effectiveness of local Volunteers, it was program restrictions in policy and funding that led to their increased use.

Influencing the placement of more community Volunteers was the idea of eliminating radical national Volunteers and directing the program toward less confrontational positions. This policy guided the program through most of the 1970s, until decreased funding made it impossible to bring any but local volunteers into service.

Ted Wilson said local Volunteers, being older and more mature, were more reasonable people to work with than the national recruits. In many cases, local Volunteers showed opposite characteristics of the national group, such as a willingness to work on projects others had established for them, Wilson said.

> The locals had no problem with the environment, and they came into the program with a clear idea of expectation. They did have a hard time conceptualizing their work as part of a process, an awareness that the problem will continue unless you train or educate someone to deal with it consistently rather than just with the immediacy.

The local Volunteer did not have the national's ability to design and initiate projects that would have meaningful impact, Wilson said. But meaningful impact was often hard to measure, and sometimes a one-to-one encounter became as meaningful as the development of an entire project, he added.

The problems in east Arkansas required the agency to give most support to ambitious national Volunteer projects and delegate community volunteers to more subordinate roles, Wilson said. Yet the success of local Volunteers suggested there were different roles for different types of people in VISTA, Wilson added.

Mrs. Delcenia Robinson agreed that VISTA offered different levels of activity for local Volunteers. Some liked the glamour of being associated with an organization, while to some it was just a paycheck, she said. Most local Volunteers were committed to their work and wished the sponsoring agency had given them greater support and encouragement to continue after VISTA service, Mrs. Robinson said.

The agency emphasis on national volunteer activities, however, gave the local Volunteers a clear understanding of their role, she said.

> The purpose of the community Volunteer was to work with and make it easier for the national. There was no way a white person would get into some of those homes. The community Volunteer was trusted by the people. The national Volunteers didn't have any problems once they knew me.

The local familiarity of community Volunteers acted as an effective balance to the special skills of the national. While the nationals might know what to do in a situation, the locals would usually know with whom it had to be done. Melvin Brown viewed this exchange at its most literal level.

> The national Volunteers had the know-how. I knew where people were. I could tell them in which yard the dog would bite and in which yard the dog would just look at you.

Brown said national Volunteers showed that things could be done locals had never thought of, even such apparently simple things as going to the local courthouse and speaking with the county judge about a problem with city services. Local Volunteers were also given specific roles by national Volunteers to keep projects going after they had departed, Brown said.

Estella Morris, a local Volunteer who worked at several projects in the Little Rock area, recognized that the complementary relationship between national and local Volunteers was many times based on expertise locals weren't aware they had. National volunteers who came into a community and identified courses of action helped Locals realize a reason for developing their individual skills, Mrs. Morris said.

> There is a lot of knowledge and resources in these communities. All you need many times is just to say "this is the need" or "this can be done."

Volunteer Estella Morris

Mrs. Morris said the most effective combination was a younger national Volunteer teamed with an older locally recruited one. The skills, energy, and daring of the young were well matched with the dedication, community roots, and hard work of the older Volunteer. Many younger community Volunteers did not achieve as much, she said.

> The younger locally recruited Volunteers were not so much aware of what had been. They didn't remember the days of segregation. Younger ones may have felt that this has always been so, that no one ever had to drag cotton sacks for 50 cents a day or scrub floors for a quarter.

Regardless of his age, the local Volunteer brought certain skills to his work that could effectively mesh with those of the national Volunteer. Foremost among these were a sense of realism and an understanding of the dynamics of his community activity. The national Volunteer often joined VISTA with the vague motivation of helping others, people he presumed to be different from himself. The local Volunteer operated under no such illusion, and poverty to him was not a distant entity, Mrs. Morris said.

> I wasn't a starry-eyed middle class kid who had difficulty believing such things existed. My eyes were already opened and working in poverty offered no new adventure, no culture shock . . . I wasn't sophisticated, but not naive either. I was part of that world, then and now.

The local Volunteer's life experience developed in him a set of realistic expectations about his world. He generally had a sense of patience and a fair degree of humility. The national Volunteer often brought opposite characteristics to his service. His naive idealism was supported by a sense of impatience and personal pride often bordering on arrogance. Working together, the ideal relationship between a local and national Volunteer allowed each to augment the other's shortcomings. The national would gain in humility and local awareness; the local would gain a sense of personal pride and expand his resource awareness by learning how to assert himself in a larger environment.

One of Arkansas' most accomplished local Volunteers was Mrs. Katherine Knight, a product of Little Rock segregated schools and a college graduate who joined VISTA in 1970. Like most community Volunteers, Mrs. Knight described herself as "volunteer oriented" with a lifelong desire to help others.

> I don't like a volunteer job that is a pay job. You have to live what you believe. Someone has to serve the people, compromise their personal time. That was my style. The appeal of VISTA to me was you weren't tied to a desk. VISTA was an opportunity to do things I liked doing and to serve.

Mrs. Knight recognized that her education gave her a different view of her community and the VISTA program than generally found in other black women of her generation. Her exposure to the black militant movement and participation in campus demonstrations had raised her consciousness about social issues, she said.

I had lived in the community and come back and recognized there was not a lot of progress in spite of laws and poverty programs. I came home and found people still starving, still not having equal rights, not knowing how to go about doing things. I was interested in helping my folks, in providing a service.

The attitude of helping people was not always displayed by the national Volunteers in the most positive manner, and they occasionally acted superior to the people they had come to serve, Mrs. Knight said. Some of the national Volunteers from the Pulaski County EOA with whom she worked also had little esteem for local Volunteers, and denied them an opportunity to contribute original direction to projects, she added.

Despite her disappointment with certain aspects of VISTA, Mrs. Knight said she believed that what she was doing was useful to others, including acting as a buffer to national Volunteers and helping them deal with situations of local hostility. As with most well-motivated volunteers, Mrs. Knight has continued her useful activities. After VISTA she was active in Girl Scouts for several years and became an English teacher at a Little Rock high school. While working on a masters degree in writing, she has served two terms as president of the Little Rock Classroom Teachers Association.

Under current policy, all Arkansas VISTA projects are staffed with community Volunteers. Project goals have changed from the days when national Volunteers were turned loose to do their best under whatever conditions they encountered. In the contemporary environment, local Volunteers are providing an outstanding level of direct service. Their commitment is what it has always been—the essence of VISTA—helping one's neighbor. In the modern context, they are literally doing it in their own neighborhoods.

SUMMER ASSOCIATE VOLUNTEERS

Program Concept & Training

In the summer of 1968, Arkansas' first Associate Volunteer program was sponsored by Ouachita Baptist University at Arkadelphia. Under the direction of Jim Ranchino, a dynamic political science professor, the program placed forty-eight college students in Arkansas communities for a ten-week service period. The program was repeated in the summer of 1969 with a larger number of Associate Volunteers from OBU and a second project sponsor, the Arkansas Council of Human Relations, which placed additional Volunteers around the state.

Associate Volunteer programs had been implemented in other states for a few years with some success. The programs allowed state residents and college students to participate in the War on Poverty in the same manner as National Volunteers, but with a much more limited training and service period. The students were expected to contribute to their assigned communities and hopefully acquire a better understanding of local poverty issues.

Dr. Fred Morrow, a sociologist from the University of Arkansas at Little Rock, saw the Associate Program as more educational than functional. Students got an introduction to the lifestyle of the impoverished and increased their sensitivity to problems.

The idea was to test their views and let them arrive at a nonjudgemental attitude toward the people they're supposed to help. The students were sent there for a time to do something that made a difference, to really get their teeth into a problem and work with organizations and individuals.

Morrow employed Ranchino to train Community Action Agency staff in an OEO program in the mid 1960s, and the outspoken and politically astute Ranchino was an ideal choice to organize and administer the first Arkansas Associate program. With assistance from Bob Riley, then head of the OBU Political Science Department and later Arkansas Lt. Governor, an OEO grant for $52,500 was received, and the program was begun.

Recruiting on Arkansas campuses and those of neighboring states brought the first Associate Volunteers to the OBU campus in June 1968. After four days of training, they were placed in their community assignments. Though he recognized the potential value of the experience to the students, Ranchino also believed the communities could gain from the program. In a memo to the OEO, he listed these items as potential long range goals: an increase in volunteerism; a raised community interest in sponsoring permanent Volunteers; and the recruitment of regular Volunteers from the Associates.

Most of those goals were achieved to some degree by the 1968 program. The program was run so efficiently and with such low overhead that only forty-six thousand dollars of the original grant funds were used. Ranchino, with a flair for challenging systems and beliefs, made an attempt to return the surplus funds. OEO bureaucracy could not comprehend such a move, and the offer threw their bookkeeping into turmoil.

Ranchino, who died in 1978, practiced confrontational techniques in his classes at OBU and was one of its most popular teachers. His widow, Veda Ranchino Morgan, recalled his ability to engage students in creative dialogues that broke down preconceived attitudes and values.

I remember Jim as an inspiring teacher, someone who would motivate the students to react with one another. He wanted people to think, to improve

Jim Ranchino

In Remembrance

It was a cool, fall day in November. The daily routine had begun for the people at Ouachita. Go to class, go to chapel, eat lunch, check your mail, class again, study, etc. But this fall day held an air of excitement and curiosity.

It was election day, November 7, 1978. In and out of class, students wre discussing the governor's race, whether Bethune or Brandon would win and if Amendment 59 would pass. Two students and two faculty members were running for the Constitutional Convention. But, despite what was going on at the polls, the college schedule continued.

That night, between studying and bull sessions, students tuned in the T.V. for election returns. There were commentators, electronic results, phones ringing, returns posted, etc. But if you were watching Channel 7, there was something missing. Jim Ranchino, professor of political science, had served the past seven years as an election commentator for KATV. He wasn't on the air and no one knew why.

But, at approximately 7:30 p.m., anchorman Steve Barnes announced Ranchino had collapsed at the studio and was taken to St. Vincent's Hospital. Ouachita students called each other spreading the dark news. Could it really be true?

Students sat glued to their T.V. sets in the dorms waiting for further news on their teacher, co-worker and friend. That news came at approximately 8:30 p.m. Jim Ranchino was pronounced dead at 7:35 p.m. of a massive coronary.

Dorm doors slung open, shouts were heard and tears were shed as the Ouachita family was stunned, shocked and saddened over the death of a close one.

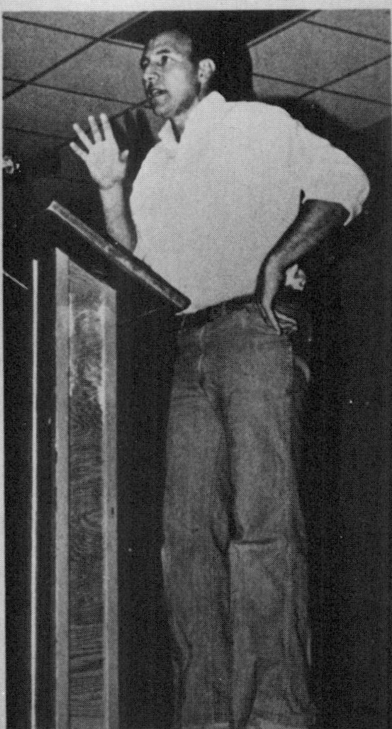

Suddenly, no one cared about the returns on the screen, the newsmen or the hard-fought campaigns.

It was a long night for friends, students and fellow professors. Many went to bed feeling as though a part of themselves was gone.

The next day the campus held an air of mourning. Students walked to class with black arm bands in his memory.

On Thursday morning, classes were dismissed for a memorial service in Mitchell Hall. It was unlike the noisy gathering during a Tuesday chapel. Instead, friends entered quickly, tearfully, to remember their close friend. Respects were paid; memories were reflected upon.

Funeral services were held at First Baptist Church. The community as well as the Ouachita Family once again assembled to pay their respects to Jim Ranchino.

He may be gone from our sight, but feelings and memories will live forever. He was special. As his sister stated at the memorial service, "His arms were as big as Texas, waiting to be stretched around someone in need." He was challenging, a rebel, loving and caring. He was a man who made you examine your own beliefs to see if they were valid. And he was a family man. As one stated in an eulogy, his wife Veda and his two children were just as much a part of his lectures as the most noted political scientists.

November 7, 1978 . . . a day Ouachita will always remember. Clinton was elected Governor, Bethune beat Brandon and Amendment 59 was defeated. And Jim Ranchino died.

emorial

Memorial to Jim Ranchino in the *Ouachita Baptist University 1979 Yearbook.*

themselves. In his sessions with the Volunteers, he would start out with a speech by Frederick Douglas—something about how you can't plant a field until you plow it all up.

Bill Meyers, an Associate Volunteer who served at Blytheville (Mississippi County), spoke of Ranchino as a person "in tune with the times and the mission of helping others, someone who knew the terrain and had a sense of what had to be done." Teresa Jackman Young, who served at Marked Tree (Poinsett County), recalled Ranchino's ability to motivate the group.

> He could inspire and indict, convince us one moment we could single-handedly cure the ills of America, chastise us the next for our arrogance and patronizing attitude. I can remember weighty sessions about community organizing and power structures and practical sessions with advice like trying to make sure the rooms we stayed in were at the back of the house because they were safer in the event of bombs which were usually thrown through front windows.

Ranchino, like other superior VISTA trainers, mixed Volunteer ideology, melodrama, and realistic advice to present the issues at hand in the simplest terms. A large man who projected a great personal energy, Ranchino became a widely known Arkansas personality. As a result, various stories about him were considered fact, including the false belief that he had played professional football with the Dallas Cowboys and was forced out of that career after being injured by Rosie Greer.

Where the stories stopped and the real man began is less important than the positive influence and commitment to human service Ranchino left all those he worked with. Mrs. Young's memory of her 1969 training session reflects the values that may best represent Ranchino's legacy:

> In retrospect, there was not really much a director can teach an 18-year-old in a one-week session. While we may not have left the OBU campus with much practical knowledge of how to end years of social ills, we left with

pure and eager hearts. If love could have ended poverty and discrimination, Jim Ranchino's little band of summer associates could have changed the face of Arkansas.

Associate Volunteer Conflicts

The reception of Associate Volunteers by the CAAS that requested them was not completely positive. In many cases, the Associate Volunteers were the first VISTA workers placed at the agencies and no clear work plan had been established for them. With only ten weeks of service, the Associates could not proceed at the leisurely pace of national Volunteers. As a result, they initiated some activities that rapidly upset CAA staff and the community status quo.

Black militant activists could easily cause problems in Arkansas, but activism did not necessarily require outright acts of confrontation. At Bald Knob (White County), Volunteer Diana Ricou was reassigned to another community for little more than having publicly associated with blacks. In June 1968, Ricou had been able to coordinate many levels of assistance in the construction of a community park, and she had established good relations with the low income community.

Ricou said that on the July 4 weekend she and another Volunteer had gotten a ride to the nearby town of Kensett, home of former U.S. Congressman Wilbur Mills, whom they happened to see watering his lawn. The car was being driven by a young black man, and the back seat was crowded with several of his younger brothers and sisters who had gone along for the ride. Ricou said she and the other Volunteer got out of the car to introduce themselves to Mills, they had a short talk while the carload of blacks waited at the curb, and then they went on.

Two days later, I got a call from Wilbur's brother, Roger Mills, who was director of my sponsoring agency. He told me to get out of town before sunset. The inference was that I had crossed racial lines and also that I had been involved with a white man who was the village idiot. I called Ranchino to find out what to do. He said don't wait till sunset.

In his summary report on the 1968 program, Ranchino wrote that many community agencies were opposed to change of any type.

The major enemy of change and the War on Poverty are those personnel employed by existing OEO agencies who are supposedly dedicated to economic and social change. . . . Until guidelines and pressures are developed which will exert the necessary force on OEO personnel to work for change, the War on Poverty remains a lackadaisical, lethargic skirmish with the status quo.

In her 1968 project review, one OBU field supervisor wrote that the "Volunteers found the agencies a complete farce, controlled by politics and destructive to the efforts of poverty programs." George Ivory, OBU field supervisor for southwest Arkansas counties, confirmed those impressions in his report, calling the CAAs at first apathetic and later hostile when they realized the Volunteer work could be confrontational. Two Associate Volunteers described their relationship with a sponsoring agency at Camden with these remarks in their final report:

The CAA . . . felt we should do slave labor for the agency . . . cooking and washing dishes, teachers aides for Head Start. They felt offended when we attempted a project of our own . . . The agency are masters at passing the buck. Perhaps they do not function properly due to an uncooperative governing board and political pressure on them by community leaders.

The Arkansas Council for Human Relations had a more direct objective for community organizing than the OBU program. Almost all CHR Volunteers were black, and several had distinctly militant philosophies. Among them, Edward Whitfield was perhaps the most well known.

A graduate of Little Rock Central High School, Whitfield was a student at Cornell University and a leader of the 1969 campus confrontation there. A photo of him and other campus blacks brandishing rifles appeared on the cover of the May 5, 1969 issue of *Newsweek.* A month later, Whitfield was in Little Rock delivering an orientation speech to new CHR Volunteers. Whitfield and some militant northern blacks who became CHR Volunteers in 1969 used African names to reduce local recognition, another CHR Volunteer said.

One of the few white Volunteers in the CHR program, Paul Williams was a Viet Nam veteran attending the University of Arkansas at Fayetteville where he was recruited by program trainer Bobby Morgan. Several of the northern blacks bought guns in Little Rock during the training program, and Williams said he was harassed by them for not sharing their militant views.

> Training was a profound racial experience, giving me a vivid first hand knowledge of what it was like to be in a persecuted minority. I'd just come back from Viet Nam and knew armed revolution in this country was nonsense. By the end of the project, many of them had accepted me for my integrity, not for my beliefs.

In addition to conflicts resulting from community or agency values, the Associate Volunteers also found some difficulty working with national Volunteers. According to a Ranchino memo, some national Volunteers were afflicted with "a strange disease—'the VISTA Image'—which infects regular Volunteers with a feeling of superiority." Ranchino suggested that national Volunteers felt threatened by Associates' activities and that the two groups should not be assigned to a common project unless the national Volunteer showed extraordinary maturity.

Associate Volunteer Achievement

Despite the barriers they faced, many Arkansas' Associate Volunteers achieved their two primary objectives: community improvement and the raising of their own levels of awareness.

In communities across the state, Associate Volunteers worked in service projects such as recreation, tutoring and consumer education, family planning and health clinics. While their achievements may seem relatively minor in a long term assessment, the efforts they made were for many communities the first attempts at change. As a 1968 report from two Associates at Blytheville states:

> . . . perhaps one of the most important things we accomplished is showing that two white girls were willing to live with a Negro family . . . the white kids are now coming to the center.

For Paul Williams, assigned to Jonesboro in 1969, community impact was achieved by helping local young people understand certain principles of organizing. Helping them overcome a reluctance to approach the power structure allowed them to demand their rights in a nonthreatening manner, Williams said.

> I felt we established good will in the minds of the blacks. I have no illusions we affected wide reaching change. We did create an awareness in the black community and white establishment that times were changing, that old ways were dying, not dead yet by a long shot, but a world of difference.

At Blytheville in 1969, Associates Bill Meyers, a medical student at the time, and Terry Healy, a nurse, chose to support a poorly organized health clinic as their summer service. They spoke at local churches, civic clubs, and at community centers, and greatly increased the clinic's level of service to the community. They trained local volunteers as health aides and coordinated nutrition and sanitation programs with area resources. In a brief period of time, they helped the voluntary efforts of a local pediatrician reach close to two hundred patients in a one-day-per-week clinic.

Perhaps the best example of personal awareness gained as a result of the Associate program can be found in a report from Teresa Jackman Young written the semester following her summer service. A student at Henderson State University at Arkadelphia, Mrs. Young enrolled in a class taught by Juanita D. Sandford, a leading Arkansas sociologist and analyst of poverty conditions, who later included Mrs. Young's report in her book, *Poverty In the Land of Opportunity*.

Mrs. Young's report is particularly significant in relation to comments by Ranchino on the topic of personal awareness. Interviewed in 1969 by the Arkansas Gazette, Ranchino identified how he hoped the Associate program would influence Volunteers and eventually bring about social change.

> In 10 weeks you're not going to break down a system which has been built up over a hundred years. Change must take place in the middle class because the poor don't have the resources. The VISTA program gives middle class students a picture of what their society is really all about. Hopefully, when they move back into their society, they're going to be very conscious of what's going on.
>
> Here's a chance to get at bedrock level. You're there where the action is. You're sleeping in a poor person's house and eating with him. You'll never be the same again.[1]

Mrs. Young's chapter in the Sandford book gives Marked Tree the name Big Slough and all persons have been given fictitious names, but the essential understanding she communicates supports Ranchino's administrative objectives. The following excerpts are from that chapter, "Profiles of Misery":

On a 75 year old black man, mentally incompetent since receiving a head injury 30 years earlier. The man had quit school when he was 13 and in the fifth grade; he had been married three times, had no family, no property and no marketable skills:

> When you look at Booker's life, you can truly say he is an example of a wasted American. His life can be multiplied thousands of times, for there are thousands like him. If for no other reason, the affluent society should try to eliminate poverty because of the tremendous cost involved—measured in terms of the loss of manpower.

On two black women, both in their eighties and widows, their children grown and living in northern states. The women shared a home in conditions of abysmal poverty little different from the lives they had known when they were working and raising their families:

> Hattie and Martha are, as Martha puts it, "waiting it out now, waiting for the Lord to take us home." It seems a harsh fate that these two old women

who labored hard all their lives have nothing to show for it but withered bodies and endless days of poverty.

On the residence and family of a seven-year-old black boy who lived in a two-room shack with his mother, five brothers and two sisters:

> The house . . . is narrow and has two small windows. The inside is dark, even on the brightest summer day. Instead of a door, there is a large piece of cardboard. It is "decorated" with crayon drawings by some of the children of some stick men and women. This gives the house an almost unreal quality—you expect a stick family to live there, not a real family of nine members. On the inside are several piles of straw with a sheet thrown over them. The children sleep on these piles of straw, two to a pile. There is one real bed which the mother and some of the younger children sleep on.

Other profiles in the chapter detail Mrs. Young's contact with white poverty families. Not surprisingly, the lives she describes parallel the poverty and ignorance found among the black families.

In the opening paragraphs, Mrs. Young states that her purpose is to "portray not only the misery of those in poverty, but also to present a picture of the closed atmosphere in Big Slough which perpetuates the conditions of poverty." The chapter concludes with these remarks:

> Big Slough is not an exceptional community. There are communities like it all over Arkansas, and indeed, in every state of the nation where people are living in conditions not fit for human beings . . . The duty of Americans is clear. We must make every effort to turn Big Slough into the exception. Indeed, where the well-being of our fellow man is concerned, we must make every effort to end the exception.[2]

Associate Contribution

The distinct limitations of the Associate program must be recognized before an accurate assessment of its contribution can be made. Primary among these factors are the brief periods of training and service, the relative inexperience of community agencies in preparing for the Volunteers, and the general level of community consciousness.

Small Arkansas towns, the same as small towns anywhere, maintain their daily levels of activity largely uninfluenced by events of the outside world. The passage of time in small towns is marked by local happenings. The affairs of the world, of the nation, and even of Little Rock, though detailed in the daily newspapers, are seen as having little influence on community life.

Arkansans in the late 1960s had been aware for more than a decade of the events at Little Rock's Central High. But the activities in the capitol did not generate much change in small towns, and the idea was reinforced that nothing would ever change. Yet change was inevitable: the Associate Volunteers entered these static environments and found many individuals waiting for it to happen. According to Carol Cantrell, OBU program assistant, the Associates woke entire communities from a lethargic lifestyle.

> For some communities, a sock hop was the herald trumpet of the 20th century. The excitement, rage, and confusion it caused was pivotal in a lot of cases. For the Volunteers to come in and say "let's do something" was revolutionary even though what they did looks so unsophisticated years later.

Though the Associates may not have done more than organize a softball team or a dance, their work provided an essential vehicle for interaction between black and white youths that likely did not exist before, Cantrell said. The Associate's activities were also a chance for small towns to assert their presence in the historical process. In Bald Knob, the community workers motivated by Ricou to construct a park thought it appropriate to name their effort the "Martin Luther King Robert Kennedy Bald Knob National Memorial Park."

The ultimate achievement of the Associate Program is more than the justification of its cost. The OBU program, one of the best of its kind in the nation, had no drop outs in the 1968 summer, and according to Ranchino, the Volunteers proved more capable and effective than had been thought possible. The total effort cost less than one thousand dollars for each Volunteer.

Federal policy changes and funding restrictions prohibited the Associate program from continuing beyond 1969. Yet for its limited time and scope, the program had its impact according to Teresa Young.

> Our contribution was not so much to the community as to the individuals we touched. We proved to young black men and women and to ourselves that blacks and whites could have a meaningful peer relationship . . . Our work may not have produced tangible results, but we did reach out with our hearts, and who can say that love itself does not create the most lasting results?

Notes

1. *Arkansas Gazette,* May 7, 1969.
2. Juanita D. Sandford, *Poverty in the Land of Opportunity,* Rose Publishing Co., Little Rock. 1978. Pgs. 37–63.

PULASKI COUNTY
POVERTY AND LOCAL POLITICS

The Early Assignments

EOA Projects: The Later Years

Highland Court

Higgins

Sweet Home

Design Co-operative

Additional EOA Projects

Later Administrative Problems

Conclusion

The Early Assignments

The Pulaski County Equal Opportunity Agency (PCEOA), incorporated in November 1965, was one of the first poverty programs to receive VISTA volunteers in Arkansas. As the state's major urban poverty program, the agency had the diverse tasks of working in Little Rock's neighborhood poverty pockets as well as dealing with the deep rooted poverty of the county's rural communities.

The empowerment of those communities and their attempts to control their own destiny match other Arkansas efforts. The PCEOA VISTA projects are distinguished, however, by the manipulative activities and desires of individuals in leadership positions.

The problems and errors that beset the PCEOA during its years as a VISTA sponsor may be due in large part to the agency's size and initial lack of experience in administering people and programs. Critics of the agency, however, have been more specific in their complaints, blaming individual staff and agency policy for failing to carry out federal mandates. Those alleged failures and a history of misused funds, the critics say, eventually brought about the economic collapse and ultimate dissolution of the agency. In late 1985, the PCEOA found itself more than $400,000 in debt with less than $1,000 in its bank account. It shut down not long afterwards.

In 1965, Pulaski County had a substantial poverty population with the expected social indicators. In the black community, eighty percent of the population earned less than four thousand dollars

VISTA workers meet the press at Little Rock. *Arkansas Gazette*

per year, and one-fourth of all adults in poverty were functionally illiterate. Substandard housing accounted for twenty-seven percent of all county dwellings, a condition largely brought on by nonenforcement of housing codes. Lack of facilities also limited the value of homes. For absentee landlords, the financial incentive of lower taxes from letting rental property deteriorate was further enhanced by a housing demand guaranteeing occupancy.

Mrs. Esther Boswell, the agency's first VISTA supervisor, spoke of assignments for Volunteers that arrived in early 1966.

> The first wave of Volunteers were just kids. If they didn't have skills in getting along with people before they came, it wasn't easy for them. If they did no more than spend time in the neighborhoods with tutoring, recreation programs or taking people to doctors, they were needed at that time. Those early Volunteers did such humdrum things, nothing really outstanding other than they cared about people. That was an accomplishment for those who were just kids themselves.

Darcy Johns and Barbara Ryder were volunteers from the original group who worked in the predominantly black Dixie addition and Hemlock Court areas of North Little Rock. Assigned as community developers, the women tutored at Shorter College (a black college in North Little Rock), organized a library, implemented sewing classes, read mail for illiterate residents, and sold sandwiches from a booth at a local park, donating the money for construction of a day care center.

"We do everything from soup to nuts," Ms. Ryder, a UCLA graduate and philosophy major, said in an interview in the December 12, 1966 Arkansas Gazette. "VISTA seemed like something that would let me do something constructive while I found myself."

Following an October 1967 meeting with Pulaski County Volunteers, OEO regional administrator Joe Bruch noted in a memo:

> . . . For the most part they gave the physical impression of being a clean cut "Joe College" type. All were attentive and responded very well. In general the Arkansas Volunteers appear to be no-problem types . . . The number of Volunteers could be increased greatly and they would be utilized as VISTA envisions they should be.

In 1968, the PCEOA had been assigned sixteen national Volunteers. Among their diverse activities, the Volunteers had organized a bail bond project, formed a tenants' rights organization to work with urban renewal, and provided extensive tutorial and recreational programs.

Two early EOA Volunteers who still reside in Pulaski County are Mary Potter and Linda Patrick; now both are registered nurses. Arriving in Arkansas in 1967, the women had their first glimpse of local culture at the Little Rock airport when a gathering of Razorback football fans began a loud chorus of "calling the Hogs." Resisting the temptation to get back on the plane, the new Volunteers soon found the agency's plans for them demanded a high degree of self confidence. They were assigned neighborhoods in which to live and told to make themselves known to the community, even knocking on doors and introducing themselves if necessary, Potter said.

> Our first Arkansas home was in East Little Rock, an area called Hanger Hill. Macaroni was about six boxes for $1, and we cooked on a single bunsen burner. We had no ice box. We couldn't rent a furnished apartment because we were supposed to live as poor people did.

The Volunteers became involved in neighborhood things and began a series of one-to-one community involvements; shopping for the homebound, assisting the elderly, visiting inmates at the women's prison. The lack of specific direction from their sponsoring agency seemed to be a distinct administrative policy, Patrick said.

> We got thrown from pillar to post to begin with. They just threw us in. We made up our own structure, set up our own projects. The agency didn't seem to care if we left the house or not.

Another PCEOA Volunteer from this period was Liz Roberts, a nineteen-year-old Colfax, Washington native who joined VISTA after her freshman year of college. Roberts later became a state VISTA supervisor and helped administer the program. She also said the PCEOA program in its early years lacked clearly stated goals.

> We arrived, were assigned to a neighborhood, told to find lodging and good luck. There was a lot of sitting around and not knowing where to

Volunteers (*left*) Linda Patrick and (*right*) Mary Potter

start. I was never real comfortable in knocking on doors and introducing myself, asking how I could help. I am a task oriented person and had difficulty finding out my job. My main impressions were frustration about the lack of direction.

Beginning in January 1967, the Pulaski County EOA came under the executive direction of W. L. "Sonny" Walker, a Pine Bluff native whose community development work earned him widespread respect and support. As deputy director of the EOA, Walker had helped organize local elections of Neighborhood Action Councils, community groups that he believed were at the core of the poverty program.

I think professionals should be on hand simply as a resource for the people in the poverty neighborhoods, not to make decisions for them . . . The poverty program is the last resort of the ungroomed, the ill-shaven, the untrained. This is the only place where they have priority. I make it a practice never to put a desk between me and a poverty person. I always sit with them.

Jim Crawford, who took over as the PCEOA Volunteer supervisor in 1968, spoke of Walker's influence on the volunteers and the agency.

The key to Sonny Walker is charisma. He knew how to talk to people, to inspire them. He could turn people on like Martin Luther King. In those times, we needed someone who could keep our spirits high. A lot of commitment to the poverty program from the Volunteers was due to Sonny's leadership.

The community development concept Walker supported was a nondirective policy that expected neighborhood people and their elected neighborhood leaders to determine the Volunteer's area of service. Walker believed that the Volunteer was there to support the neighborhood and to attach himself to the locally organized structure, and he rejected the Volunteer's criticism of lack of direction.

I would disagree there was a lack of structure. Most of the Volunteers were into community organizing. You can't prescribe that. You don't send them out and say here's what you do and where. We designated for them a neighborhood and people to contact. They were to respond to the community, not carry out the mandate of a director. That was by design.

College Station, a black neighborhood in southeast Little Rock, offered a good example of Walker's ideas in application. Prior to the VISTA program, that community had attempted to solve its local problems through a grass roots organization, the College Station Progressive League.

Under the leadership of Annie Mae Bankhead, the League's founder and director for many years, the College Station Progressive League worked diligently to better community life. Volunteers assigned to College Station were quickly and quietly absorbed into its on-going efforts, Mrs. Bankhead said.

Whatever we tried to do, they would help us get it—bolts of cloth for our senior citizens sewing class or food for our community banquets. They would go to stores and businesses would donate it. When the Volunteers came in with some ideas, it wasn't hard for the people to join in and pull together.

Mrs. Bankhead recalled the Volunteers helping some of the young women put on a "Miss Personality" program, an evening's entertainment that raised about seven hundred dollars for the community. The funds were eventually used to buy a kiln and help establish a ceramics shop that continues to function at the local senor citizen center, she added.

Several community centers were established during Walker's tenure as PCEOA director. For the most part, these were multipurpose centers where Volunteers were able to offer tutoring or recreational programs. The centers were more socially acceptable locations for integrated activities than the Volunteers' homes. Racial tensions were high at the time, and a group of black youths regularly visiting a household of white females was not well accepted in the late 1960s in Pulaski County.

Within the PCEOA itself, racial and sexual problems developed between the primarily all white Volunteers and the all black agency staff, but conflicts there did not match the racial tensions exhibited outside the agency.

In February 1968, rumors of photographs depicting two white female Volunteers in bed with a black man brought Liz Roberts, then a state supervisor, to the Jacksonville community center to investigate. The actual photo showed one Volunteer sitting on the edge of a bed with a black boy, but community members had so exaggerated the story there was great concern about the media picking up on the alleged scandal.

Involvements between black locals and white female Volunteers seem relatively harmless from the modern perspective, yet at the time that type of racial mixing was considered scandalous.

One Volunteer who informed her family she planned to marry a local black man found that her two older brothers were sent down to escort her home. Returning to Little Rock, she received word her mother was critically ill, but that turned out to be another ruse to remove her from the southern environment. The Volunteer defied her family and eventually married the man.

Black/white relations were not always of such a trivial nature. White female Volunteers were exposed to some danger living in black neighborhoods, and several faced the threat of rape. Liz Roberts recalled occasions when their homes were broken into by local men who assumed the girls were prostitutes. On at least one occasion, a white female Volunteer in Little Rock was raped.

In August 1968, the streets of downtown Little Rock were patrolled by more than five hundred national Guardsmen, and a curfew was imposed following violent protest rallies concerning the beating death of a black youth by a white trustee at the county penal farm.

Jim Crawford recalled one afternoon during the rallies when local blacks forced entry into the PCEOA offices and attacked white volunteers. On another occasion shortly afterwards, Volunteer Harold Penwell walked out from the offices while the black protesters marched by. He too was attacked and received a concussion. Dazed and nearly unconscious, Penwell was mistakenly arrested and jailed on charges of public drunkenness.

Beyond the racial problems, the PCEOA experienced local and federal administrative difficulties. Conflicts developed from interfacing with the Little Rock Model Cities Program, an urban development project. In 1967, a funding crisis tested the Volunteers' resolve to remain in service for an undetermined period without pay.

That funding crisis foreshadowed efforts by the Nixon administration to abolish VISTA by cutting off transportation allowances in the spring of 1967. The Pulaski County Volunteers reacted to that plan by sending a letter of protest of the White House. The letter, signed by seventeen Volunteers and Supervisor Goforth Coleman, questioned the President's integrity and referred to earlier remarks promising administrative support of VISTA. The Volunteers asked how the elimination of transportation funds could be considered an example of that support.

Mike Watts, one of the signers of the letter, sent another mes-

Volunteer Mike Watts

sage in April 1972 to his VISTA and ACTION superiors. In his personal letter, Watts stated his refusal to cooperate with the administration, including the writing of reports. His reasons were that the administration was completely unwilling to respond to Volunteers and that it had no concern for them or the people supposed to be served. Watts' letter ended in clear defiance.

> VISTA is welcome to take any action against me that it feels necessary. I will not, however, respond quietly. If VISTA is to die, then let it be with a bang, but I'll be damned if I'll let it die with a whimper.

Volunteer complaints about administrative neglect were a preview of what was to come in the mid 1970s. Under Walker's direction, however, the PCEOA VISTA program received a sincere inauguration. Following his 1969 resignation to become State OEO director, the agency adopted a new style of leadership during the fifteen-year tenure of Dean Goldsby, a former director of program operations, who took over in September 1970.

EOA Projects: The Later Years

Similar to other large community action agencies during the 1970s, the PCEOA sponsored a variety of VISTA projects throughout its service area. The many grass roots agencies that would later replace it as VISTA sponsors had not yet gained sufficient internal organization to apply for and support their own Volunteers. Many of the agencies had not yet been created.

This situation gave enormous power to the EOA. In its time, it was the main channel of federal anti-poverty funds, and it had administrative control over which projects would receive those funds and how the money would be spent.

According to conservative VISTA philosophy, the success of a project can be measured in part by its duration. A successful project should create a level of community involvement and support sufficient to maintain the work for its necessary life span.

This criterion does not account for projects that solved a specific problem and were then justifiably phased out. The "long range impact" assessment also fails to give credit to Volunteer assignments that closely meshed with on-going community affairs, assignments that assisted in the development of community centers, post offices, Head Start programs, medical clinics, and other local service operations.

In College Station, for example, Mrs. Bankhead and other community leaders spoke warmly of the Volunteers' personal efforts, but could only recall in a very general manner the projects in which the Volunteers worked. In College Station, and likely in many other areas of Pulaski County, Volunteers were so closely involved with local projects their identities and personal contributions were never given distinct recognition by anyone beyond the persons with whom they worked and lived.

One College Station resident who served as a PCEOA Neighborhood Aide for seventeen years recalled only the first names of three national Volunteers assigned to her community. She spoke of their contributions in this manner:

> The Volunteers did some research to help people pass the postal test . . . they helped in the community clean up . . . helped me and my son get to the hospital . . . did some tutoring in adult education . . . helped establish Head Start . . . helped us get gas lines and water supply . . . helped people fill out forms for social service.

The key word in her recollections is "helped," a concept more significant than the identity of those who served. These were national Volunteers who did not stay on after their VISTA time. Their semi-anonymous role is fitting and proper, particularly in an urban environment where change and new faces are a part of daily life.

In Pulaski County, and probably throughout Arkansas, VISTA history can be learned in the living rooms and church meeting rooms of poverty communities, from individuals whom the Volunteers directly assisted.

This chapter's partial review of PCEOA projects is a reflection of the agency's almost twenty-year association with the program. No complete history exists or can be created.

Highland Court

Highland Court, also known as Highland Park, is a low-income housing project in central Little Rock that utilized Volunteers for youth recreation and sports, tutoring programs, counseling, legal aid, senior citizen assistance, and other projects.

The area's problems were due to a population density of young and elderly residents and a lack of facilities and planned programs for their benefits. Early Volunteer efforts attempted to establish tenant councils and develop in the people a sense of their collective strength when dealing with the Little Rock Housing Authority and other providers of service.

Volunteer David Stewart gained the assistance of the Little Rock Jaycees in a 1974 program that helped with senior citizen transportation to grocery stores. By 1977, Volunteer Rebecca Brown had coordinated a tutoring program that solicited children from the area schools, recruited volunteer tutors from local colleges, and utilized the facilities of the nearby campus of the University of Arkansas at Little Rock.

A Volunteer who gained recognition at Highland Court was Beverly Boswell. Nominated by her VISTA supervisor for a 1978 Community Service Award, Ms. Boswell organized the first tenant council in Highland's twenty-five year history. She also increased parental involvement in a summer tutoring program by sending home those children whose parents failed to attend the planning meetings.

In an April 1978 report, Ms. Boswell wrote:

> This is my last week as a Volunteer. I feel our involvement in Highland has had a positive effect on the community. There is involvement where there wasn't before . . . the youth and parents are starting to work together . . . I am leaving with warm feelings in my heart. I have learned a great deal in these past 14 months and I believe I have helped in some ways the development of Highland Park youth.

The Volunteer who achieved the most measureable results in Highland Park was Estella Morris, a locally recruited VISTA who during a four-year period also served in the Granite Mountain area near College Station and at the Veterans Hospital in North Little Rock. Mrs. Morris worked in many programs in Highland Park, including a legal aid project where she served as a lay advocate to represent children in juvenile court.

A 1979 letter from the Highland Tenant Council to the PCEOA praised Mrs. Morris for her work and leadership, citing her assistance in working out a budget and by-laws to obtain funds from the city housing authority and the State Board of Education. The letter stated that as a result of Mrs. Morris' efforts "we have become much stronger and are working together much better as a community." Mrs. Morris said that at Highland she recognized a need for an adult population who could "take the reins and start working for themselves."

> I still look at Highland and feel like a lot of what was started is still being carried on. Now the city is renovating the whole area. One thing those folks were pushing for was input into the housing project administration. After the Tenant Council, they began to be heard.

Mrs. Morris also helped the area children get a school bus route assigned, eliminating their daily crossings of busy University Avenue. Yet for all her accomplishments, the project she takes most pride in was the most elementary of all.

In the middle of the Jefferson Street playground, a huge pile of dirt had been dumped there and ignored by city officials despite pleas by Highland parents to have it removed. Rain washed muddy streams off the sides of the pile, and the entire playground was alternately muddy or dust covered.

Mrs. Morris decided to pursue a different course of action. She recruited a local photographer to take photos of the dirt and the playground, and sent copies of the photos with letters to Arkansas Congressmen and Health, Education, and Welfare officials in Washington, DC. Within two weeks, the dirt was removed.

All it took was people banding together, saying we are voting age people. Once organized, the parents became a feisty bunch. Once they found out what they could do, they were willing to jump right in and tromp on. The Tenant Council made me feel good about myself.

Higgins

In the southeast corner of Pulaski County a string of small black communities are located in the flat bottom land close to the Arkansas River. In Higgins and other nearby towns, the city life of Little Rock seems much further than the few actual miles traveled. Pecan trees and plowed fields, gravel and dirt roads leading up to worn wooden homes are the details of this rural landscape.

The first Volunteer assigned to Higgins was Joann Violo Rose, a New York City native who spent most of 1970 helping the community organize a Head Start program and raise the funds to purchase land and build a community center. Ms. Rose, who currently lives in Little Rock and teaches elementary school in another low income community, spoke of a number of projects she established in Higgins, including organizing the people to sue the county water department for high costs and poor services.

I remember when I first got there I taught in a one-room shack with no water, no toilets, and 20 preschoolers. I remember the little wooden chairs. The kids would go pee out back. That little shack was like a VISTA poster. It actualized every fantasy I had.

Attending community meetings, Ms. Rose said her personal motivation was augmented by the energy and dedication of the locals, people who worked for low wages all day then spent hours in meetings to get things others already had. In her recreational work with a girl's softball team, Ms. Rose saw examples of poverty-related problems such as teenage pregnancy. At the time, she felt "the cycle could be broken."

According to Pat Jackson, a Higgins resident and PCEOA community development aide, Ms. Rose freed the people from dependence on the agency for local services and instilled in them the idea of depending on themselves. In return, the community accepted her and later Volunteers as their own.

Mrs. Jackson, who became something of a surrogate mother for many of the Volunteers assigned to her area, recalled Volunteers living in her house and how she outfitted them in her children's clothes to make them more presentable at local church services.

Penny Lewis was a Volunteer who served in Higgins for a short while in 1971 after Joann Rose. Lewis, who later went on to work in Head Start and preschool programs at other locations in Pulaski County, said she could never determine exactly what her role in the community was supposed to be.

After a few days of training at Philander Smith (a black college in Little Rock), I was shipped down the road to Higgins and lived a week with Mother Rivers, a black woman in her 80s. Her house had a commode, but for baths I went down the road to her daughter's, Sister Walker. Beside mother Rivers' house was a cinder block church and on the front lawn was a scummy, fenced-off cement hole for baptisms. In August, it was hot, dusty and smelly. The man behind the house raised hogs.

After many weeks as the Higgins Volunteer, I still could not figure out what I was supposed to do. Every day my roommate in Little Rock would drop me off at Pat Jackson's house. Pat had faith in me and my ability to take care of things.

"Penny, you go talk to Leo about his drinking. He'll listen to you. You've been to college," and the unsaid "You're white." If I had been Leo, I would have been drunk too. I did not talk to Leo or any of the others Pat suggested.

After a while, I got a bike so I could get around the community better. The people in Higgins thought this was hilarious—an adult on a bike.

How can one account for the immediate rapport and success of one Volunteer while another could only perceive a lack of worth-

Grand Prize Winner

WASHINGTON, D.C.—Former VISTA volunteer Arthur Clifton, 33, of Sarasota, Fla., has been awarded the grand prize in the VISTA tenth anniversary photo contest sponsored by ACTION.

Clifton's black and white photo of a mother and child, taken while he was serving with VISTA in North Little Rock, Ark., during 1968 and 1969, was the unanimous choice of a panel of judges. The panel members, including Associated Press White House photographer Hank Burroughs and Sandra Eisert of the White House photo staff, considered more than 1,500 entries submitted by 150 current and former VISTA volunteers.

Frank Williams, deputy associate director for VISTA and anti-poverty programs, presented Clifton with the grand prize—a Leitz Pradovit slide projector—during a reception at the agency's Washington headquarters. The photo contest marked the tenth year of operation for VISTA.

Clifton's interest in photography dates back to his senior year in high school. "Someone showed me what could be done with printing, and that started the whole thing," Clifton recalls.

After graduating from high school, Clifton enrolled in the Brooks Institute of Photography in Santa Barbara, Calif. He left Brooks to become a member of the pictorial unit of the U.S. Army and for the next two years "took photographs from Scandinavia all the way down to Africa."

Following his discharge from the service, Clifton returned to Brooks and received his bachelor of photographic arts degree. "While I was out there, I met the chief of the Chumash Indians who lived on a reservation near Santa Barbara," Clifton says. "He said, 'why don't you become a VISTA and come work with us?' "

Clifton applied to VISTA and was assigned to the Economic Opportunity Agency of Pulaski County in Little Rock, Ark., where he worked with youth groups. During his year with VISTA, Clifton also managed to make use of his photographic talents. At the invitation of a Little Rock ecumenical council which sought to involve local church groups in relevant social issues, Clifton presented slide shows to area churches illustrating poverty "in their own backyard."

In his final months with VISTA, Clifton traveled throughout the state to develop a photo essay which was used, in the form of a slide show, to introduce VISTA trainees to the conditions they might encounter as volunteers in Arkansas.

"At that time, so many of the volunteers were from white middleclass backgrounds and here they were, plunked down in the middle of a poor rural area of Arkansas. They hadn't known what to expect and often they found they just couldn't cope," Clifton says.

The photograph which won the VISTA tenth anniversary photo contest was taken in Scott, Ark. "It's an old plantation area. Houses along the side of the road still belong to whoever owns the plantations, which were really big cotton and soybean farms. There wasn't any work for many of the people, who lived in the houses rent free. The photograph was taken in one of these houses in February, 1969."

Photograph by Volunteer Arthur Clifton and article in 1975 issue of *Interaction*, a federal publication concerning volunteer activities while involvements? Certainly the Higgins community itself hadn't changed significantly in one year's time. The answer may lie in the varying personalities of the Volunteers, but that is just one of many factors that influence VISTA service.

Penny Lewis was clearly no shirker. Her later work was highly praised by community leaders in Sweet Home and defended by her VISTA supervisor. She currently works as a licensed foster mother in Washington, "honing and using the skills I first learned in VISTA."

Perhaps it was her decision to live in Little Rock and car pool each day to Higgins that established the distance she felt. Perhaps it was the demands of the PCEOA area director. Whatever the reasons, the lesson from Higgins is that VISTA service and results can never be predetermined. VISTA is a distinctly human effort, subject to the many variables of time and place, personal and community character.

Sweet Home

A visitor to Sweet Home in the late 1960s and early 1970s would have no trouble identifying the structure that served as the focal point of that south Pulaski County community. Near the center of town, an old wooden schoolhouse, abandoned by the county school district, would have been bustling with adults and preschool children.

That one-room schoolhouse had stood vacant for six years before it was purchased in 1968 by the Community Workers Organization, a Sweet Home grass roots agency. The CWO used the aging structure for its community service efforts—cooking food for a senior citizen hot lunch program, holding community meetings and recreational programs, and establishing a much needed preschool.

At the time, Sweet Home evidenced poverty symptoms common to many Arkansas communities: sixty-five percent of its population was below poverty guidelines, a high percentage of single parent households were unable to obtain work because of lack of day care facilities, and many families were financially unable to provide their children with adequate meals.

The situation was changed with the PCEOA assignment of Volunteers and a determined community effort led by Mrs. Zelma Miller, a long time Sweet Home resident described by Volunteer Karen Waldner as the "backbone of the community." The Sweet Home preschool became an early example to the community that it could achieve significant levels of self improvement, Waldner said.

Children in playground at Sweet Home Community Center

We accomplished the goal of setting up quality educational, recreational, and social preschool programs. We held yearly graduation programs, complete with little caps and gowns for the children. The parents of the preschoolers, mostly single mothers, were very involved in fundraising and in our trips. We were well accepted by all residents.

The old community center required constant maintenance, yet its drafty walls and leaky roof never seemed to dampen the spirits of the Volunteers or community workers who made the preschool program there so successful. Mike Fixler, a Volunteer who started teaching at the preschool in March 1975, recalled a progressive learning system and educational testing for the children that he and other Volunteers were able to implement.

With the success of the preschool and the deterioration of the building, plans for a new community center and fundraising efforts were launched. Those plans took on an urgency after a fire in September 1975 completely destroyed the old structure.

The loss of the building clearly did not limit the aspirations of the community nor the commitment of the Volunteers. Mrs. Miller took the initiative and moved the entire preschool program into a house in the rear of her property. Karen Waldner recalled Sweet Home parents working to prepare the temporary structure and much of her own time after classes spent telephoning around the county for donations of supplies.

Other PCEOA volunteers assisted in the efforts. Accountant Mike Watts established a bookkeeping system, and architect Jim Mercado helped design plans for the new community center. Mercado, however, mentioned Mrs. Miller's tasty sweet potato pies and admitted his visits to Sweet Home were frequently arranged to coincide with servings of the Hot Lunch program.

The new Sweet Home Community Center did not take long to become a reality. With some seed money arranged through County Judge Frank Mackey, ground breaking for the new center took place by the end of 1975. The center continues today to serve the community through the preschool and other activities.

From a VISTA perspective, the Sweet Home story offers these insights: it illustrates what can be achieved when a community sincerely welcomes all Volunteers and incorporates their efforts into an active project with strong citizen support.

Sweet Home also reveals the influence of a dynamic local personality upon a community and Volunteers. For Mrs. Miller, VISTA was another vehicle in her lifelong commitment to community service. Volunteers who were able to locate such individuals and allow those persons to direct their service found their efforts aligned with true community needs.

Design Co-operative

If Pulaski County was to have a showcase VISTA project, the Design Co-op would have been it. This gathering of national Volunteers, most of them "specialists" in some professional field, set out to revitalize communities by focusing on public and private dwellings.

> The Design Co-op is a group of architects, urban planners, landscape architects, engineers, economists, community developers and other professionals who volunteer their talents to produce a more livable, *people-oriented* physical environment for Arkansans. [from the Design Co-op brochure.]

In 1972, when the Design Co-op was incorporated, there were approximately seventy similar organizations around the nation. Some were sponsored by University architectural programs, some by various municipal governments, and almost all of them received federal support in one form or another. The goals of these co-ops were to improve the physical environment of a poverty community and to increase residents participation in the planning process.

During the four years the Design Co-op of Little Rock functioned, it completed a large number of worthwhile projects in Pulaski County and across Arkansas. By the time the Co-op failed, however, it had become a flamboyant arena of confrontation.

Design Co-op Volunteers had no reservations about placing the blame for the failure of their organization directly on the PCEOA

Cover of brochure published by the Design Co-operative

staff and what the Volunteers perceived as the manipulative policies of the agency. In its attempts to disengage itself from the PCEOA, the Co-op hired a local black man as its director. Ironically, it was the new director who more than anyone else hastened the ultimate collapse of the organization.

According to Goforth Coleman, Volunteer supervisor for the PCEOA during the 1970s, the original idea of the Co-op was simply Volunteer assistance to communities. Most poverty communities were in clear need of better physical facilities, but few had the capability to transform that need into a concrete project. The Volunteer could provide that expertise, but more than skillful planning or design was often needed, Coleman said.

> Our plan was to get the Volunteers into those environments, but we couldn't get them to interpret the long range plans for the areas. Some may have felt they knew what poor people needed. That wasn't true. Maybe the folks just wanted a gravel road instead of the dirt one they had. The Volunteers wanted it to be paved. You've got to learn to move people from where they are to another level. The Volunteers could get very impatient.

Impatience, outright arrogance, and defiance of the accepted systems—these were some complaints directed by PCEOA staff toward selected members of the Co-op. To some degree, those criticisms were accurate, for many of the Co-op staff brought into their service role a noncompromising attitude.

Bill Peters, for example, was a twenty-two-year-old Berkeley graduate who established the Co-op with two other VISTA architects, Gilbert Gullaksen and Stanley Kozinsky. Peters said he arrived in Little Rock in 1972 with "a silver BMW and my liberal ways" and immediately tried to sue the city for repairs on his vehicle after it was damaged by running into what he says was an unmarked construction ditch.

The three Co-op architects achieved some notable results in their early efforts. They designed clinics, parks, and playgrounds; rebuilt community fire stations and churches. With community assistance, many of their design projects were constructed. It was

Volunteers at the Design Co-operative. *Front row (left left to right):* unknown, Mary-Ann Ellenbecker. *Middle Row:* Janet Dunwoody, Chris Entis, unknown, Jim Samsel. *Back Row:* Tony Bozynski, Jim Howard, Jim Mercado. *1975 photo by Pam Sheen.*

Peters' attitude, however, that upset his VISTA supervisors, an attitude Peters admits may not have been easy to deal with.

> We set out to do things that hadn't been done before, and we got most of them done. Coleman accused me of being arrogant once when we were screaming at each other in the hallway of the federal building. And he was correct. I had no problem with it, though, and used it with my ideals and persistence in a caring way to accomplish things which mattered more than any rules or risks I thought silly or irrelevant. Arrogant? Yes!

Peters, who later became a Pulaski County Justice of the Peace, said that in his VISTA days radical action was required. He said the burdensome system in effect at the time would require him to personally visit the old courthouse and wait for an appointment with the county judge just to request a repair crew be sent to Sweet Home roads.

I was young and impatient. There were correct and slow ways of doing things, and there were more expedient ways. Some upset supervisors and other officials, but they got the job done.

At one public meeting I spoke and was quoted in the papers. This sort of attention was not allowed. Coleman and Crawford were furious, yet the result for the people of Little Rock was they learned they had influence over design of the Wilbur Mills Freeway, and they got a better deal from it.

Peters' attitude toward expedient ways of doing things probably influenced those who came after him. In a 1973 memo to the PCEOA, the Co-op staff stated their refusal to produce daily reports on activities because they believed writing the reports would interfere with more tangible achievements. A request for daily work reports seems an overly detailed demand, but from an administrative point of view it may have been attempted as a means of drawing in the reins on a headstrong group. Despite any such administrative restraints, the Design Co-op staff was able to accomplish an extraordinary amount of work.

This is a partial list of projects the Co-op was involved with from 1973 through 1975:

— Publication of *Arkansas Taxpayer's Guide,* a reference booklet for the low-income taxpayer and property owner.
— Financial counseling program for low income families.
— Work with Broadway Neighborhood Association to transform vacant lots into playgrounds, gardens, and public space.
— Landscaping, home construction, and sewage facility treatment plans at Scott.
— Renovation and weatherization of low-income housing.
— Study of Pulaski County public transportation problems.
— Community centers at Dick Jeter Community, Sweet Home, and others.
— Playground and park construction projects at McDermott, J. C. Cooke, Marche, Paragould, Lake Village, Hampton, and many Pulaski County schools, churches, and day care centers.
— Work with North Little Rock Stark Bend Water Commission.
— Renovation of Gaines House, a boarding home for women's rehabilitation; Gyst House, a drug abuse house; and a home for teenage runaways.
— Creation of posters for Social Services to help welfare recipients.

DICK JETER COMMUNITY PARK

A PLAYGROUND SUCCESS STORY

Residents of the Dick Jeter Community, a sparsley populated area near Jacksonville, Arkansas, have a history of organizing themselves to obtain local improvements. Previous to their park project, the community had successfully formed the Dick Jeter—Valentine Water Users Association which received Farmers Home Administration funding to install a community water system.

Their first task in developing a community park was obtaining a piece of land. The residents found some land which they felt would meet their needs and convinced the owners to hold the land until the community secured financing. After much time and red tape the community received a committment for fifty percent of the purchase price from the Bureau of Outdoor Recreation. The remainder of the financing was supplied by a monthly fee assessed to each family.

The Design Co-op was requested by the community to prepare site development and playground construction plans. After the plans were approved and the residents agreed to supply the labor, the community approached the Pulaski County Judge for funds to purchase materials. Funds were provided to construct a playground, picnic shelter, basketball court and baseball field. With some supervisory assistance from the Design Co-op and the County Parks Department, donated materials from business firms, and heavy equipment from the National Guard, the first phase of the park was completed in 1974. The community now plans to expand the play area and begin fund raising for a new community center.

Page from "Children, Play, and Playgrounds In Your Community—A How-To Guide for Neighborhood Groups"—a pamphlet published by the Design Co-operative.

— Work with Minority Contractors Association to provide educational seminars on construction business skills.

Perhaps the most visible of the Co-op's projects are the many playgrounds which staff members designed and helped construct. These playgrounds, composed primarily of recycled or minimal cost materials such as telephone poles, railroad ties, and tires, were built throughout Pulaski County and across the state as a result of Co-op Volunteers organizing community planning and work days.

The Co-op also published an excellent "how to" guide for neighborhood groups on playground planning and design.

Despite these and other worthy achievements, Co-op Volunteers spoke of an extremely loose internal organization that allowed staff to select or ignore their individual job responsibilities. Under PCEOA sponsorship, the Co-op never had a director to coordinate its many projects. The assignment of new Volunteers rarely allowed an overlapping period essential to a smooth transition, as a 1975 report from Volunteer Christine Entis indicates:

> . . . time to decide. Extend? Re-up? Terminate? The Co-op is in a crisis situation. It is necessary for me to extend for at least two months to help orient new Volunteers. Overlap is essential. Poor planning created a situation of only one Volunteer remaining here in March. If new ones come in and leave in a year, the situation will be repeated.

Pam Sheen, a Volunteer who served two years beginning in 1974, said the disorganization at the Co-op allowed her to choose her own area of service.

> With its humble ramshackle exterior, the old gray house at 1424 Center Street could be expected to sell homemade crafts or even auto parts . . . Without adequate money for a director's salary, the daily dynamics of the office were chaotic. Since it was up to me, I chose to be a nonprofit "broker" and assist in loan applications. I saw the daily gaps between the haves and have-nots with respect to the basics of life, such as shelter. In processing a loan, I tried to avoid being a case worker. Instead, I tried to plug people into institutional arrangements so they could effectively tackle similar problems again.

Though many individual projects were accomplished, administrative problems continued to create friction between the Co-op and the PCEOA. On one level, the specialized skills of the Co-op Volunteers did not always mesh with the communities they served, Mercado said.

> The Co-op concept, to provide the technical assistance to neighborhoods, was ahead of its time. Many communities couldn't utilize our expertise. They were just gaining confidence, getting incorporated. We were ready to

build. They needed legal and organizational help. I went to meetings where I had to take the minutes because I was the only one there who could write and read.

Mercado's patience could make the best of those situations, and he is credited with providing a high level of internal order to the Co-op during his 1973–1975 service. Other Volunteers were less willing to sacrifice what they saw as their primary VISTA responsibility.

In his letter of resignation from the Co-op and VISTA, architect Frances Mercedes stated that long range urban planning was not developing from playground projects.

There is no process for identification and solution of urban scale problems. The people in these communities must be made aware of their problems and that a framework that can help them actually exists . . . I see no position or process I can plug myself into to practice or develop my urban planning skills.

Mercedes' remarks are crucial in understanding the dissatisfaction many specialist Volunteers felt. Brought into the program with definite skills, they felt misused in not being given the chance to utilize those skills as they saw fit. Many of them also refused to engage in the long range preliminary work with communities and prepare the way for a similar specialist to follow them and perform his specific duties.

Another Co-op Volunteer who left the program with hard feelings was James Howard. In a sixty-one-page letter of resignation, Howard detailed his frustration with the PCEOA for its interference with his housing and weatherization work. He also strongly criticized the PCEOA Neighborhood Directors for using the agency for self gain and the EOA as a whole for attempting to take credit for Volunteer and community projects.

Mercado, who agreed with most of Howard's criticisms, put it more succinctly.

The Co-op was its own project, but it was tied to the PCEOA because we had to be. They gave us minimal support and caused us lots of problems. We spent more time with their bull than doing work . . . Our projects made

A Pulaski County home before renovation by Design Co-operative staff

The same home following work by Volunteers

the EOA look good and they wanted to take credit for them. We had to go along with it because we needed a CAP sponsor.

By the fall of 1975 the Volunteers began taking steps to disengage the Co-op from the PCEOA and establish it as an independent VISTA project. A five-year plan was proposed for expanded and improved Co-op services, and a funding application for the first year was submitted to a private foundation.

To assist in fundraising and other external affairs, the Co-op hired a CETA worker, Bob Sterley, a local black man with public relations and speaking skills. Sterley was originally hired as a program coordinator, but by June 1976 he had acquired the title of Co-op director.

The last Volunteer assigned to the Co-op was Phil Quandt in February 1976. Quandt recalled some bitterness among the Co-op staff toward Sterley, sentiments he said he did not understand at the time. As Volunteers began terminating or requesting transfers to other projects, Quandt said he was able to see things more clearly.

> Bob seemed a gentle type of person, but as he assumed more power his true personality came out. He liked to manage things, to be in control, but the Volunteers knew more about the Co-op than he did, and this stymied him. As they left, he was able to assume more power. His job was to handle the money. I had no idea of how he did it until after the fact.

Beyond his financial manipulations, Sterley also alienated the remaining Co-op Volunteers until all had either quit or transferred out. Finally, when only Quandt remained on staff, friction between the two began to build. Quandt recalls his final conflict with Sterley concerned a playground model he was building for a show at the city convention center.

According to Quandt, Sterley had already paid some architectural students to make another model, which angered Quandt because their work wasn't as good as his. The evening before the show, Quandt said he was putting the final touches on his model when Sterley came to take it from him.

> We fought over it, both holding either side. I finally put my hand on it and said "If you take it, you'll destroy it." He pulled it out and broke it. That was my end. I was bull headed, but he had no respect for me or any other VISTA because they had all subverted him before.

Sterley's attempts to control the Design Co-op did destroy the organization. In a June 1976 letter to the Co-op Board, Quandt and two other former Co-op Volunteers called for Sterley's resignation, charging him with alienating the former staff, refusing technical assistance, and placing the Co-op's financial accounts in his name alone.

The Volunteer charges against Sterley were partially substantiated when he was arrested in November 1976 for illegally receiving checks for $8,325 from Pulaski County Revenue Sharing funds. Sterley claimed he did nothing wrong, simply paid himself $6 an hour for 1,296 hours, including overtime, for his work on the Sweet Home Community Center.

On this occasion, Sterley received a five-year suspended sentence. He was arrested again in 1979 for theft by deception, in

1982 for embezzling and converting federal funds to his own use, and in 1984 for fraud. The Design Co-op board fired Sterley after the first arrest, leaving them with an agency with no staff and no administration. They had no choice but to close it down. They hired former Volunteer Tony Bozynski to make the final arrangements, and the Co-op officially closed its doors by the end of 1976.

Additional EOA Projects

Throughout Pulaski County, EOA Volunteers were assigned to projects that revealed the day-to-day needs of the scattered poverty communities. These projects did not require the highly refined talents of specialists, just a basic commitment to human service and the ability to solve problems.

In Scott, locally recruited Volunteer Sharon Pettus served a variety of community needs, and her compassion for people is evident in her July 1979 report:

[Original spelling retained]
Ive been tring to help get some assistance for the Willie Thomas family that got burn out July 31. In the incident the family lost there six year old daughter. she was the baby girl. she was trap inside the burning six room burning home. the family lost everything they owned. the procession's were not limited. Assistance from the red cross could not be surrended because the family had not found a place to live. I, Sharon, and my family help with funeral arrangements and foods, money and other assistance that were accepted . . .

An equal degree of human service can be found in the monthly reports of Anna Gottlieb, a national Volunteer who helped establish Arkansas' first female residential drug rehabilitation home. Grateful for whatever contributions the home received, Gottlieb commented in a 1975 monthly report:

Lots of physical improvements made in the drug house through donations. We now have a sink to wash our dishes instead of a bathtub . . . I find counseling to be very challenging, and I realize how careful I have to be. Most of our girls are young and impressionable, will listen and take our word as final. My goal is not to run their lives, only to help them see all alternatives and realize decisions are in their hands. This concept is hard to get across because most seem to want direction and would let me do their decision making for them.

Other projects around the county focused on youth education through extensive tutoring and recreational programs. The file on 1981 Volunteer Lorraine Kelley documents her enormous range of activities and the community support she was able to raise. In addition to personally tutoring at several intermediate schools, Ms. Kelly also coordinated volunteer tutors from local high schools and colleges, worked in energy assistance, summer recreation, and senior citizen programs. These and other accomplishments noted in her file indicate that VISTA was what the Volunteers made it. The self-starter, the Volunteer who would not passively wait for assignments to be passed along, always seemed to find worthy things to do.

In food and nutrition programs, the file on 1980 Volunteer Mary Mordhurst offers another example of extraordinary achievement in establishing community gardens and other related activities. Another 1980 Volunteer, Sharon Reid, assigned to the Pulaski County Council on Aging, was able to recruit more than 350 merchants in a senior citizen discount program.

These names and recorded activities only hint at the volume of activity undertaken by PCEOA Volunteers in the later years of the program. The activity itself implies at least a working relationship with the agency, but it does not offer an accurate assessment of the PCEOA VISTA sponsorship or the administrative attitudes which Volunteers encountered.

In almost every Arkansas project, Volunteers complained about unsafe GSA vehicles or a lack of funds to make vehicles available. In Pulaski County, lack of transportation resulted in a five thousand dollar wasted effort in Scott when Design Co-op staff could not be on hand to correct the improper placement of sewage lines. The lack of transportation funds was especially disturbing to Volunteers who believed executive staff at the agency were misusing allocated federal money.

Comments in Volunteer Edward Kaul's 1980 file offer more than a general expression of discontent:

> August 20—Helped with the EOA election. What a farce! Next time I'm not going to do EOA's dirty work just because I'm a VISTA. You are a poll worker to make sure the elections are honest, not make them a fixed, ballot stuffing disgrace.

Later Administrative Problems

To gain an impartial assessment of VISTA projects, ACTION evaluators would occasionally make site visits to interview sponsoring agency staff and assigned Volunteers. A 1975 ACTION report on a site visit to the PCEOA reveals a remarkable distance between the Volunteers' and the agency supervisor's perception of their common problems.

The report states that Volunteers perceived the PCEOA as mainly trying to keep its ship together, with limited interest in the Volunteers and low communication and trust levels with them. The Volunteers also believed the PCEOA set up programs designed to fail, then blamed the Volunteers when they did fail.

On the other hand, supervisor Goforth Coleman believed the Volunteers were not responsive to agency ideas or programs, did not understand the PCEOA system, and were not sufficiently sensitive to the people's actual needs.

Regardless of its accuracy, a perceived reality is the reality dealt with. The Volunteers who vented their frustrations had no reservations about putting the blame directly on the PCEOA.

The most pointed and vehement accusations came in James Howard's letter of resignation from the Design Co-op and VISTA. In a sixty-one-page tirade sent to President Ford, Arkansas Congressmen and Senators, and the local and national press, Howard called VISTA and the PCEOA one of the worst frauds since Watergate and the Teapot Dome Scandal, saying the agencies used people as a means to justify their own existence.

Howard's letter describes in detail his work in a self-help housing project in Wrightsville and his utter disgust at the manipulative attempts of the PCEOA and its local area director to control and take credit for his efforts. The letter eventually offers some good insight into VISTA administration, but its length and derogatory tone severely reduce its impact. The letter reads more like a vendetta than a rational criticism. Yet Mercado, a level headed, successful Volunteer who worked with Howard at the Design Co-op, supported those views.

> Howard's letter was true. You never knew when the EOA needed some publicity and would call in the television cameras. Howard didn't need that bull and wasn't going to put up with it.

Mercado explained his lack of respect for the PCEOA by his claim that it "ran a scam" in the city by being the "only show in town" when federal anti-poverty funds were spread around, a show he said the agency made worse by being incompetent.

> My personal frustrations were not with the projects or communities. I knew what had to be done and how to do it. It was with underdeveloped community leadership and poor sponsoring agency support.
>
> I'm out there totally alone from Detroit in rural Arkansas trying to get nails to build a project. I have to fill out forms in triplicate. You wait for nails for three weeks, then go out and buy them yourself.

According to Goforth Coleman, Howard was obsessed and much of his letter was a fabrication. Answering the charges that community members attempted to gain credit for Volunteer work, however, Coleman admitted that it may have happened.

> People that have been out here all their lives, they've been used. If you can present a situation to them where they can see any progress, where they feel they've accomplished something, they tend to grab it. Sure they had egos. Many had bad attitudes. The Volunteers had egos, too.

As to the delays in ordering supplies, Coleman did not deny that bureaucratic red tape at times created a "hurry up and wait" situation. It was hard for some Volunteers to understand why they had to go through the process, but a delay permitted them to reassess a situation and gain a better perspective, he said.

Other factors which negatively influenced the Volunteers' perception of their service was inadequate preparation for the degree of poverty they encountered, Coleman said. Volunteer remarks such as "How could people live like that?" revealed a lack of sensitivity to the poor, he said.

> Sometimes they felt people weren't as grateful to them as they should have been. That they had given up so much to come here. Folks were grateful, but they didn't have a parade for them. Some were disillusioned by that. Others adjusted. Most felt they weren't adequately trained.

Tony Bozynski related an anecdote whose lesson falls somewhere in between the Volunteer limitations and criticism of the agency attitude. As a Design Co-op planner, Bozynski had been helping the Woodson and Hensley communities with some plans for a playground. After meeting with them several times, Bozynski told his community group they needed to make their presentation to PCEOA Director Dean Goldsby.

> We got there and Goldsby stayed behind the huge desk in his office, putting an immediate wall between us. He asked questions but there was no community response. They were so intimidated, they were overwhelmed. They all were talking prior to the meeting. I thought we had it licked. Where did I go wrong? They knew he had the money. Why didn't they talk?

Bozynski's error may have been in pushing the community too far or going too far with them himself. Nevertheless, by his account, Goldsby made no attempt to decrease the tension or formality of the encounter. In light of Walker's vow to never put a desk between himself and a poverty person, the encounter can be especially revealing.

As PCEOA Executive Director, Goldsby's attitude affected the entire agency. In a 1977 letter to him, seven Volunteers expressed their frustration at the lack of basic support and professional cour-

Volunteer Joann Rose and her son Chris

tesy they had received. The letter said one of the group had been six months on her assignment without any administrative meeting, while another had finally received a GSA car after ten months of service only to have it break down the second day.

Lora Kennel, one of the national Volunteers who signed the letter, resigned from VISTA later that year, three months after re-enrolling for a second year of service. In her letter of resignation, she charges the agency with lying and misrepresenting information to the poor.

> . . . My reasons for terminating all spring from one crucial problem; the EOA uses people and grossly neglects the needs of the poor persons they are funded to serve . . . I can no longer work where politically expedient decisions prevail which negatively effect the lives of poor people.

Volunteer Tony Bozynski

The same sentiments are repeated by Volunteers who completed their periods of service. Joann Rose said that the EOA forced her to overcome the illusion that working at the "business of the people" would make an agency more competent.

The folks in Higgins were into social action. Those at the EOA were out for themselves. Driving their cars. Raising salaries of top administrators and keeping community workers at substandard levels.

Phil Quandt further expressed the Volunteer criticism:

> My feelings to the EOA as an agency are all negative. The money was not being channeled toward agency work, more to administrators and padding. All the money was at the top.

These feelings were not limited to national Volunteers. Locally recruited Volunteer Melvin Brown of Sweet Home said the philosophy under Walker was to go in, show the people, then vacate, get them to the level where they could do for themselves. "In recent years, taking credit for things is their game," Brown said.

For Pam Sheen, the conflicts between the Design Co-op and the PCEOA exposed the agency's overall attitude.

> Through self-serving enterprise, the EOA has exemplified the loss of ACTION goals at the local level. The issue is magnified at the Co-op where many Volunteers feel personal obligation to its purpose over technical accountability to the EOA.

Pulaski County EOA: Conclusion

To some Volunteers, community services were rendered despite the PCEOA's role as sponsoring agency. This attitude is reminiscent of the arrogance Bill Peters admitted. There is no harm in desiring an agency to be better than it is, but that should not create a wholesale rejection of necessary support mechanisms that only local structures can provide.

On the other hand, the actual degree of the agency's corruption may never be known beyond Volunteer and former PCEOA staff accusations. Details of the 1985 financial failure certainly give some credence to those charges, but it is unlikely that agency executive personnel would leave themselves open to criminal investigations as did Robert Sterley.

For Goforth Coleman, characterized by one Volunteer as "a man in the middle," positioned between the Volunteers and the agency, the biggest problem was Volunteers wanting to be totally independent of the agency. Some Volunteers wanted to respond to other needs without answering to the sponsoring organization, Coleman said.

> Some Volunteers didn't learn there were limitations. A lot felt they were placed in a box and didn't have the freedom to move. Also a lot came up with the idea they could change the system overnight. A lot of times we had to pull them back and explain you can make progress, but not total change, not in one year.

Coleman sees the effectiveness of the PCEOA Volunteers in the traditional role of change agents—they were to provide information to help people develop their own communities and decide what was good for them. The success of that effort can be seen in the contemporary emphasis on generalist Volunteers, Coleman said.

VISTA became more specific in areas of expertise in the 1970s. Now we're kind of going back to the original way. Most programs are now a service kind. They don't need a specialist.

The mid 1970s were the primary VISTA years of the Pulaski County EOA. It was a period that brought the agency more specialized and motivated Volunteers than it seemed capable of handling. Those that succeeded were able to create their own environment, Mercado said.

There was no system to work with, so we drew our own. We put the shortcomings in the back of our minds. Just try to make it through the day and get some work done. The people before us were into the civil rights of the 60s. We were into nuts and bolts.

For Pam Sheen, those changes were more style than substance. Regardless of the issues, the VISTA motivation was clear.

The civil rights Volunteers, the cautious anti-war politicos were gone. I flew to VISTA training in Dallas on a champagne breakfast flight. For roughly two weeks I was indoctrinated with ideals only a little more impossible than my own.

A VISTA DIARY

JOHN LEWIS IN LITTLE ROCK

John Lewis was a twenty-two-year-old volunteer from Panama City, Florida who kept a daily record of his VISTA service. His observations on VISTA training and his personal role as a Volunteer illustrate the psychology he and many others brought into their service.

Lewis' comments do not provide a detailed account of the actual work of a Volunteer, but a personal diary would not serve as the best medium for recounting a daily work schedule. What the book does offer is a view of VISTA life from the inside; its ambiguities, frustrations, revelations, and moments of joy.

Reading these comments years after they were written, it is possible to see in them the idealism which characterized Lewis' generation and the difficulty he felt in accepting many of the social norms of the time. These descriptions are in the voice of a young writer with an ability to clearly document what he saw.

FEBRUARY 15, 1969—[Following six weeks of training in Austin, Lewis is taken to a low-income household in the Longley neighborhood where he will make his first Little Rock residence.] Down a clay road, through mud and slush and arrived at "home" of Mrs. S. She will keep using her own luxuries—electricity, TV, telephone. All that's missing is an indoor bathroom or running water.

FEBRUARY 25—Afternoon visit with County Judge, former sheriff of Pulaski County for 30 years. "We're going to get that road paved in Longley as soon as the weather clears." I bet!

FEBRUARY 28—Visited all the industries in the Industrial Park on the other side of I-30. Million dollar industries in view of houses with no running water.

MARCH 1—Tour of Negro Boys School at Wrightsville . . . in rec hall over 100 boys of all ages seated in auditorium fashion, enjoying the vigorous recreation of sitting, nothing else, just sitting. They were to eat lunch, then sit some more. And this was an improvement from 10 years ago!

MARCH 9—I woke up because I was alive and cold. A warm fire feels good. Church at Union AME Church, Rev. Cecil Cone said "Let Go and Let God." Gospel choir sang "Step by Step, We'll Make This Journey." Perhaps they were trying to tell me something about the year to come.

MARCH 10—Looking at an Arkansas map. Little Rock is about 200 miles from Success and about 120 miles from Hope. I guess you could say we are closer to Hope than Success. I wonder?

MARCH 12—Met Jim Ranchino, a young professor at Ouachita Baptist College in Arkadelphia. I said he must be doing something right because last week his wife received the first threat on their lives. Jim talked about politics in Arkansas. They're getting rid of people at that good Baptist College—and possibly Ranchino.

MARCH 13—I'm watching the recovery of the astronauts of Apollo IX. Isn't it amazing how we can send a man to the moon, but still can't get along any better. These poor people around here don't really understand the moon and space and why America is spending billions for space when people on Earth are hungry. Who can?

MARCH 15—Woken up by a telephone call from Mrs. B. I had (?) to take her to the grocery store and dime store. What can be done (or not done) to convince people that VISTA is not the "Do Good Taxi Service?"
[By this time, Lewis had been issued a GSA car and had rented a house with other Little Rock volunteers]

MARCH 28—On the way to the house, we stopped by Walgreens. While parked, a red neck type (bastard) stopped the car, read the writing, looked in and asked, "Is this a government car?" No, it's a Sherman tank. "Are those groceries? You know it's illegal to use GSA cars for this." He took down the tag number and we drove away.

MARCH 30—Church day again. I went to the big downtown First (United) Methodist. Another church full of "good, Christian folks." I think I'll use them as a target and try to mess up some of their middle-class minds.

MARCH 31—The Eisenhower funeral on television. It is indeed amazing what Americans go through when someone dies. Four days worth, this time. And think of all the money that was wasted.

APRIL 2—More Eisenhower funeral. How long does it take to bury one person?

APRIL 20—A trip to 1505 Chester (EOA offices). On the way, I saw something interesting. A black woman and a dog. The dog was jumping up, loving and licking the woman. The dog didn't know that the woman was black and probably didn't care. He just loved her for what she was—someone who returned his affection. Perhaps us white folks just have too much sense. Maybe if we just had the brains of a dog, we'd be a lot better off. Absurd?

JUNE ?—[Lewis' letter to the Arkansas Democrat newspaper, winner of the $5 prize for "Letter of the Week." His letter is in response to a Democrat editorial stating the "ideal poverty program would provide one wise, concerned person to work with each poor person, but that would cost us too much." Lewis' letter begins by challenging the equating of income and education.] People who have little money have to be smart merely to survive . . . Poor people can be concerned . . . Middle class ought to offer more help than concern . . . People should work with poverty because they may be part cause of it . . . Perhaps the US doesn't have a problem with poverty but a problem with wealth and affluency . . . Cost? If only we could readjust our values and priorities. Until we do, we'll have to be content with sending men to the moon and putting artificial turf in a stadium instead of caring for our sick and feeding our hungry.

JULY 10—Amos (a neighbor) brought the fellow across the street to meet me. Amos was finishing a half pint of whiskey. He was about to leave when John drove up. Then he proceeded to finish a second 1/2 pint and tell us about his wife, 5 kids, divorce, beating by the police at the jail, and how he wants to kill his wife. We listened. What could we say? Little by little, we're beginning to find out what's bothering Amos. What can we do to help him?

JULY 19—[Lewis is awakened about midnight by sirens in the street] I opened my eyes and saw blue lights flashing on the walls . . . Through the window I counted at least 10 police cars, but there were more in both directions . . . Cops were walking around in groups of 4 or 5 with rifles . . . I heard shots, sort of muffled, popping sounds, that came from a block or two away. Rifle-carrying policeman ran toward the sound. People screamed . . . One cop told a group of on-lookers to "get out of here—all of you" . . . I heard one of them tell his friends, "It's gonna be a long, hot summer" . . . Someone on a porch across the street was yelling "They can't come in here with those guns and kill my kids." The cops went over, banged on the door, told the people to turn down their television. After that there was relative quiet. So I returned to bed, not knowing what happened, or why.

JULY 20—Today the first man set foot on the moon. It took us $24 billion, but we did it! A man on the moon and an outhouse in Longley.

AUGUST 12—The highlight of my social career arrived—I joined the picket line. For about two hours I carried a sign. All day passing motorists shouted insults from their cars. That didn't matter. We just wanted to show somebody that we were white folks who were not in favor of "alleged police brutality." . . . At present, LR is tense and sizzling. It may explode soon.

AUGUST 13—In the Gazette this morning, the black picketers were warned about shouting obscenities at policemen and passersby. What about all those good white folks who shouted obscenities at us white pickets all day?

SEPTEMBER 6—Turned on the television. First it was an all-American football game. Then came the all-American of all-American shows, the Miss America Beauty Pageant. It does represent America after all. Beautiful, all white, pleasant, artificial, removed and unrelated to the rest of the world. "There she goes, Miss America. There she goes, our ideal."

SEPTEMBER 29—Time for our daily visit from Eddie M. and Alice. . . . Aretha Franklin sang on the stereo. We were sung to, touched, laughed at, and then it happened. Eddie went into my bedroom and took her blouse off. She took her blouse off!! What was she trying to do? Why did this 14-year-old child do it?

OCTOBER ?—[Descriptions of some neighborhood residents] Then there was Amos, Korean War veteran, two years of college, pill pusher, divorced, father of five, usually full of wine and beer, always wandering up and down the street. Often, Amos would drop by, sometimes for as long as two hours, nothing but talk. So we listened. Some of his choice quotes: "People is 'ignant', you think I'm 'ignant', don't you?" "Sheeeit, what the hell is soul, anyway?" "C'mon brother, I'm gonna take you down to Mac's and get you drunk!" Amos told us that he almost killed a blind man and wanted to kill his wife. What could we do? Listening seemed so little, but maybe it was a lot for some one who wanted to talk.

Younger girls have found us, too. Eddie Mae and Alice Ann, in particular. Two sisters, 13 and 14, who come in, dance to Aretha Franklin records, sing to us, tell us of their sexual exploits, rub our heads and tell us how soft our hair is. What do you do when a 14-year-old-child parades around and takes her blouse off? Tell her to get dressed, wonder why she did it and what kind of life she has to look forward to.

NOVEMBER 11—Veteran's Day—all of these brave Americans who served and defended their country with a gun in their hands. Serving your country by shooting people—sounds typically American.

JANUARY 26, 1970—Today I think I reached an all time low of depression. Mainly because it's really dawned on me that I haven't done one damn thing to directly help anyone in poverty. It's the not ever knowing that's bad. In addition, the waiting has begun for Local Board 6 to make a move. Helplessness.

JANUARY 29—Clarksville, College of the Ozarks, for a folk music festival and folk culture display. The entertainment wasn't until evening so we headed north into the Ozark National Forest. High in the mountains on narrow unpaved roads. Lakes and streams. What a beautiful country. Mountains and valleys. So few people and houses—unspoiled countryside. Back to the C of the O. Two hours of pure, unadulterated folk music by real mountain people. Guitars, banjos, zithers, and dulcimers, played by people who really enjoyed it. Their music is part of their lives and part of America. 100 miles back to the big city after a good day in America.

FEBRUARY 17—What a day of opposites it was. First to 1505 to take a woman someplace. We eventually went to the Salvation Army.

The poor woman was confused about her story and problem, but she said she only received $26 a month and needed groceries. And the Salvation Army can not help anyone between 12 and 1. They eat while others wait for groceries.

Back home again and a trip to Hot Springs and the horse races. People. Rich, poor, black, white, young, old. Money to throw away. Betting is contagious. I should have quit when I was ahead, but I didn't.

APRIL 7—Out to the Air Force Base to pick up a couple more beds. Then to East Gate to deliver and assemble them. Children alone, no windows open, flies, the smell of human defecation and heat. How long will the beds last? Will the people ever know any other way of life? A man came up and told Jim to move his truck off the sacred and valuable grass (which seemed to be more important than the people).

MAY 1—May Day. Help—VISTA! A meeting of volunteers and Joe Bruch. The Nixon administration is trying its best to do away with OEO and VISTA. No national director and no intention of appointing one. No planning or recruiting. The regional office is slowly being changed and demolished. Most pessimistic prediction? No more VISTA in 6 months. Why bother? Don't ask. For some reason we do.

MRS. ZELMA MILLER
"SOUL" OF SWEET HOME

A short, elderly woman opened the screen door of her house and walked out toward the car that had just parked in her drive. Her gray hair was pulled tightly into a bun at the back of her head, and the apron she wore around her waist had sewing thread and scraps of cloth in its front pocket.

Afternoon sunlight shone on her bright yellow dress and in its reflected glow, her brown skin seemed even fairer. On her dress, a large white button boldly proclaimed "I Support Community Action." Mrs. Zelma Miller reached out and quickly engaged her visitor in a robust, soul brother hand shake, three quick movements of the hand she performed with an energetic style.

Inside the old wooden building, possibly a log structure beneath the white sideboards, she sat in the front-room rocking chair with her large quilting loom before her, pulling her needle through its colorful starburst patterns.

"Why didn't you stop in here when you first drove by?" she asked, occasionally directing her eyes to the windows that faced her quiet street.

Her curiosity was sparked on learning that her visitor had first driven by the Sweet Home Community Center and had taken some photos of children in the playground. Who was there, she wanted to know. Just some kids, she was told, some teenage boys shooting baskets, some older folks playing cards at a table beneath a tree across the street.

Sweet Home community leader Mrs. Zelma Miller

"Used to be I knew everybody that had a car on this street, but now there's so many new people, I just go out and ask them who they are," she said. "Better that way I get to know 'em and they get to know me."

Getting to know folks and having them remember her never seemed to have been a problem for the dynamic Mrs. Miller, a woman whose personal energy is matched only by her selfless commitment to her community. She speaks proudly of her recent eightieth birthday, and one gets the impression that Mrs. Miller has been radiating the same human warmth and compassion all her life.

When VISTA Volunteers first came to Sweet Home in the early 1970s to work in the preschool, meals for the elderly, the Head Start programs, it was Mrs. Miller who introduced them to the community and helped focus their desire to serve specific community needs. Volunteer Karen Waldner called her "the backbone of the Sweet Home Building Committee" and said she considered herself lucky to know such a dedicated woman, someone willing to give up so much of her time and effort.

"The Voluteers made a wonderful contribution," Mrs. Miller said, repaying the compliment in her characteristically modest way. "All of them that came to Sweet Home, as ragged and disorganized as this community is, they all enjoyed themselves immensely."

Sweet Home, perhaps more than the other primarily black communities on Highway 365, the old Pine Bluff highway, no longer seems to fit Mrs. Miller's description. The fact that the rural poverty which once held the town has loosened its grip is evidenced in the clean streets, in the small but brightly painted houses, and in the flowering gardens that abound through the neighborhoods.

These signs of community pride reflect community character. Mrs. Miller credits the Volunteers and their sponsoring agency, the Pulaski County EOA, as major influences.

"Had not been for the EOA, we wouldn't have had any of this. The state, the county wasn't doing nothing for us," she said emphatically. Then pointing to the button on her dress, she added, "You see that button? I wear it where ever I go, church, anywhere. Oh yeah."

The EOA was designed to help one help himself, Mrs. Miller said, and the Volunteers were a means of getting that process started. She spoke of their bringing meals and visiting with elderly shut-ins, she told of their work in the preschool program, and of their help in getting contacts with "the money people" and their writing fund-raising letters for the community.

"The VISTAs never did have any kind of trouble, no black-white problems here. They were welcome here just like we welcome anybody," she said. "That is our way of doing. We opened our doors to 'em right away. They came on in and went on going."

A conversation with Mrs. Miller rapidly becomes more than just a simple exchange of words, for her colorful expressions and animated gestures are modern reminders of the storyteller's timeless tradition.

"Folks always tell me I say things they remember," she said. "Bill Peters said I once told him some food was 'tender as a baby's hug.'"

For Bill Peters and other Volunteers who served in Sweet Home, a woman with Mrs. Miller's natural warmth and inspiration could make the difference between a year of effective service and one of just filling in time. Many former Volunteers still keep in touch, asking about the community and the people with whom they shared their year of service.

With her basic understanding of people and events, Mrs. Miller is rarely unprepared to offer her comments on a subject. Her remarks somehow cut through layers of pretension and strike with a simplistic honesty at the heart of the issues she addresses.

In the recent history of Sweet Home, no single issue has provided a stronger base of pride than the Community Center. Originally located in an old wooden schoolhouse, a structure that was totally lost in a 1975 fire, the center was described by Volunteer Mike Fixler in a monthly report.

> The building epitomized everything I have been working for and with the town . . . Of course the building was in great disrepair and presented all kinds of problems in its utter inadequacy as a public structure. Yet it meant so much to so many. One hardly met anyone who grew up in Sweet Home who did not walk through the portals of the old schoolhouse to a grade school class at one time or another . . . Mrs. Miller is a carpenter of sorts and practically holds that turn-of-the-century structure together with her own hammer and jar of nails.

Mrs. Miller admitted she did perform some radical repairs on the old center. When roof leaks persisted despite her efforts to keep the cracks stopped up, she said a more practical course of action had to be taken.

"I had them bore holes in the floor so the water would run out and keep the boards from swelling up," she said.

With no glass in the windows nor the money to buy any, the window openings were covered with any materials on hand. "We'd just raise up the paste board and see who was passing by," she recalled.

When the old center burned, Mrs. Miller said she didn't get discouraged, she just went to work. She moved the preschool program and other community activities into her own home and a second building on her property, then began the fundraising campaign to finance construction of the new center.

"I have a BM degree," she said. "That's 'Begging for Money.' If one said no, I'd just go to another. Hardly ever be turned down. I tell folks I was born in a town called Poverty, but Momma raised us on Economic Street."

Mrs. Miller's striving has earned her state-wide recognition, including the Governor's Award for Volunteerism. Little Rock architect Jim Mercado, a Volunteer who accompanied Mrs. Miller on some of her fundraising escapades, recalled driving her about the city and stopping at her request to go into businesses and solicit contributions.

"We stopped one time at a Sterling 5 & 10 store, and she walked in and found the president," Mercado said. "She told him many of his customers were from her neighborhood and how important the new center would be. When the moment was right, she had me pull out the architectural plans and explain them. We walked out of there that day with a check for $500."

Mercado added that Mrs. Miller was still effective as a fundraiser, and that he had just received a request from her for twenty dollars to purchase new cots for the day care program.

"When Mrs. Miller asks for my $20, I know those cots wouldn't be there without it," Mercado said. "If the EOA asked for $20, I'd tell them where to put it."

The negative attitude Mercado and other former volunteers expressed toward the Pulaski County EOA is based on their dissatisfaction with that agency's administration and policies toward VISTA. Mrs. Miller, on the other hand, expressed no ill will toward the agency or any of its past involvements. One quickly gets the impression that it is not her way to speak poorly of anyone.

"Time is like a wagon wheel, constantly turning. Some of those times suitable, some not," she said. "Right now we're working on relocating the Sweet Home post office. We got to shake, rattle, and roll to raise that money."

When asked about her influence on the Volunteers who served in Sweet Home, Mrs. Miller looked up from the busy stitching on her quilt which she had maintained throughout the conversation and gazed out the window in thought.

"I can't figure that out," she said, at last. "They tell me they think of me all the time. I was just me. I never had any children of my own, but I raised many of 'em around here. Maybe that's why I wasn't to have any of my own."

WARREN

POVERTY AND COMMUNITY VALUES

The VISTA project sponsored by the Bradley County Community Action Corporation lasted a little more than one year. Yet in that brief period, incidents occurred that made Warren, a south Arkansas town known primarily for its tomato crop, infamous.

Related in Volunteer training sessions as an example of Arkansas small town reaction to VISTA activity, the Warren episode was received with outright incredulity by newly enlisted Volunteers being trained in Austin in the early 1970s. Some laughed at the story. Others took it as a personal challenge.

On December 31, 1968, four national Volunteers were taken from a New Year's Eve party at their residence in Warren by city police. They were fingerprinted, photographed, and released without formal charges. On January 3rd, based on signed complaints, they were arrested. The official charge was disturbing the peace, but that was not what broke the local code of ethics. The Volunteers had black guests at their house that night, and black males danced with white females at the first integrated party ever held in Warren. The Volunteers were arrested for race-mixing.

On the surface, such action evokes images of oppressive and racist southern stereotypes. Yet behind any label is a more complex truth about community identity, a truth that goes deeper than established racial divisions.

Warren, like much of rural Arkansas at the time, had little or no involvement with outside organizers prior to the Volunteers. Eddie Colen, former deputy director of the Bradley County CAC, said that in the late 1960s, forty-eight percent of Bradley County lived in poverty. There were more whites in that group than blacks, but proportionally black poverty levels were higher.

Warren was not making great strides in fighting local poverty, yet neither was the issue totally ignored. Close to half of the thirty-six board members of the Bradley County CAC were black, and three neighborhood centers had been established by the agency to help organize local communities, Colen said.

The status quo was first disrupted in the summer of 1968 when Summer Associate Volunteers sponsored by Ouachita Baptist University at Arkadelphia were assigned to Warren. The Associate Volunteers accomplished little that summer, but the town took large notice of them, mainly because one white female was repeatedly seen walking with a local black male. In the OBU files, a note on this assignment states ". . . three Associates spent a miserable summer, frustration ruled most days. Unless there are changes here, federal poverty funds are wasted."

The first National Volunteer, Robert Fleming, was assigned to Warren in the fall of 1968. By December four others had also been placed. They were Larry Kressley, a nineteen-year-old from Allentown, Pennsylvania, Ellen Smith, a registered nurse, Kathy Lynch, and Anne Roberts.

In a college report written in 1973, Kressley described himself as the model recruit—young, idealistic, and with a firm belief that "if we only committed ourselves to the task we could achieve social justice in the United States."

After what he felt was an unproductive training session in Norman, Oklahoma, and an equally frustrating four weeks of field work at Menifee (Conway County), an all-black community in central Arkansas, Kressley was assigned along with the others to the Bradley County CAC. He arrived there totally unprepared for a tense racial situation and with very little in the way of skills or training to offer, he said.

> Our first and continuing mistake in our work in Warren was to decide too quickly that we were going to work with blacks rather than poor whites—despite that more than half of the county's poor people were white. All of us, I suppose, had sort of a mid-1960s civil rights worker's mentality about our work. We identified the poor whites—the rednecks, we called them—as our enemies.

James Rogers, agency director at the time, said the newly assigned Volunteers tried to accomplish too much too quickly and were overzealous about their work. They wanted to use classrooms in the local schools for some of their projects and felt that the buildings ought to be unconditionally open to them. The Volunteers didn't consult the agency because they felt it was the "establishment" and wasn't moving fast enough for them, he said.

> They met the system head on and felt that was the way to do it. They didn't consult with the black ministers, but just aligned themselves with black youth. They wanted instant freedom without responsibility, the same with all civil rights things. Change is not accomplished in a way like Central High but with people gradually accepting an idea. You've got to take the community along with you.

Like other Volunteers assigned in similar situations, the Warren group quickly became identified with the black community, adding to the suspicions already evidenced toward VISTA by local whites. Disregarding these feelings, the Volunteers decided to have a New Year's Eve party at Kressley's house in an effort to get to know some of the local black high school students with whom they wanted to work. Kressley's house was located in one of Warren's few racially mixed neighborhoods. Next door were poor whites Kressley had never made an effort to meet. He also invited no local white people to the party, nor did he inquire if having such a party would offend anyone.

Throughout the evening some thirty or forty black youths, mainly males, circulated in and out of the house. At times, the two female Volunteers (one had gone home for the holidays) danced with some of the young black men. Unknown to them, all of this was being watched through a window by one of the white neighbors.

In a report to VISTA Program Officer Joe Bruch a few days after the incident, Kressley described the subsequent events:

> At 10 pm, a city police officer entered the house and brought the four Volunteers out onto the front porch. Being informed who they were, the officer said, "Now, maybe you can do these things where you come from, but down here people don't go for any of this race mixing. If you know what's good for you, you'll pack your bags and get out of town and break this up right now or they'll be big trouble.

The officer said he would be back soon to make sure the party had broken up. The Volunteers, not advised they had been doing anything legally wrong, turned the music down low and allowed the party to continue. The officers returned within an hour and brought the four Volunteers to the city police station where they were told the "Chief" wanted to talk with them.

At the station, the police chief told the Volunteers a complaint had been lodged against them for disturbing the peace, and if the complaint was signed the group would spend the night in jail. The complaint was not signed that night and the Volunteers, after being fingerprinted and photographed, were released. Before he allowed them to go, the police chief had this conversation with Kathy Lynch:

> CHIEF: What exactly is VISTA and what is the job of a VISTA Volunteer?
>
> LYNCH: It's a domestic Peace Corps. We're Volunteers in service to America.
>
> CHIEF: Who is your boss?
>
> LYNCH: The federal government.
>
> CHIEF: Who could I contact in reference to you?
>
> LYNCH: Call your Congressman.
>
> CHIEF: Don't you have a local boss?
>
> LYNCH: We're sponsored by the CAP agency, but they're not our boss. They are simply our sponsor.

The police chief stated that people in the area were not used to race mixing and he would appreciate it if the Volunteers let him know before they had any more such gatherings. He asked them to bring the fifth Volunteer by his office when she returned to town, then told them they could return to their party and that he didn't care how much noise they made.

On January 2, the four Volunteers were having breakfast at a cafe in town when Kressley was stopped by the police chief who was sitting at the cafe counter. The chief said he had a warrant for their arrest and that they should stop by the police station sometime that day and see him about it. The following day, the complaints were signed by the local prosecuting attorney, the Volunteers were formally arrested for disturbing the peace and immediately released on their own recognizance. Their hearing was scheduled later that month.

Upon reading Kressley's report, Bruch went to Warren to form his own impressions. His description of the situation and what he learned there illustrates the easily exploited nature of the community and how predictably it would react.

> I set up a meeting with the chief at the local cafe. He introduced me all around. After we talked for a while, the cafe emptied out until there was just the two of us there. I finally asked him what he really arrested them for. He rises up. I rise up. He looks both ways. "We got 'em for race mixing," he said. Since we were now comrades, I had to keep a straight face.

Bruch said the neighbor who originally called the police later admitted she could not hear the party and was informed of it when another neighbor came by and told her of the race mixing at the VISTA residence. That second lady was the one peeking in the windows of the house that night, Bruch said. The complaint was brought through the neighborhood by police, and one of the five who signed it acknowledged she knew nothing of the party but was simply against race mixing. One who signed wasn't even home the night of the party, Bruch added.

The charges against the Volunteers were dropped after an aide to Gov. Winthrop Rockefeller intervened on their behalf and convinced local authorities that the state could not afford the negative publicity such a case would bring.

But the damage had been done, and according to Kressley, during the next two months the Volunteers were constantly harassed by a small group of whites. The female Volunteers, taunted as prostitutes working for the government to encourage interracial sex, were more frequent victims. Projects the Volunteers tried to start were carefully watched and older members of the black community became cautious about getting too involved, Kressley said. He also recalled when he and Fleming were invited by a teacher to speak and show a VISTA film at a local school but white students blocked their entry. The school principal finally came out to escort them inside, Kressley said.

School integration was being implemented across Arkansas at this time, and in Warren the local school board was scheduled to vote on district consolidation and closing of the all black school. Freedom, Inc., a freedom of choice group organized in Texarkana, had its supporters in Bradley County, and the Volunteers became convenient scapegoats for the group's effort to maintain separate school systems.

A final incident convinced regional VISTA officials that the Bradley County Volunteers should be removed before physical harm was done. Kressley said that in February, 1969, a drunk white man came to the female Volunteers' house with an axe and attempted to break through the door. Kressley and Fleming happened to be there at the time and convinced the man to back off, but not before he unloaded a vocal barrage of venom and hatred. Warren police were called to the scene by those inside the house, but they didn't arrive until half an hour later. Kressley said police explained their late arrival as a result of having gotten caught in traffic.

Over the next month, one of the female Volunteers resigned from VISTA, and others were transferred to different projects. Kressley traveled the southwest region doing recruiting work. He kept pressuring program officers to let him complete his year at Warren, and with Rogers' permission, he returned there in March. Rogers admitted there was some risk in bringing Kressley back, but he believed the young Volunteer could help the community.

> I felt Larry was the most sensible and open to discussion. I felt our agency benefited from his tenure with us. I went to bat for him, said I'd like to keep him for the year. I stuck my neck out and was never particularly disappointed. We communicated. I suggested things to smooth the way and accomplish what he wanted.

Kressley knew that upon returning to Warren he would have to make deliberate attempts to work with whites. Yet his remaining nine months were haunted by the events of New Year's Eve, and he was unable to make contact with the white poverty community. He became involved in typical VISTA projects, however, helping organize neighborhood councils and youth recreational projects, driving people to medical offices, tutoring adults for their high school equivalency diplomas, and other activities.

Kressley said his most important and successful work was the organizing of twenty black students who chose to attend the white high school in Warren under the Freedom of Choice plan. This plan was widely used in the South until the Supreme Court ruled it unconstitutional in 1970. No white students in Warren wanted to attend the black school and most blacks knew all too well the intimidation they would likely receive if they attended the white high school, Kressley said.

> Nonetheless, twenty black students requested to attend the previously all-white Warren High School. From the beginning they received harassment and intimidation from both teachers and students. It was around this treatment that we organized a group called Black United Youth to try to change the situation. The group met with both success and failure, but most importantly it provided a chance for the first time for young people in the black community to come together and take action on their common problems. It was the one success of my year in Warren.

Kressley completed his service year in December, 1969, and like most Volunteers, cut his Arkansas ties and went on to other involvements. He completed college and graduate school, worked as an organizer and with community based organizations. He is currently program officer for a private, grant-making foundation in Washington, DC.

As one who never left Warren, Eddie Colen is in a better position to judge VISTA success there than Kressley. Colen said Kressley had some impact on the town and his staying on through the year eased some of the tension that followed the ill fated party. Seventeen years later, these events seem trivial, and Colen laughed as he recalled them.

The Bradley County agency has grown since Kressley's time to include a five-county service area. Colen, currently its director, said a family planning program the Volunteers helped get started is still functioning. In 1978, another Volunteer was assigned to Warren, a young white man who provided excellent assistance to the whole community through his work with a local housing development corporation, Colen added.

From a state-wide perspective, the Bradley County VISTA project did not generate exceptional results or failures. If not for the Volunteers' party, the project would have probably gained only slight attention. Yet the situation in Warren offers a lesson in humility, both on the community side and by the Volunteers. It is an example of shortsightedness resulting from inflexible and shallow positions. More than anything else, it shows that Volunteers had to adapt their priorities to the real needs of each situation. In Bradley County, this meant changing the minds of those who opposed them more than rallying those whose support had already been gained.

ARKANSAS VISTA ACHIEVEMENT

Approximately 1,300 Volunteers, the majority of them Arkansas natives, have served low-income communities and individuals in the twenty years since Arkansas received its first VISTA workers in 1965. Their projects have focused on virtually every facet of community life.

In the early years, most Arkansas projects were somewhat ill defined. With no preceding group to offer guidance, the first Volunteers generally had to assess community needs and initiate their own programs. Yet by 1970, Arkansas VISTA projects were credited with some extraordinary accomplishments. VISTA had either established needed community programs or else publicly exposed the opposition forces that refused change.

VISTA had a significant effect on Arkansas. Richard First explained Arkansas VISTA success as a result of the limited exposure and involvement many state residents had with the rest of the nation.

> The Volunteers were the only outsiders to come in during the days when a large amount of oppression for blacks and the poor was unchallenged. Under the control of county judges, there was a heavy dimension of keeping people in place. The Volunteers represented an external influence. The low income communities began to see there was support from the outside for their problems, and they began to draw on it.[1]

The major confrontation between Arkansas Volunteers and community power groups occurred between 1969 and 1975. Highly publicized community resistance in 1970 to VISTA projects in the eastern delta counties and Texarkana (Miller County) heightened statewide sensitivity and awareness. Prior to 1969, however, the state program had generated only scattered community resistance.

At a December 1967 in-service training workshop attended by thirty-five Arkansas Volunteers, Joe Bruch commented that Arkansas was in good shape with less VISTA problems than other places. Rural Volunteers especially enjoyed contact with others and the relative luxury of a motel with running water.

A national report on hunger broke the calm of Arkansas' early VISTA years. In April 1968, the Citizens Board of Inquiry into Hunger and Malnutrition released a report stating that four Arkansas counties were among 256 "hunger" counties in twenty states where chronic hunger and dangerous levels of malnutrition existed. Three Delta counties were named—Crittenden, Lee, and Mississippi—and Stone County in the north central area. Lee County would soon gain additional notoriety by being listed among the ten poorest in the nation.[2]

Arkansas officials were skeptical about the report. They admitted hunger existed in the state, but they said the problem was affected families not being well informed enough to take advantage of available welfare aid. Robert Sandstead, director of the Lee County Welfare Office, bluntly said the report stated an untruth.

> Assistance is available even to the penniless. So I don't see where there is any hunger here. I certainly haven't seen any.[3]

Sandstead added that if hunger did exist in Lee County, it was due to ignorance. Other county welfare officials voiced similar reactions, and shortly afterwards the state welfare commissioner stated his belief that no widespread chronic hunger existed in the four listed Arkansas counties.[4]

Despite the local denials, hunger became a leading issue in the structuring of Arkansas' Volunteer effort, especially among Health

Advocates projects in Delta counties. Resistance to that group's work, particularly in Lee County, set into motion a host of false rumors and speculations about Volunteers across the state.

Events were also taking place in Little Rock that rapidly changed community reception of VISTA projects from one of cautious approval to outright suspicion. Following a 1968 summer of racial tensions and street violence, Volunteer activities in black communities came under a much harsher scrutiny. Community organizing work also generated more local criticism because younger and more politically opinionated Volunteers began to replace PDPs and older Volunteers.

With a new wave of Volunteers coming in and the state reaction growing increasingly turbulent and complex, Bruch drafted a memo on training requirements for Arkansas VISTA placement. Preference would be given to rural and southern applicants, particularly married couples, with a minimum of two years of college and experiences applicable to the skill slot. "No ego bags or missionaries" would be tolerated, and a large percentage should be black, Bruch wrote.

> Arkansas is a particularly hostile environment for outsiders, do-gooders, and ne'er do wells. . . . Volunteers serving in the state must have an extra measure of commitment, without martyrdom. They are required to get up early in the morning . . . They do work long hours. They have little support. They are often extremely isolated. They are constantly being scrutinized in their personal lives, and they more often fail than succeed in the programs they attempt.

For Bruch, 1969 was a banner year in the state VISTA program. More than 140 Volunteers served in Arkansas and approximately forty government vehicles and half-a-dozen rented cars were in use. Locally recruited Volunteers were first being used in projects at Harrison and Little Rock. Permission was first being given to organizations other than community action agencies to sponsor VISTA projects.

As the decade ended, so did a distinct chapter in VISTA history.

The early, unstructured days of OEO and CAA sponsorship were gone. A more conservative federal agency, ACTION, imposed new requirements of measurable goals and clearly identified plans for achieving them. The state's first ACTION director was Dr. Amos Bennet, who commented in 1974 on recent changes in the program.

> The traditional image of VISTA people and other volunteers—outsiders, radicals with long hair—no longer holds true. We are trying to use more local people because they know the area better . . . More closely monitored programs to meet specific . . . goals.[5]

Bennet was not a popular administrator with state VISTA staff and Volunteers. Some spoke of his odd behavior—sudden personality shifts and a difficulty relating to the program staff during his tenure. His attitudes about VISTA, however, fit squarely within the dominant Republican policies that guided the program through most of the 1970s.

By 1977, Freeman McKindra said that eight years of Republican administration had removed the romantic appeal of changing the world for most Volunteers. The shift was most visible in recruiting. Locally recruited Volunteers working on specific topics had replaced an earlier emphasis on a young, nationally recruited group, McKindra said. Veteran project supervisor Lou Vitale of Dardanelle shared that opinion, stating "what we look for today is technical skills. No more wide-eyed kids that just want to help out."[6]

VISTA emphasis has changed over the years, but specific Arkansas problems have not. Hunger continues to be a major problem in the state. A 1985 study by the Harvard School of Public Health listed six Arkansas counties among 150 nationwide "hunger counties," areas defined as having less than one-third of eligible residents receiving food stamps. The problem was a result of restricted access to food stamps and a failure of federal assistance programs to reach the needy, researchers said.[7]

Could a more aggressive VISTA program over the twenty-year period have placed Arkansas counties above the level for the study's definition of a hunger county? Former state program officer Jim

Crawford believes Arkansas had one of the best programs in the nation, that it designed and implemented creative traditional projects, that it used Volunteers well and fit them into appropriate roles.

After twenty years, however, there is justification in seeking a measurement of achievements. Each major Arkansas project brought beneficial change to its community. Projects with lesser impact or media attention, with a shorter life span or lower Volunteer numbers, also influenced change. But those changes cannot be counted like bricks in a wall, not even when the VISTA effort was a construction project.

Social analysts seeking a "bottom line" should keep a tally of those projects that served communities across the state without significant media attention. This chapter identifies several such projects. To understand the ultimate contribution of VISTA, however, the program must be recognized as a catalyst to social change, not a vehicle of change in itself.

Those who seek to measure program results must include long term, residual affects on a community. Unfortunately, at that point original VISTA influences have often become too indistinct to accurately assess. Successful VISTA projects help create on-going grass roots efforts. The Volunteer influence, essential to the origin of these projects, has a decreasing impact as time goes on. The ideal end result is a vital, self-sufficient community service organization.

No plaques or honorary markers for early VISTA work are likely to be found at these organizations. Community members and current staff may not even be aware of what went on. What VISTA offers is an analysis of community development demonstrated through community progress and human interaction. Arkansas progress is measureable through economic, health, education, and other clearly defined factors. Just as clearly, the level of VISTA involvement in the state has significantly decreased from its 1969 peak.

In 1980, 72 Volunteers were working with 13 sponsoring agencies. In 1985, approximately 65 Volunteers were assigned to 20 active projects across the state. From a strict policy analysis, the balance of decreasing Volunteer support and increasing project independence and growth is altogether fitting. This can be interpreted to mean the state is decreasing its need for VISTA workers.

Bob Torvestad, current state program officer, has a backlog of community requests for Volunteer approval that contradicts any such interpretation. Based on the current demand, Torvestad said he sees no reason to publicize the program's limited resources.

> Just through word of mouth, we now have two or three times the proposals that I can fund. We're already committed through 1987. Arkansas Volunteer assignments are now twice as high as allocated resources based on state poverty levels.

Resources for Arkansas Volunteers are coming from unused allocations from other states. As a result, recent Arkansas Volunteer assignments have been higher than in California and Texas. Torvestad said successful current projects are at small community organizations with approximately three Volunteers assigned, because those organizations are better able to respond to the Volunteer and increase his impact on the immediate community. That is the direction VISTA has to go in the future, he added.

Current Volunteers are locally recruited from low-income communities. Their VISTA training has been reduced to half a day on program logistics. Project sponsors take over from there. About eighty percent of current Volunteers want to stay on for a second and third year of service. Outstanding modern Volunteers are often hired as staff members of their organizations. This is a new challenge older programs rarely had to face. Current projects have adapted by moving Volunteers out of a service role after their first year and letting them recruit or train others. The modern Volunteer is developing new skills as his project grows.

Two contemporary Arkansas VISTA projects are achieving excellent results in this manner, Torvestad said. They are the Literacy Council of Jefferson County and Neighbor-to-Neighbor, both at Pine Bluff. The Literacy Council has former Volunteers directing the program from key staff positions. The three current Volunteers were chosen for their abilities in fundraising, office administration, and literacy tutoring. The project is expected to continue expanding with limited Volunteer assignments.

Neighbor-to-Neighbor is a community organization serving the poor through a variety of church groups. It provides food, clothing, shelter, counseling, and crisis assistance. Locally recruited Volunteers have "people skills," Torvestad said, and after a first year of direct service they are trained to recruit supplies for the project. The success of those efforts has allowed Neighbor-to-Neighbor to grow faster than any community organization he has seen.

Arkansas communities continue to state their demand for Volunteers, Torvestad said, but projects now receiving Volunteer approval are past the need for an organizing role. Successful programs are using Volunteers to serve the needs of the low-income people, not just empower them. Torvestad said his current concern is that Volunteers are well supervised and provided the proper structure. The focus has changed, he believes, and empowerment won't work now or ever again.

More than a hundred VISTA projects have served Arkansas communities at some time during the program's first twenty years. It is not the intention of this book to provide a comprehensive listing of them all. Projects selected for this chronological review are some that have had distinct long range impact within a specific area.

Many worthwhile VISTA projects are not included here because of the diverse nature of their success—for example, a home weatherization program sponsored by the state Division of Community Services used Volunteers and community workers to upgrade more than nine hundred Arkansas homes in the early 1980s.

Similar widespread results were achieved through the Arkansas Nutrition Coalition, which assisted in a variety of food programs. Effective programs to decrease the state's high illiteracy rate continue to be implemented by the Arkansas Literacy Council and spin-off literacy councils sponsored by individual counties, such as those in Pine Bluff and Little Rock.

An "umbrella agency," the Human Service Providers Association assigned Volunteers to a variety of smaller state projects in the early 1980s. In its 1981 annual report, the HSPA stated its Volunteers had generated $480,000 worth of resources in Arkansas and recruited more than 1,300 community volunteers to work in local programs. Various Legal Services offices across the state sponsored VISTA lawyers. Councils on aging used Volunteers to design and implement their service programs. The list of direct service and organizing projects goes on.

Two large scale projects deserving of mention were Arkansas Consumer Research (ACR) and Arkansas Community Organization for Reform Now (ACORN). ACR was dedicated to consumer representation in utility and other citizens rights issues. ACORN, a national organization that originated in Arkansas, and its subsidiary CORAP (Community Organizing Research and Action Program) were involved in political issues and community organizing efforts across the state.

Arkansas VISTA achievements are as widespread as state communities and organizations are diverse. No single review can encompass them all. The following projects represent just a few of those outstanding efforts:

Job Corps Conservation Centers

Established in 1965 as one of the first four VISTA projects in Arkansas, Job Corps Conservation Centers were located near Hot Springs at Royal (Garland County) and at Cass (Franklin County). The two centers, sponsored by the U.S. Forestry Service, provided a residential program for teen age boys from across the country. Few Arkansas youth were placed there. Volunteers at the centers performed academic, recreational, vocational, and counseling duties.

The Arkansas JCCC attempted to provide new opportunity and guidance to low-income youth while assisting in the initial develop-

Volunteer and Crowley's Ridge VISTA supervisor Loren Ivener

ment of the Ouachita and Ozark National Forests. The young men alternated weeks of academic and vocational training programs. In their physical work periods, they helped build roads and forest trails, fences and cattle guards, and maintained recreational centers. Many of their projects are still in use in the two national forests.

Loren Ivener, one of the nation's original twenty Volunteers, served his first VISTA year at the Royal Center in 1965. He recalled a camp of approximately 120 boys, perhaps three-quarters of them black, and a daily atmosphere of racial tension and easily triggered fights. A 1966 article in the *Arkansas Gazette* described the center as looking like a summer camp with baseball and swimming, yet upon a closer inspection, JCCC residents were older, small for their age, and many had nicotine stained fingers. The average educational level among the youths was fifth grade, the article said.[8]

Ivener credited Horace Henry, an older Volunteer from Texas, with providing an outstanding moral role model for the JCCC boys. Ivener, twenty one at the time, said he didn't have Henry's grandfatherly maturity to help him. Instead, weekly trips into Hot Springs, the site of a similar program for girls, worked as effective leverage for keeping the youths under control, Ivener explained.

Ivener served a second year at a VISTA project in St. Louis, then returned to the Royal JCCC to work as a staff member. In 1969, he became Volunteer supervisor at the newly established Crowley's Ridge Development Council at Jonesboro.

Crowley's Ridge Development Council

Serving four northeast Arkansas counties (Greene, Craighead, Jackson, Poinsett), Crowley's Ridge Development Council at Jonesboro has used national and locally recruited Volunteers since 1969 when the agency was incorporated and its first ten Volunteers were assigned. Over the years, CRDC has provided a range of outstanding services with little controversy or community resistance.

Several agency projects started by Volunteers are continuing as on-going community efforts with strong local support. Credit for this continuity and effective performance is due in part to agency director Bobby Yopp, who has held that role since 1969. With the backing of a confident agency director, CRDC Volunteers were spared much interference in their work.

In 1971, when VISTA programs across the state were being strongly criticized, a CRDC newsletter credited the agency Volunteers with bringing significant help to the area. Their continued work in the area was urged, and residents were invited to express their support in letters to the governor's office. Criticisms or suggestions for improving the CRDC VISTA program were also solicited in the article.

With agency support and supervision, CRDC Volunteers have successfully dealt with a range of low-income problems. Early work at Marked Tree (Poinsett County) helped overcome established racial barriers as white Volunteers initiated health and recreation programs in the black community. Another successful project was Camp Crajasett, where Volunteers raised funds and helped administer a summer program for low-income youth in Craighead, Jackson and Poinsett counties.

An overall need for health services, particularly among the elderly, had CRDC Volunteers working in an innovative program of senior foster care. Placing isolated and temporarily disabled senior citizens in homes where they received caring companionship helped prevent premature institutionalization. At one point, the entire Poinsett County health service was administered by a CRDC Volunteer nurse.

Yopp said that an alcoholism program begun by a Volunteer in 1973 now serves seven counties and maintains three residential centers. The Jonesboro Hot Line, a twenty-four-hour telephone service for emergency counseling and assistance currently funded by the United Way, also began as a VISTA project. Another on-going

CRDC project is a local food bank eligible for Second Harvest contributions. In addition to helping establish the first food bank in the state, Yopp said CRDC Volunteers helped the agency overcome personnel costs and other difficulties of the start-up phase of many projects.

> With the Volunteers help, we could begin a project, show what it could do, and then seek ongoing funding. We now have a broad base of community support and get more from the United Way than most community agencies in the state. We have a good reputation in the community, and people realize our interest in doing things for them.

Black River Area Development

A community action agency serving three northeastern counties (Clay, Randolph, and Lawrence), the Black River Area Development Corporation at Pocahontas was fortunate in having PDP Volunteer William Louis Bookheim assigned in 1968 as its first national Volunteer.

Bookheim turned his solo assignment into something special. Beyond the traditional PDP role of assisting the agency in creating future plans, Bookheim helped create a detailed application to the state Commission of Education that lead to the area's selection as site of a new vo-tech school. The long range impact of the Black River Vo-Tech School on the area is virtually too large to measure.

Not many Volunteer efforts at BRAD could compare to Bookheim's achievement. Problems resulting from later Volunteer service were listed in a memo intended as a recruiting article for the agency newsletter. The memo also reveals the value of humor in a healthy agency-Volunteer relationship, a quality evidently possessed at BRAD.

No one seems to want you? VISTA might! Sign your name and you gain instantly:

1. enough wages to get by on . . . almost
2. a bad reputation with half the population
3. work no one else wants
4. unending questions as to why an educated person would do it to himself
5. head-on confrontations with sooner or later every Bircher within a radius of 100 miles
6. everybody saying what you *can't* do, nobody saying *why* you can't do it and nobody saying what you can do
7. the companionship of other VISTAS—hopefully non-violent
8. parents asking, "What did I do wrong to deserve a kid like this?"
9. other equally satisfying rewards

BRAD sponsored national and locally recruited Volunteers for close to ten years, applying their expertise and commitment to community problems in medical services, senior citizen programs, transportation, and other needs. Jim Jansen, the original and ongoing BRAD director, said the results of Volunteer efforts include the establishment of twelve senior centers in the three-county area.

Jansen said a national Volunteer assigned to BRAD who remained in the area was Donnie Peterson Martin. Originally assigned to Clay County to work with retarded children and Head Start, by 1985, Ms. Martin has become executive director of the Community School for Exceptional Children, a Pocahontas (Randolph County) facility with unquestionable long term contribution, Jansen added.

A 1974 agency report listed 4,700 meals to the elderly served. That same year, national Volunteer Martha May, a widowed mother of three children, began work at BRAD. Two years later, the New York native was honored by the agency for service to the area. Mrs. May had established thirty-two health clinics and personally trained twenty-nine staff and Volunteer workers.

Locally recruited Volunteers were no less important to achieving agency goals. In 1975, when all but one Volunteer were locally recruited, an ACTION evaluation report said BRAD Volunteers had a mature and positive perspective on their jobs and were given the full responsibility of professional people in carrying out their duties. Local Volunteer Dora Walker was the subject of a more personal endorsement when a lady from the tiny community of O'Kean (Randolph County) wrote to her congressman.

> . . . VISTA workers help to make life for the rest of us real and good and not just exciting. But three cheers for Dora, the sweetest, best and hardest working of all. Please do see we get to keep her. She is an inspiration to all of us in countless ways and means . . . a tireless worker . . . So, hurrah for VISTA, long may we have them with us.

Washington County Economic Opportunity Agency

The first Volunteers to gain attention in Washington County were a husband and wife team assigned in 1968 to the Washington County EOA at Fayetteville. Joe Bruch rated the couple as some of the most promising Volunteers in the state program, but by the fall of 1969 the two had been reassigned to another project, and the agency had its VISTA sponsorship discontinued by the regional OEO office.

An agency "shot through with corruption" was the reason for this abrupt reversal, though investigations were unable to prove any illegal activities had taken place, an OEO memo stated. The agency director at the time was the son of the incumbent county judge, and conflicts had developed concerning the agency's relationship with local power groups at the expense of low-income people. The director resigned in 1969 and Charles Johnson was appointed in his place.

Johnson, who directed the Washington County EOA until he was elected County Judge in 1978, recognized that agency leadership contributed to some of the early problems, but he said that VISTA projects as a whole had difficulty working in the area. Washington County's diverse low-income community, low percentage of poverty, and relatively small ghetto areas caused the difficulties, Johnson explained. The area's relatively low level of VISTA accomplishments can also be blamed on a more common problem—project administrators' shortsighted understanding of what the Volunteers were supposed to do.

The Boston Mountain Co-op, a Washington County agency that administered rural schools, was project sponsor for an ambitious 1971 undertaking. The Co-op placed Volunteers skilled in arts and special education at county schools in an attempt at curriculum enrichment. The program was discontinued by its second year because local school administrators preferred to use the Volunteers as teachers' aides and adjunct staff. Perhaps the only positive result of the discontinued program was that many of the talented Volunteers stayed on in the Fayetteville area, adding their cultural and human service expertise to that community's diverse character.

Not all Washington County projects ended in total dissolution. The EOA placed Volunteers through the 1970s in direct service projects of home weatherization and food cooperatives. For a temporary period, Volunteers achieved some success through the Tenant Landlord Organization, an advocacy project for renters.

In the mid 1970s, an independent agency, People for Awareness and Community Action, used locally recruited Volunteers in an effective program that provided free school lunches, recreational activities, and counseling services. In 1980, Volunteers from the Mari Spehar Health Education Project initiated the first health counseling program for women at the Washington County jail and later expanded its women's services to local foster girls and the community at large.

Perhaps the most tangible result of VISTA activity in Washington County is Youth Bridge, an on-going program of residential, counseling, and other services to young people. In 1972, national Volunteer Steve Anderson arrived in Fayetteville and began the youth service work that had motivated him to join VISTA. With the sup-

Volunteer Steve Anderson. *Photo by Drew Kilgore.*

port of the local juvenile court and members of the city council, Anderson established Indian Trails House, a residential program for problem youth.

The success of Indian Trails House motivated other community groups to start similar programs. Another Fayetteville youth home and a rural residential program eventually merged with Indian Trails House to form Youth Bridge. Anderson recognized that his VISTA role was only to initiate the program, to show that it could be done. "You do what you can, take it to a point and hand it to someone," he said. "If you've done a good job, it works."

Anderson is also an example of VISTA's long range results on the Volunteer and the community in which he lives. Following his year of service, Anderson taught in a rural Arkansas school, graduated law school at Fayetteville and was elected a Washington County Justice of the Peace. For some years he worked in Washington, DC as a special assistant to an Arkansas congressman. He is currently involved in Caracen, an advocacy organization for Salvadorean refugees in the U.S.

Graduate School of Social Work—University of Arkansas at Little Rock

Using graduate students as VISTA workers was an attempt to break new ground in techniques of social work. Students enrolled in the School of Social Work at the University of Arkansas at Little Rock would gain first hand experience of poverty conditions while they earned academic credit. The encounters with real poverty, not textbook case studies, would expand their understanding and abilities to deal with such situations.

The idea of such a program came through Richard First, who joined the faculty of the UALR Graduate School in Social Work early in 1969. First had seen a similar program in effect at the University of Maryland. He also had a comprehensive background in community organizing and Volunteer training. First developed the graduate school curriculum in 1969, and students enrolled and simultaneously entered VISTA service in 1970. Bill Bookheim, having completed his year with BRAD, served a second VISTA year and helped First establish the program at Little Rock.

First said his curriculum trained the student/Volunteers in community organizing, giving them a better exposure and value stance than if they had been regular Volunteers placed directly in community agencies. The UALR Volunteers had to spend twenty hours a week on VISTA work as well as carry the necessary academic load required for the Master of Social Work degree. The program was attractive to the state OEO because it provided extensive work beyond the normal short term VISTA service, and it developed careers in organizing, First said.

Bob Frank, currently a professor of social work at St. Mary of the Woods College in Indiana, was one of the UALR Volunteers. Frank initially served as youth director at the Little Rock St. Francis House. Others in his group worked on a variety of projects through the Pulaski County EOA. Later in 1970, the UALR Volunteers worked across the state, and Frank recalled being involved with the Saline County food stamp office, a council on aging at Malvern, and community organizing work for the Lee County Clinic at Marianna.

VISTA involvement through the Graduate School of Social Work created in his group the attitude of social workers as change agents, a self-assessment few professional social workers maintain, Frank said. The UALR program only lasted a year, but it helped a group of human service professionals expand their sense of service. The Volunteer's awareness of techniques for achieving social change was mixed with the social worker's understanding of psychology and immediate community influences. More astute and resourceful professionals were the result.

Watershed

The College Station area of Little Rock is the site of one of Arkansas' most persistent and accomplished communities. Through the determined organizing efforts of community leaders, College Station was one of the first areas in the state to receive VISTA workers in the mid 1960s. Through Volunteer and community efforts several on-going community projects have been established, yet the most significant chapter in the College Station VISTA history did not begin until 1978.

That year Watershed was established, and the agency began to deliver a variety of services in support of community projects. Programs were staffed by community volunteers with help from assigned VISTA workers. Among its services, Watershed provided a medical clinic, adult education, youth programs, a library, a clothing exchange, a community newspaper, and other programs. The agency based its long range goals on direct services, Rev. H. D. Stewart, Watershed director, said.

> What Watershed is all about is changing the lifestyle and destiny of people from one of hopelessness to one of hope and moving into self-sufficiency . . . a program devoted to helping people do better . . . we're into the total life of people.

In 1980, Rex and Neva Erickson, two new Volunteers, significantly raised the level of service at Watershed. The Ericksons were in their 40s, parents of eight children, and Rex had been a Michigan YMCA director for the past 16 years. The couple had the attitude and skills needed for successful community efforts. In addition to bringing new energy into on-going programs, the Ericksons revitalized the local Boy Scout troop, helped senior citizens with tax issues, and visited the sick. It was an immediate assimilation, and the middle aged white couple soon became part of the College Station community, Rev. Stewart said.

> In an oppressed community, there is an oppressed mentality you must understand before dealing with the crises people face daily. Rex and Neva didn't seek to raise people above their level but to move them from level to level.

The Erickson's success began to attract notice when the couple enrolled for a second year of service. An article in the Arkansas Democrat stated:

> The Ericksons have blended so well with the community they serve, it is difficult to pinpoint how much credit goes to them, the community members already involved when the Ericksons arrived, or to other community members recruited by the couple as neighborhood volunteers.[9]

It was the Erickson's initiative to establish the College Station YMCA. They received a grant to renovate an old College Station barn and create the youth program they continue to direct more than five years after their VISTA service ended. The Ericksons were

Volunteers Rex and Neva Erickson

fortunately placed in a community with a strong foundation in group activity. But their success results from more than a chance assignment. It is directly related to their uncompromised human compassion.

That emotion is evidenced in a journal Neva maintained during her VISTA years. In one journal entry, she described an old black man whose poverty was so extreme he could only burn paper for heat in his home. After his wife died from burns when her coat caught fire, the old man was placed in a nursing home fifteen miles away, Neva wrote. Having wandered away from the home several times, the man finally disappeared, and several months later his skeleton was discovered in a wooded area. In her journal, Neva wrote:

> Tomorrow we will stop by the cemetery for a grave side service. They found him the day Princess Grace was killed and all the world mourned her passing, and I doubt there will be five people at Mr. Lane's funeral.

But I have a feeling that the Lord won't see all that much difference between the beautiful princess and a little old black man who couldn't even write his name.

Rev. Stewart, who continues to direct Watershed from its expanded offices in a second College Station facility, spoke of the lasting value of VISTA workers in things "unseen and immeasurable," the realities that produce an Eagle Scout or better grades in school. The Ericksons and the College Station YMCA are winning the battle against social crime by creating jobs and levels of awareness significant to the development of the community, Stewart said.

A Final Sermon

In a final assessment, VISTA life values support a metaphysical ideology. They elevate what is real by working to achieve what is sublime. VISTA is built on paradox and contradiction. It represents the tenuous merger of church and state, and it succeeds only when a profound understanding of society forms the base of its efforts.

Rev. Stewart saw the results of VISTA relatively late into the program's history. His agency's first Volunteers, Rex and Neva Erickson, were assigned in 1980, but their outstanding efforts revealed to him the strong similarities between VISTA goals and the spiritual ideology of his ministry.

The VISTA organization is like a well organized missionary group, Stewart believes, because it performs the functions that God greatly approves of, those of loving and caring for your neighbor. Volunteers embrace the philosophy of self help, Stewart said.

> The magic here is that insignificant mothers can produce significant children. The Volunteers need to see more than their skill and talent in the community. They must love people. That is the only way to do any human service or volunteer work. Without that, you won't last.

Stewart understood the frustrations felt by federal administrators who looked to VISTA for specific and measureable results. They would not find what they were looking for because VISTA was never designed to fulfill that type of expectation, Stewart said.

> VISTA is a liability that creates assets. It is not an economic piece. The government wants tangible results. If they want VISTA to be a construction company, they should say so. If they want an organization to plant seeds to change life and change attitudes, those seasons are much longer. You can't measure these things in one fiscal year. VISTA operates on love of people, not on dollars. VISTA says, "Here's what I love. Now watch it grow."

To gain a better understanding of the tangible results of VISTA programs and results, Stewart suggested that program administrators participate in Volunteer groups for a few weeks. They would see how VISTA has saved lives and how in the long run it has even helped wealthy people by steering young people away from crime.

Stewart did not seem troubled by the diminishing emphasis the federal government was placing on volunteerism or what seemed to be the approaching end of the Arkansas VISTA program. VISTA results would emerge and exert their influence long after the actual program had ended, Stewart said.

> Anytime there's a seed planted with the truth in it, that seed must die for the truth to live. VISTA must die for the truth to emerge. VISTA has too much resurrecting power. As time passes, the crucifixion will be great, but the resurrection will be glorious.

Notes

1. Richard First, personal interview.
2. *Arkansas Gazette,* April 23, 1968.
3. *Arkansas Gazette,* May 6, 1968.
4. *Arkansas Gazette,* June 13, 1968.
5. *Arkansas Democrat,* April 7, 1974.
6. *Arkansas Gazette,* September 22, 1977.
7. *Arkansas Gazette,* January 14, 1986.
8. *Arkansas Gazette,* March 29, 1966.
9. *Arkansas Democrat,* February 15, 1981.

A LETTER FROM BILL BOOKHEIM

Louis William Bookheim was a New York native who joined VISTA in 1968 at the age of twenty-two. According to Joe Bruch, Bookheim was the "ideal VISTA Volunteer." The success of Bookheim's efforts was due to an ability to use ingenuity in relating with all groups of people and his creative approach in finding solutions, Bruch said.

In his initial northeast Arkansas assignment, Bookheim assisted in creating a successful application for a vocational technical school and federal funding for a local hospital. In his second year of VISTA, Bookheim helped establish a special scholarship program for poor blacks and whites at the University of Arkansas Graduate School of Social Work at Little Rock. Bookheim also showed an exceptional ability to facilitate communication between low income communities and organizations whose resources were to be tapped and utilized.

Bookheim currently lives in San Diego where he works as a law librarian.

"At Oberlin College (1964–1968) I was interested in social change and societal justice. I belonged to local and national civil rights organizations. At the same time that I applied to VISTA and the Peace Corps, I applied to the Columbia School of Social Work. I was accepted to all three, but joined VISTA.

I was trained in Colorado by Howard Higman's group. We were supposedly an elite bunch with most of the candidates coming from Ivy League type schools. We were trained as Program Development Planners (PDP). We were later referred to as Super-VISTAS. Higman's group had the reputation of being tough, no-nonsense people. The basic lesson was to keep your personal opinions to yourself and work your butt off helping the community to organize around their own needs.

I was assigned to Black River Area Development (BRAD) which covered three rural counties in northeast Arkansas (Randolph, Lawrence, and Clay Counties). The area was probably 90–95% white. BRAD's main office was in Pocahontas. I lived in Pocahontas for the first month, then moved into an old quonset hut at the former WWII air base at College City, located halfway between Pocahontas and Walnut Ridge. College City was the site of a Southern Baptist junior college, a municipal airport, and an industrial park.

As a PDP, I helped BRAD fill out federal funding proposals. I helped with the full planning process. I met with local groups in our neighborhood offices. I met with all the BRAD community aides and visited their communities.

The project I am most proud of was the coordination of an application for the construction of a vocational-technical school. There were over 20 applications for the three schools the state would build. We were one of the three chosen. Our application was the only bi-county request. We had the elected officials, "power brokers," and businesses in Randolph and Lawrence Counties cooperating and concentrating their efforts for the same goal.

We told the Department of Education, in effect, 'We want the school: here are several sites in our two counties; you pick the site, but give us the school.' While working on the vocational school project, I met State Assemblyman Leroy Blankenship. At one point he invited me to visit the Capitol in Little Rock. I did, and on that visit I registered as a state lobbyist. The school was approved and built after I left BRAD.

I tried to become involved in community affairs to get to know people in the community better. I was invited to join Kiwanis, and did. I joined the College City Volunteer Fire Department and held the rank of lieutenant. I caught for the Brown Shoe Company softball team in the local league. Because I was an energetic Northerner, climbed stairs two at a time, and worked as quickly as I could, my co-workers sometimes called me 'Wild Bill.'

There were no other VISTAS in my area. I was "isolated" in so far as I was working without direct contact with other non-Arkansans. I was the first VISTA to be placed in that area of Arkansas. Every couple of months I would meet with Charlie Deknatel, a VISTA PDP with whom I had trained. He was working in Blytheville, about 80 miles away. We would get together, have a meal out, and exchange 'war stories' about the people we were working with.

When it was my turn to bring a speaker to a Pocahontas Kiwanis lunch meeting, I spoke myself and presented a program or explanation on what BRAD was doing in the community, and the purposes of OEO. Before the program, I read an excerpt from a letter my father had written me. He wrote that his father, my grandfather, had been very active in Kiwanis for many years in Albany, New York, and would have been very proud to know that I belonged to Kiwanis. It was an emotional moment for me. I had to wipe away a tear.

My regional supervisor was Joe Bruch. He was very supportive. He made me feel he was one of 'us,' on the side of the VISTA workers and social progress. I remember on his first visit to BRAD that instead of talking with me in BRAD's office, we went for a walk around the old courthouse square. He spoke softly, and it seemed as if he hardly moved his lips. It gave me the impression that he didn't want anyone to overhear him. That helped the feeling that he was one of 'us' (outsiders).

We weren't there to impose unwanted change, but to learn their local needs and concerns and help them organize around them so they could use local and federal resources to meet their local problems. We were to keep our own opinions private to avoid unnecessarily alienating local people. And that could be difficult at times.

Soon after I arrived at BRAD, I remember a Clay County coordinator commenting about the demonstrations at the Democratic Convention in Chicago. He complained that the police didn't use two hands on the clubs. I kept my mouth shut. There was that certain air of conservatism present in northeast Arkansas.

On one of my first days at BRAD, the coordinator for Randolph County invited me to lunch. On the floor of his pickup was a note to the effect, 'Hey Jim, let's go coon hunting tonight.' My reaction was a vision of racial violence. So much for cultural shock. I quietly and quickly determined that it is the sport of many men in the mountainous areas of Arkansas to hunt raccoons at night with their hunting dogs (which they raise with much pride).

During my year with BRAD, VISTA/OEO sent an evaluator in to review my performance. My evaluator was a former nun, a native Bostonian. She was accompanying me while I did my work, and we stopped for lunch at a Razorback barbecue stand. I ended up acting as an interpreter. The man behind the counter asked her what she wanted. She asked me, 'What did he say?' She told him what she wanted. He looked at me and said, 'What did she say?'

Eldridge Cleaver (*Soul on Ice*) had a theory about the relationship between sex and power—basically, those without power spend their time involved in the pursuit of sex, and those without sex spend their time amassing power. At that time, I could understand it. I did not date any of the 'locals,' nor was I very 'socially' involved with them. Although I bought a country-western 'best hits' record in case any of my colleagues or neighbors dropped by, I basically kept to myself.

But I was very active when it came to working on projects and helping local people with their problems. All my energy was channeled into my work. There was a minimal time and effort for 'personal gratification.' I adopted a kitten which I named Roger Williams [after the colonialist who struggled for religious freedom], and later I got a puppy from Marianna VISTA Jan Wrede whom I named Joshua [after the Biblical figure].

I tried to get to know all of the BRAD employees by name and to visit every community in the three counties we served. I particularly remember Warm Springs, an unincorporated little community in Randolph County on the border with Missouri in the Ozark foothills. The backwoods road to Warm Springs passed over several low water bridges that would be covered with water after heavy rains. Most of the local men there seemed to work in the lumber industry, cutting trees or making pallets. One of the fellows raised a wild orphaned fawn which would come out of the woods when he whistled. However, despite the appeal and the aura of the photographs in *The Family of Man,* poverty is not quaint. Not from what I saw.

I learned that there was a small Jewish congregation in Jonesboro (Craighead County). They had services every couple of weeks when a student rabbi would come in from Cincinnati. On the weekends the Rabbi was there, they would also have a forum or discussion group. A liberal Christian from the local university would also attend. I enjoyed the warmth, intellectual discussions and community feeling that they gave.

Somehow I learned of a work-training program run by Mary Prentice in the bootheel of Missouri. I called them, and then went over for a visit. It was a marvelously conceived and well run program. They gave remedial training to the uneducated to prepare them for work. I believe they went so far as providing alarm clocks to all who needed help to get them up on time. They taught too, and trained them at it. They provided meals during training to take the trainees mind off of hunger. It also provided another job training: the kitchen. I tried to pass on word of Prentice's program to as many others as I could in Arkansas.

I re-enlisted in VISTA for a second year and was assigned to Little Rock. Before I left BRAD I was made an honorary lifetime member of the Pocahontas Jaycees and given a little 'money' tree full of singles by community people at the Walnut Ridge BRAD center. One of the community aides gave me her favorite Dave Brubeck record. I still have it.

The Walnut Ridge Chamber of Commerce invited me back in December 1969 for one of their luncheon meetings and presented me with a plaque for 'outstanding services.' I was later invited to consider becoming the manager of their Chamber of Commerce. I declined since I had already made plans at that point to study abroad the following year.

In Little Rock I was assigned to work with Dick First at the University of Arkansas School of Social Work. The purpose was to help encourage and help support native Arkansans to matriculate there and to place them in community work projects. Those were the days when Rabbi Palnick was removed from the board of the Pulaski County EOA because he was so outspoken against the private power brokers. And he was immediately selected by a local poverty group to continue as an effective spokesperson for the poor. I enjoyed Rabbi Palnick's services and sat in on one of his discussion groups.

When my second year ended, I left VISTA and Little Rock to undertake rabbinical studies at Hebrew Union College in Jerusalem. I dropped out of that program, and instead spent the next year working on kibbutzim in Israel. I returned to the States and got my law degree. I worked for an industrial outfit in Brooklyn for five or six years. Got my Masters of Library Science and am now a law librarian at a law school. Married, two kids, and an Israeli dog named Tat-Aluf."

“WILLIE” FERGUSON

THE ARKANSAS FOOD STAMPS LADY

On a narrow street in Eureka Springs, the modest home of Mrs. Wilma Ferguson seems much the same as the residences of other senior citizens who have chosen the north Arkansas town for their retirement. Mrs. Ferguson, however, is no ordinary retiree. A former Volunteer whose energy and commitment brought her national attention, she is one of those rare individuals that has made service to others a permanent vocation.

I've been called "Crazy Willie" and the "Arkansas Food Stamps Lady" because I believe people should eat and shouldn't be given a hassle about it. I don't talk; I preach. Inevitably, I would get publicity on me, perhaps because I was convinced the food stamp program was so important.

Mrs. Ferguson's efforts were aimed at a better public understanding and larger participation in the state food stamp program. To accomplish that goal, she served in VISTA for two-and-a-half years and worked as director of a state-wide nutrition project. Her emphasis today, as it was then, is on an often overlooked aspect of the food stamp program. Besides putting food on the tables of the hungry, she is convinced the program makes a significant contribution to the state and local economy.

In the middle 1960s, Mrs. Ferguson, then in her late 40s, found herself suddenly a widow, the mother of three children grown and gone from home, and living in a small town in Iowa. Faced with the

Volunteer Mrs. "Willie" Ferguson

choice of "being just one more widow in Iowa or going out and doing something," she enrolled in the University of Iowa. Despite never having graduated from high school, she earned a degree in English in three and a half years.

So what do you do with a B.A. with the first half-century behind you? A career was obviously out, so I looked around for something I could do that would be meaningful.

The opportunity presented itself through a campus VISTA recruiter. Mrs. Ferguson joined the program and spent her first six months working in a Texas senior citizens center. Not adequately challenged there, she requested a transfer and was reassigned to the South Central Arkansas Community Action Agency at Camden (Ouachita County).

In Camden, I was working in a poverty program, and there was a lot to do. Most of the other Volunteers were social activists who wanted to change the system. I was 51 years old. I didn't expect to live to see the revolution. I wanted to see the best parts of the system work. I wanted to see the people eat, and I saw the food stamps program as the way to do it.

With memories of much food being wasted in Iowa, Mrs. Ferguson realized that any effort to bring that lost resource to positive use had to begin with an organized outreach program. She met with the Camden Chamber of Commerce to explain the economic advantages of the food stamp program and supported her efforts with articles written for the local newspaper.

> . . . We, the American taxpayers, have been supporting the price of farm products since 1933. We have paid for the slaughter of surplus pigs, the plowing-under of growing crops. We have built corn cribs and grain bins for on-the-farm storage of the ever-normal grainery, and we have torn them down again. We have transported our surplus foodstuff halfway across the continent to fill leased warehouses, and the rats grew sleek and fat at our expense.
>
> For thirty seven years we, the American taxpayers, have provided money for agricultural price support programs. We are committed to continue this support, for American farmers can no longer operate without some kind of government subsidy. There is no way to reduce the level of spending for this price support program, but we do have a choice of method. The Food Stamp Program is the one method that channels the surplus food produced on American farms through the local retail outlets and onto the tables of American families.
>
> For thirty seven years we have shared in the cost; at last we have an opportunity to share in the benefits.
>
> [*Camden News,* August 10, 1970]

During her service at the Camden agency, Mrs. Ferguson completed a study on the food stamp program and the state economy. Her research showed that the bonus value of food stamps (the difference between the cost of the stamps and their face value) could add an additional 2 million dollars in sales tax into the state treasury if all eligible families participated in the program.

With only thirty-five percent of eligible families then receiving food stamps, Mrs. Ferguson urged the state to add an advertising program to the Food Stamp Division of the Department of Public

Welfare to inform the public about the program. Her report refuted the view of food stamps as a "welfare handout" and portrayed them as an opportunity for low-income families to make significant contributions to the community economy.

Having convinced Ouachita County officials of the validity of her plan, a local media campaign was implemented. The results were overwhelming. An increased participation by eligible families brought the county level up to fifty percent. On one occasion a near riot occurred in the food stamp office when an overworked issuing clerk tried to leave early one day, Mrs. Ferguson said.

The report also included Mrs. Ferguson's concerns about what she felt was a humiliating interview and income-verification process applicants had to endure. It is a process still largely followed to this day, she said.

> It has now become a humiliating process to qualify. It's written into the law. You have to bring in a large sheaf of papers as if you would be getting a bank loan. You have to interview. The difference is a bank really wants to lend you the money. That's its business. The certification person's job is riding on his being able to protect the roles.

Having gained attention for her report, Mrs. Ferguson followed her year in Camden with another nine months of VISTA service traveling the state as a teacher of the food stamp program. She later became director of the Arkansas Nutrition Coalition, an organization concerned about the problems of hunger and malnutrition. She followed that role by joining VISTA again, this time as a locally recruited Volunteer for the ANC.

During her last phase of VISTA service, Mrs. Ferguson was invited to Washington, DC to speak before the Senate Agriculture Committee. In her testimony, Mrs. Ferguson argued for a program reform to abolish the purchase requirement that forced low- or fixed-income recipients to purchase food stamps. The purchase requirement, despite the stamps' bonus value, at times forced recipients to do without other necessities, Mrs. Ferguson said.

. . . The purchase requirement makes a mockery of the stated purpose of the food stamp act. By withholding food from those who cannot afford to pay the price, it punishes alike the improvident, the unfortunate, and the unlucky. It is the old and the very young who suffer the most from this regressive requirement.

I first became involved in food stamp outreach in 1970, as an idealistic and naive VISTA Volunteer. As a survivor of the Great Depression, I knew about poverty. Knew it all. The food stamp program, with its purchase requirement, was an excellent tool to teach household budgeting. I clung to this illusion for a year, then saw it crumble under the harsh realities of jobs dependent on the weather, of charge accounts at the company store, and of the omnivorous automobile, that indispensable transportation.

Sadly, I had to concede that for the most needy of our people, budgeting was impossible, and the food stamp program with its purchase requirement and its bright promise of adequate nutrition was out of reach. It still is, and will continue to be out of reach, until the purchase requirement is abolished.

[*Press Argus,* Van Buren, AR—April 29, 1978]

Mrs. Ferguson said she considered herself a Jewish mother, an honorary title she explained did not require a person to be Jewish or even female. One only had to believe that all the problems in the world could be solved with enough chicken soup well distributed, she said. Mrs. Ferguson's "soup" was food stamps, and her Arkansas VISTA service more than confirms her resolution to feed the hungry.

I don't regret anything except the six months I spent pouring punch at the senor citizen domino parties in Texas. If I had my way, old socialist that I am, I would have expanded food stamps to include everybody. It's an agriculture project, but its benefits are to the farmers and the people. I told the truth, selectively, but I always told the truth. You have to know the right thing to say at the right time.

POST-SERVICE PSYCHOLOGY

Post-Service Psychology

Success, Failure, and Personal Fulfillment

A "No-Win" Situation

Post-Service Psychology

Complex emotions and social involvement left a mark on Volunteer personalities in a way few other experiences could have. Former Volunteers generally view their service from one of two perspectives. It is either shadowed with impressions of guilt, doubt, and unfulfilled expectations, or it is viewed as a singularly enriching period with clearly accomplished objectives, a period when daily activity reaffirmed a sense of purpose. The Volunteers' relative youth contributed to this dichotomy. Not having experienced the major dramas of life, most Volunteers were unable to view things from a holistic perspective. Many expressed greater feelings of guilt during their service than they do now from a more mature perspective.

Volunteer impressions were necessarily influenced by their own definitions of success, fulfillment, and failure. In addition, these definitions can often be markedly different when applied to personal or community goals. Post-service psychology is a profound indicator of who the Volunteers were and what experiences they encountered.

Volunteer Earl Anthes recalled distinct character types that ultimately influenced the VISTAS' self-assessment. He listed them as:

1. Those who entered the program without a predefined goal to essentially go out and do good. For them, even helping one person was a net gain.

2. Those who desired major social change, a group with strong residual feelings of frustration.

3. Those who entered the program with a basic cynicism, who mistrusted personal idealism and its glorified rhetoric. These Volunteer often became the real long term problem solvers because they realized their year of service was just a first step for the community.

4. Those who failed to achieve any relationship with their communities because of an "embassy mentality of us versus them."

Another type might be added to this list—the overly zealous Volunteer whose personal insecurity about what he was doing created a sense of one-upmanship, a "my poverty is worse than your poverty" attitude, Anthes said.

These character types were largely defined prior to VISTA exposure. One theory holds that guilt or discomfort with a well provided economic status brought many young people into the program. This view confuses economic security with emotional stability. The successful Volunteer has been identified as a good listener. A person overwhelmed with his own problems will not possess the qualities that allow him to be a good listener.

Yet many Volunteers came into the program with the less-than-joking ambition of wanting to change the world. If the Volunteers were, as program services officer George Ellis called them, entrepreneural types willing to take things on, what was in it for them?

Some Volunteers became depressed because the world remained unchanged despite their efforts. Others took the attitude that hard core poverty people didn't want to be saved. Some could never understand the hatred or ridicule that was vented upon them for their siding with the disadvantaged. For the individual who mixed personal insecurity with a misguided sense of social service, VISTA offered an ideal self justification.

Ellis mentioned two Volunteer groups who demonstrated a healthy understanding of what they were capable of doing and why they were doing it.

The professional Volunteers, those with definite skills, were able to apply their skills, and generally came out pretty well. The group that went in to

> do basic services—teachers and others—didn't go in to change the world or redistribute power. They went in to teach some Head Start kids how to read. This did not change their lives, but it was a meaningful thing to them.

The properly motivated Volunteer can often be identified through his expression of a commonly stated regret—the feeling of having personally gained more than he gave to the community. Or as Anthes said, a person who realized self-gain from working with a community that's been ripped off inevitably begins to wonder if he too is ripping them off.

This idea troubled Volunteer Francis Woods for some years. Only recent contact with a former member of the east Arkansas agricultural co-op she helped establish has given her a new perspective, she said.

> Toward the end of my stay and a lot since then I began to worry and wonder if we had somehow raised false hopes, had started something that could not become institutionalized, become a permanent fixture. And in doing so, had we perhaps ruined something for the future, done something that would stop people from getting involved in a more permanent change effort? I remember thinking this in later years in other organizing efforts, and asking myself whether I was willing to stay permanently, be a part of the community and see something through to the very end, whatever that is.

For Volunteer Gene Richards, VISTA time is associated with his youth, a period he said was spent as well as possible but one that left no specific or measureable achievement. Richards' VISTA group, the Health Advocates, has not maintained much contact over the years, he said.

> It was not enough for this group to feel better and learn more than VISTA. We wanted to accomplish something. Not enough to be a great learner or to grow up through VISTA. That spirit of guilt. Why should we want a reunion of mellow disappointments? Others could have a cause for celebration. In a couple of years after VISTA, the brashness had gone off. We became the oldest group of young people I'd ever met. There was some heavy damage.

Woods suggested those remarks were overstated as a result of Richards' individual experiences. Contemplating her VISTA exposure, Woods said her only "damage" would be in having no inclination to join superficial community groups that lacked a dedicated commitment to change.

Volunteers who can accept personal gain as a result of VISTA service have an additional affirmation of their activities. They are able to identify a distinct result, even one as open ended as allowing themselves to continue making life better.

Volunteer Penny Lewis believes she achieved more personal growth and learning than she was able to impart to her assigned community. Lewis said she has been able to reconcile that gain through her current involvement in foster child care.

> The thing that appeases my guilt is what I took from Arkansas, I gave back here in Wisconsin. The skills I started learning in VISTA I am still honing and using. With time and patience, I finally became a good listener. I am learning to hear what people wanted, not what I thought they should have. And I guess I'm still giving back.

Success, Failure, And Personal Fulfillment

Most former Volunteers realized too many variables existed in their projects, their communities, and in themselves—too much was beyond their immediate control—for any sense of total achievement to dominate VISTA memories. The passing years have softened their idealism and increased their willingness to compromise. Yet in summary descriptions of their service, Volunteers often return to memories of their inability to deal with a situation or change the downward course of events.

In one way, this relates to the essential humility of the true Volunteer. Starting in training sessions, the Volunteers were told that providing effective community assistance was a self-effacing role. Successful Volunteers kept themselves out of the front lines. Their VISTA recollections, however, often begin with comments on what they failed to do rather than what they were able to achieve.

Sandy Smegelsky spoke of the malnourished and undersized babies she saw at the Gaylor Clinic, a Memphis facility that accepted destitute Arkansas patients.

I remember holding a baby with brain damage from malnutrition. The doctor had examined it and was mad. He blamed the mother and refused to speak with her. I had to go out to the waiting room and explain. I remember a whole ward of undersized babies. I can remember being so drained, going home at night and collapsing.

The lack of medical services for the poor in east Arkansas in the late 1960s was more than deplorable. It was an outrage that destroyed the human spirit as thoroughly as it ruined the physical body. The situation had so degenerated that Smegelsky found herself questioning her daily activities for their lack of long range impact. She recalled taking youngsters for treatment to St. Jude's Hospital at Memphis.

For those kids, it was like going to Disneyland. They got lunch there and special attention. There were flush toilets. They'd talk about it all the way home. I used to think what those days meant to those kids and if it was doing any good to bring them. Would it give them bitterness or hope?

Volunteer psychology seems to inhibit taking solace in short term or single moments of achievement. Yet Lucille Warren, a community leader in the tiny Mississippi County town of Birdsong, defined successful Volunteer work as helping just one family that didn't have a house or food to eat. That in itself would justify a VISTA year, Warren said. There was no way to erase poverty all at once for the whole county, she added.

This practical understanding seems obvious, yet it was a recognition many Volunteers never seemed to wholeheartedly endorse. One Volunteer group that accepted the limitations Warren referred to was involved in physical projects—architects, carpenters, and others in construction projects.

While physical projects could be stymied by a continual lack of needed materials, and Volunteer satisfaction could be eroded by administrational conflicts, completed projects did leave something that could be touched, climbed on, or used by communities for future activities. Physical projects produced measureable results.

Volunteer Tony Bozynski recognizes the satisfaction gained from working on physical projects. As a Volunteer in 1975, Bozynski helped build school and park playgrounds using Design Co-op plans for recycled materials such as tires and railroad ties. Ten years later, most of those playgrounds are still in use.

Bozynski, currently a Little Rock city planner, has the advantage of having stayed in the community he served and having continued a similar function. Yet perhaps most significantly, his daughter attends a public school with one of his VISTA-constructed playgrounds in its yard. With such continuing personal fulfillment, Bozynski's impressions of VISTA are understandably positive.

Many VISTA assignments could not produce Volunteer satisfaction similar to Bozynski's because the long range impact was impossible to determine. For Ted Wilson, time has been a key factor in his service analysis.

> I am fully cognizant of the transient nature of my VISTA accomplishments in the delta. I think some of the Volunteers literally saved lives, but we did not change history there. We left only the tiniest footprints, and those will get fainter as time moves on.

Volunteer John Clark had wide exposure to Arkansas VISTA service through community organizing assignments in the delta and as a teacher in Washington County. In his view, teaching is an intangible activity with no means of measuring long range impact. The only lasting result he can assess is the influence the program had on him, Clark said.

> VISTA turned me into more of a cynic. I had nice liberal values when I came to east Arkansas, and then was truly shocked at the racial issues there. It was time well spent, but it left me with less faith in the ability to bring about change. We can do things, but maybe not that way.

Volunteer comments are often directed at how problems personally influenced them. Frances Woods recalled a "kind of despair" from immediately seeing the human effects of poverty. For her, it was the kind "where you'd go home and cry, not a hardening or bitterness type of despair."

The emotional detachment required for a successful professional effort was lacking in many Volunteers. Many linked themselves too closely with assigned communities and people. This was a detriment Volunteer Jim Mercado realized when assessing his service and sponsoring agency.

My only regret would be to spend more time on the poor system we had to deal with. We felt vulnerable, away from home, tied to minimal support. I look back and think we shouldn't have let the Pulaski County EOA get away with what they did. Problems we knew were there but the community didn't. We didn't like to badmouth the agency in front of the community. It was all they had. Yet we may have done a disservice by not showing them that.

Mercado achieved success for several reasons. He was an architect who had the satisfaction of dealing with physical projects, and he had the proper attitude to recognize that personal idealism could interfere with effective community work. Having remained in Little Rock, he has been able to see long range results, Mercado said.

I saw a few people as they started and grew, how they gained a certain confidence. To see someone become a community leader and not just a resident is a fulfilling thing. That makes you feel good. Sometimes you get more personal mileage from building a little playground than a whole community center. It depends on what people do with that resource.

Bozynski recalled a state architect's meeting he and Mercado attended where the guest speaker showed slides of enormous Denver skyscrapers he had designed. Mercado followed that presentation with slides of the Design Co-op's work—small single family houses and playgrounds created from recycled materials, Bozynski said.

To Bozynski, both presentations were basically the same—individuals doing the best they could in their chosen environment. Yet the Volunteers were able to gain an additional fulfillment from their group indentity. Working in conjunction with others of the same spirit gave their roles a higher meaning. It reinforced their concept of what was right, Woods said.

There was an incredible intensity of emotion and commitment set in such a foreign atmosphere. The contrasts were so stark. I remember the Nixon election in 1968, feeling that the rest of the world was going to hell but we were trying to do something.

That group identity could not appease the guilt and secret unhappiness Woods said her group shared. She has lost contact with all but one other Volunteer because of those feelings, emotions similar to what a war veteran might feel, she said.

Volunteer group identity has not always served as a positive psychological fulfillment, especially in east Arkansas where most VISTAS saw little or no results and almost all have moved on. Yet some individuals can draw satisfaction from the effort alone, such as these recollections of Jerry Hornsby:

> On one level, West Memphis vindicates my existence on the planet. The collective experience of east Arkansas, though of such brief duration, represents the one moment in my life when I can say without reservation that I did try to interfere with "wrong."

A "No-Win" Situation

The Volunteers' best results were most often achieved when they established a presence in the community and developed their skills. In many cases it was clearly a no-win situation.

Yet time and again the Volunteers were reminded that VISTA was not established for their convenience. Once they realized that their ideals could not be applied, frustration and guilt from having pursued a righteous though futile course of action overtook them.

Such are the emotions of the former Volunteer whose project did not achieve established goals. Because he is no longer in his original service community, the frustrated Volunteer has no way of knowing if any advancement resulted from his efforts or presence. Christel Brellochs said that following her service she gained an awareness that would have served well at the time.

> We were arrogant enough to say we would create something to change the local economy and improve people's lives. I've learned since then you need long term commitment to develop leadership. Some great idea—open the co-op doors, hire a manager, then walk away and never go back. I feel real guilty about that too.

Volunteer John Boyle said many VISTA projects failed not so much because their social analysis was wrong but because of a limited understanding by program administrators. Just because people agreed to something didn't mean anything had been fundamentally changed, Boyle said.

What keeps most Volunteers from becoming depressed over project results is the satisfaction they gained from being part of the experience. The emotional highs and lows of their service year generally balance out to positive feelings. Volunteer Greg Prestamon recounted his emotional journey after a year with Community Energy Futures, an unsuccessful project that tried to develop community interest in low-cost energy systems.

> I went from feeling euphoric to utterly depressed to feeling pretty good despite huge loads of anger I feel toward CEF administration. Their unwillingness to be careful and precise with the program left me with the feeling that I was being used, a pawn in someone else's game, the victim of a bad practical joke.

Despite these negative emotions, Prestamon's final judgment of his VISTA service was mixed. In his year end report, Prestamon wrote he would not do it again, but he also suggested the year was worthwhile for the friends and memories he gained.

A final psychological assessment of the VISTA experience must include those Volunteers who forced situations on themselves, or who were impersonally used by project directors. Ellis said that some Volunteers' pristine naive idealism let them drop possibilities that nobody dared think about before and opened up new courses of action.

> They also became a little bit of cannon fodder in the process. They were expendable and were used by some project directors that way. Other Volunteers forced some radical moves and the fallout was great on them, too.
>
> In maybe two ways, the whole experience did damage them. Some did what they did and the whole project just folded. Others just had an awful experience or they were assaulted or raped. Those were the tragedies.

Ellis said another variety of VISTA "fallout" that still hits former Volunteers is the lack of intensity and dedication since their service ended. While many of them have gone on to careers in human or social service, the VISTA experience can not be duplicated. Some of them have not found anything in their lives, families, or careers to replace the cause to which they were once so committed.

Hornsby, though not a Volunteer himself, was as committed to social change as anyone in the program. Despite the belief that VISTA represented his most dedicated effort, Hornsby is convinced more could have been done.

> On a very personal level, I feel I have betrayed the whole class of have-not people with whom I expressed solidarity. I feel the only true revolutionary is either dead or in prison. I am neither. Therefore, I have stopped short of the total commitment required if one is to live with an easy conscience.

VISTA LIFE VALUES

Community Life Values

Volunteer Life Values

Disillusionment, Apathy, and "Street Smarts"

Community Life Values

One unique facet of VISTA as a government program was its recognition of attitude change as a prerequisite to community development. In the early years, the emphasis was on organizing-type projects, and the program supported Volunteer efforts that achieved little more than an enhancement of individual pride or community awareness.

The shift in program emphasis over the years has positioned VISTA securely in the opposite camp. Now projects must have clearly defined and measurable goals. Yet beneath these current guidelines, the same principles are at work from the program's origin.

The target of projects aiming toward financial development is not money itself. It is psychological security and the release from unnecessary suffering which freedom from poverty can bring. In west central Arkansas, for example, a folk crafts co-operative sponsored by the Arkansas River Valley Area Council has brought hundreds of thousands of dollars directly to local artisans by marketing their work across the nation.

That program could not be considered a success if its participants had not shown over a long term some decrease in the levels of illiteracy, substandard housing, and poor health that characterized the region. Better schools, roads, medical treatment, and other services are the inevitable results of an elevated community income level.

The second ten years of Arkansas VISTA history has promoted

materialism not for its own sake but rather as a means to an end. Both early and later philosophies are open to criticism. It may be said that early techniques gave poor people an awareness of a better life but no means of acquiring it, while the later philosophy can be faulted for a lack of value orientation during the rise from poverty.

Joe Bruch said VISTA, as he knew it, centered around programs or individual projects. Volunteers had to realize what they could do, learn community resources, and find the manpower to accomplish that objective.

> The Volunteers had to hang in there and do something. Sometimes that just meant surviving. We hoped the Volunteers would leave something behind, affect someone's life, and change in themselves. This was an attitude change. We were absolutely not into bricks. An attitude change on both sides—the bad guys and the voting populace. A greater good is accomplished by this. How it's done takes different forms.

Bruch's three VISTA goals summarize the unpredictable mixing of Volunteer and community. At best, the experience would lead to real change in the community. The least acceptable result, but nevertheless one with a recognized value, was of Volunteers alone coming away with an increased understanding.

As in most conceptual projects, the ideal goal is the most difficult to achieve. The VISTA impact on Arkansas is no exception. Since 1965, the state has shown significant advances in many areas addressed by VISTA projects, but there is no distinct way to link present conditions with past efforts nor to separate VISTA influence from the spectrum of issues that forced a state-wide maturity during the same twenty-year period.

Additionally, while a project may have originated through Volunteer assistance, the bulk of the credit for its achievements belongs to the community that carried it along over the years. Volunteers initiated community improvement clubs, co-ops, and associations around the state, but those projects would have eventually solely on projects, the "bricks" that Bruch mentioned. The real VISTA legacy are the life values VISTA was able to impart, the intangible gains both in-state and wherever national Volunteers have gone.

In West Memphis, for example, where former Volunteers Earl and Cherie Anthes continue to reside, significant changes have come about. A city whose municipal government was once rooted in an unchallengeable white power base has had in recent years a black mayor and alderman. A significant part of the first steps toward bringing about this change is related to Volunteers "opening a door here and there," Anthes said.

Anthes also spoke of major improvements in the east Arkansas health delivery system since Volunteers from his group worked in the area in the early 1970s. This view was supported by John Clark, former director of East Central Arkansas Community Action Agency, who spoke of a "turnaround" in Crittenden County welfare and education services as a result of Volunteer efforts.

> It was impressive the way the Volunteers handled the local services—welfare, food stamps, health and education. Poor blacks and whites had a hard time, were treated like dirt. The Volunteers worked with a lot of finesse. They made people angry but didn't alienate them. The Volunteers changed the slavery mentality of those offices. They changed the attitudes of the officials, too.

Clark believes the need still exists for Volunteers, those with a spirit of adventure and willingness to take risks for the common good. With larger numbers of poor residents now than twenty years ago, financial assistance has not gotten at the core of the problem. Generations of welfare people have lived with the thought of being stuck, and money doesn't change those attitudes, he said.

What can and did change those attitudes was the exposure to alternative solutions Volunteers were able to impart. At times, those alternatives took shape in real projects. More often, the influence was of a less discernible nature. Elijah Coleman, former director of the Arkansas Council for Human Relations, commented on this influence on young people.

The Volunteers left seeds. They taught a lot of the young people. Many of the youth didn't even know things were supposed to be different. It created some disciples that have not quit yet.

VISTA trainer Neal Blakely described the Volunteer presence in many low-income black communities as those areas' first positive encounter with white people. This was a new exposure and one that influenced their lives in many other ways, Blakely said.

The Volunteers would give a sense of hope about their lives, about people. That all white people were not trying to rip them off. So they would work with others. The community got that spirit from the Volunteers. They didn't get it from the agency staff.

Blakely's remarks are less a criticism of community action agency staff than a recognition of the potential results a new perspective can bring to a static situation. Some agency staff lived in the poverty community, and like locally recruited Volunteers, they may have known the area needs. What locals didn't have was the knowledge of how to do things. That knowledge, combined with the national Volunteers' new attitudes and style, partially explains the spirit of hope they were able to create in the community.

Mrs. Pat Jackson explained how that spirit was passed on:

Through the Volunteers, the community people realized they could do things for themselves instead of having things done for them. They could raise money and build a community center. The Volunteers not only told them, they showed them how and helped them. They told us we needed to do it for ourselves. They really motivated us. They had what we needed. It was up to us to get it by accepting them.

Higgins, Sweet Home, and other small towns across the state built their community centers as a result of Volunteer initiative. An invaluable inspiration has been achieved from these projects and from the more dramatic successes of major projects such as the Lee County Co-operative Medical Clinic at Marianna. If community self-management was the goal, a VISTA-fostered attitude of confidence was one means of achieving it. While it may be fruitless to pose "what if" questions about history, Arkansas community history would certainly not be the same had these events not happened.

Like a chain reaction, one success leads to another. While all can not possibly have the presence of a community center or medical clinic, the personal confidence community members gained from Volunteers brought them a new understanding of opportunity. Melvin Brown recalled that influence on himself and on Mrs. Zelma Miller.

> When we got money to do something, we done something. We got so little, yet we done so much. Once Mrs. Miller found out she could get a dollar by asking, we went everywhere. Through the Volunteers, I met people I thought I was supposed to cross the street to get out of their way. They would give us money.

Confidence creates a call to action, a call that for many is still being heard. Mrs. Jackson said that had she the chance to speak with former Volunteers she would explain that the groundwork they laid is still in the minds of the people, still playing a part in getting folks results.

In low-income communities, the Volunteers represented unified action, Blakely said. Seeing them, people thought about togetherness and knew they were fixing to have a meeting or do things, he said. Poor people, once they get the right information and learn they can do things, are ready to do them, Blakely added.

A willingness to do things, to maintain the struggle despite clearly perceived obstacles, is the ultimate VISTA life value for the low-income community. Few Arkansas communities showed this determination more than Birdsong (Mississippi County). Mayor Robert Johnson said it took twelve years to get his town incorporated, but it was a continuing effort inspired by the two Volunteers assigned to the area in 1969.

> They taught us never to give up, that there wasn't a victory given in the middle of a race. You got to keep on running. Francis taught that to me and to a lot more people. You don't find people willing to come down. Once you get them started, they always want to go further. They got us started. You can't take that away.

Volunteer Life Values

Living in poverty communities, the Volunteers influenced local people as no other group had previously done. In return, Volunteers received exposure to a more profound reality than many had known before entering the program. The Volunteers were influenced by unsophisticated local personalities, those who had never known more than the stark honesty of their impoverished surroundings.

Through these encounters, Volunteers achieved a moral growth that affected their personal views. That exposure continues to influence their decisions about poverty, charity, and personal involvement. Jerry Hornsby wrote a 1984 article for a Nashville, Tennessee newspaper illustrating that continuing influence.

Hornsby's article tells of his refusing to give money to a derelict who wanted to buy a bottle of whiskey. The incident reminded Hornsby of Roosevelt Thompson, a homeless black man in his 70s who lived by his wits on the West Memphis streets. Thompson could not receive welfare or Social Security benefits, Hornsby wrote, because he could not prove his age.

Impressed with Thompson's courage and optimism, Hornsby helped the man verify his military service and qualify for VA benefits. Thompson received a retroactive settlement of seven hundred dollars and a monthly stipend of one hundred dollars, the most money he had had in decades. Hornsby helped him set up a bank account and lectured him on how to judiciously use the money. In a short time, however, Thompson had spent it all, and Hornsby was left to sort out his own emotions. The article concludes with these remarks:

> What right had we to dictate to Thompson the conduct of his life? What gave us the mandate to control how and when he could enjoy his own money? Who appointed us his moral guardians? . . . We had tried to teach, to guide. In the end, it was he who taught us something about life and ourselves. . . . [to the derelict] Thompson would have shared with you anything he might have had, with no conditions attached. He would have wanted your heart to sing, your clouds to lift, if only for a little while.

Memories of local encounters have stayed with Volunteers over the years and have shaped their life values. For young, impressionable Volunteers, their exposure to individuals, especially older, low-income people who had preserved a strong personal character despite their surroundings, was almost mythic in proportion. These meetings shaped the Volunteers' concept of basic human dignity and put them in touch with local history.

Harry Conard recalled such an encounter that helped form the style he has continued to this day in a career of community planning and development. A VISTA training visit brought Conard to his first black area in the south, Lowndes County, Alabama, where Martin Luther King walked nearby in the days of the Selma Freedom March, he said.

> All the white/black agitation had left a torn community. I'll never forget the words of one of the remaining black community leaders, who said "When it's all over, we'll still be living together with the same people in the past, and the outsiders will go on to their next effort." I realized we had to build effective local movements around an identified need and act as a facilitator. Above all, do not impose your ego or will in the local effort. Do not build a monument to your own ego.

Most Volunteers do not have a single individual or incident as the primary symbol of the moral growth they achieved through VISTA. Instead, their service represents a period of personal growth where survival skills and self-determination flourished in the most challenging of circumstances.

While some guilty feelings resulted from this personal gain, it also transported Volunteers to a higher level of social awareness. Volunteer Larry Kressley said he somehow salvaged rewarding experiences despite the strong community resistance to his project at Warren. Yet Volunteer moral growth would only come when one stopped seeking good experiences for oneself that disregarded others, Kressley said.

A large number of former Volunteers have followed careers of human and community service. Former VISTA director William Crook saw this as a logical extension of the psychological influences that originally brought them into the program. In *Warriors of the Poor,* Crook wrote that Volunteers were essentially "critics of the current social scene" who would have never joined the program unless they felt there was something wrong that needed to be corrected.

The Volunteers' critical sense would be enhanced by their service, and they would seek to continue to express their opinions once that service was over, Crook wrote.

> VISTA experience offers a postgraduate course in practical politics. The Volunteers learn about the power structure and how to use it . . . The former Volunteers will assume active roles in their communities because they now know the remedies that cure a number of social ills. It is doubtful that former Volunteers will be awed by the local establishment.[1]

As practical politics or hard core reality, VISTA was an educational experience that taught the Volunteers things they would never learn in school. John Boyle said his service was like getting a graduate degree in "All That's Wrong with America That We Were Neglected to be Told." Boyle helped initiate the Boston Mountain Co-op, an educational program in Washington County rural schools. The program never overcame its administrative problems and was disbanded. Boyle said his style was not to publicize the "good ole' boy deceptions" he believed caused that failure but to acknowledge them as "the good and bad, as life as we know it."

Boyle reflected the impressions of most national Volunteers when he said he could not do the same work again because he now knows too much. Instead he has built on that knowledge by starting and directing The Pebble Project, a child abuse prevention project for low-income people at Austin, Texas.

Few if any Volunteers left the pogram with their personal ideas unchanged. Many of those who went into the prgram to "save the world" came out with a deeper understanding of what that meant. It meant strengthening their social values. For the most part, this change was a general shift to the political left or toward actions focusing more on community service than personal advancement. Joann Rose, who worked as a VISTA recruiter after her year in Pulaski County, explained it in the following manner.

> When recruiting, I'd tell people that if they went into VISTA as a conservative, they would come out as a liberal. If they went in as a liberal, they'd come out as a radical. And if they went in as a radical, they'd come out and go live on a mountain top.

The changes Volunteers went through were not solely due to the impact of the program. As Crook implied, many Volunteers were already headed in that direction, so the program's impact and the support Volunteers gave each other naturally felt good. With VISTA providing the last bit of thrust, many Volunteers either deliberately or unknowingly moved into service careers.

Almost unanimously, these former Volunteers have identified their VISTA service as the single most influential event in determining their career directions. Their exposure to a range of knowledge—the social, racial, bureaucratic, and personal curriculum of their VISTA education—has created an internal momentum this group seems compelled to continue.

Bob Frank is an Indiana college professor with extensive involvement in alternate education, community organizing, and other social affairs. "What I got out of VISTA is that you DO something," Frank said.

The career-directed Volunteer has learned to expand his professional role beyond its immediate concerns. Architect Jim Mercado has served as board member of several community organizations. Winner of a state competition for solar home design, Mercado spoke of the VISTA influence in his life values.

> I feel a greater sense of wanting to educate and distribute the information, the technical knowledge about solar homes, not just keep it to myself. By sharing that in some way, I could further distribute the knowledge.

In Fayetteville, psychologist Francis Woods recalls her VISTA year as "absolutely germinal" in forming her values, work habits, and goals. Woods' extended professional role includes involvement in local women's support groups, child abuse projects, and a residence program for pregnant women.

Beyond directing Volunteers toward service careers and a wider parameter of service within their specialty, VISTA life values have also helped these individuals do better what they have chosen to do.

For Christel Brellochs, this means using organizing experience from east Arkansas in her recent professional role of establishing a series of community health centers in urban poverty neighborhoods of The Bronx. The principles behind both challenges were remarkably similar, Brellochs said.

> VISTA gave me a real appreciation of how much in life is all support. People arrive in situations with similar talents, and it is the environment that nurtures or thwarts that . . . I've learned that when you negotiate, you must have some power base to get something . . . Just doing something is not necessarily the best thing. One has to evaluate action, not only to satisfy an agenda but for its impact on people's lives.

Sandy Smegelsky said she still applies the lessons of fear and frustration from her VISTA service. These are effective motivators in her work.

> VISTA helped shape my views on how to help people help themselves. An organization from the top means nothing to them. But give them the tools to help themselves. You need frustration to maintain your goals and per-

spective. Understand fear in your gut, and it will help shape your response. It's a good place to start.

Understanding fear is one way of overcoming it. The Volunteers learned to overcome not only their own fears but those of the people with whom they lived and worked. The relationships they built within the poverty community allowed them to see how people survive under adverse conditions. Ted Wilson spoke of the knowledge which came from those encounters.

> I learned to understand people, the realities, difficulties, problems everyone encounters on a day to day basis. Perhaps more graphically or visibly, I came to understand the beauty, strength, and intelligence which large numbers of poor people exhibit in their day to day thinking. People from poor communities are as supportive and caring and helpful to one another, if not more so, than any other element of our society.

Disillusionment, Apathy, and "Street Smarts"

Wilson's praise for the integrity and social interaction found in poverty communities sounds much like the idealized optimism which many Volunteers brought into the program. Yet just as the Volunteers' false world view was rapidly overcome by the realities of their situations, Wilson's and others' respect for the poor was accompanied by an understanding of the overwhelming difficulties and injustices they continued to face. Larry Kressley commented on that disillusionment.

> After a year in VISTA, I was beginning to have doubts about things getting better in America. I was convinced that helping individuals only served to pacify them, to make poverty more tolerable. I was a year older, no longer so idealistic, and cynical about our ability to achieve social justice in this country no matter how hard we tried.

Kressley's criticism is based on the presumed failure of one-to-one contact. Other Volunteers have expressed similar emotions but more in relation to the administrative structure of the program. They see their idealism as having been used by the federal government to address problems for which no defined solution was available. They consider the concept of reducing poverty through federal assistance as a worthwhile goal, but they fault administrative channels for ineffective operation.

The views of Joann Rose fall between the personal and objective disappointments that have emerged from VISTA. Among her several Volunteer duties, Rose taught Pulaski County grade school children. Her later career as a grade school teacher in that same area has provided her with a fifteen-year perspective on local problems and efforts to solve them.

I never stopped doing the same work, always taught poor kids and spent half the time doing social work. My tolerance is lower now. I have less hope it will change. During VISTA I had all the hope in the world. Today, kids in my class come in hungry because there is no free breakfast program. Fifteen years ago that was just starting. We thought it would solve the problem forever.

Carried to an extreme, the loss of optimism and disillusionment with the value of attempted change can create a dramatic reversal in an individual's world view. One Arkansas Volunteer confirmed that her experience changed her, "not for the better, but for the bitter."

I listened well to the black side, but not the white side because I felt what they had to say was despicable. And this perhaps leads me to the biggest regret of my VISTA days. I started out being very prejudiced against my own race of white people and I left being full of prejudice against the blacks.

When I first arrived, I was so moved about the injustices that I felt all black people were wonderful and in need of anything I could do to help. I felt a great brotherhood existed among the people we worked with. Yet as time went by, I knew that if a real race riot occurred, we would be among the first they stabbed (literally) in the back. If it came down to a situation where they had to choose between us and their own, there was no doubt in my mind they would have shot us down with all the other white-skinned people, including those they hated the most.

I guess I was so blinded by my efforts . . . that I did not realize prejudice can exist on both sides. I left feeling very prejudiced against all blacks. It has taken me a long, long time to get over that feeling, and I am not completely over it yet.

This Volunteer was a victim of her own false idealism and the impossible demands she placed on others to uphold her world view. The frustration of not having those values confirmed led to a reassessment of her views. She spoke of poor people not desiring change and of their contented state among houses infested with rats and roaches as long as they had welfare, food stamps, and some money for beer and gambling.

Her unsuccessful attempts to change their lives brought her to the realization that "they didn't want to be saved." She stopped trying to help them because it seemed a waste of time, the Volunteer said.

> From my experiences in Arkansas . . . this is probably my biggest regret, that I have become so apathetic. Since I left, I do not have that burning desire to help people like I once had . . . I guess the problem is that I'm blaming them when it's myself I should blame.

This Volunteer made fundamental errors in her assessment of VISTA and black poverty communities. Her idealism did not allow for character flaws on both sides of the color line. The rejection by the poor of her assistance and her friendship has lead to her condemnation of both the people and program with which she worked.

Negative experiences must be understood before they can be overcome. Some fifteen years after the service period, she has made the intellectual adjustment necessary for a revaluation. Her emotional healing may take even longer.

Most Volunteers have a healthy mixture of cynicism and idealism, a commitment to service but a lack of patience with administrative procedure. Mary Potter, an early Pulaski County Volunteer and currently a registered nurse, has a "damn good bedside manner" and an admitted dislike for filling out forms.

For Mercado, the summary result of VISTA is what he called a fuller outlook on life and a greater respect for the efforts of grassroots organizations.

> You just can't turn down those appeals when you know how valuable a $20 bill can be. I know who's jiving and who isn't. These are the kinds of things that really develop street smarts.

Notes

1. *Warriors of the Poor,* William Crook & Ross Thomas, William Morrow & Co., 1969, Pages 180–183.

ARKANSAS IMPRESSIONS

A person who turns from the mirror and asks his companions "How do I look?" puts his personal impressions at risk. Arkansas Volunteers, never hesitant to state their feelings or act on them, were given the unique opportunity of answering that question. Volunteer impressions, particularly those from the early years of the state VISTA program, reveal much about Arkansas people and culture.

Like photos in a family album, Volunteer impressions serve as a record of the state's recent past. They highlight aspects of Arkansas culture that often go unrecognized. Because they were "outsiders," Volunteer impressions did not always match the Arkansas self-image. The many differences and occasional similarities partly account for why projects succeeded or failed. They provide a glimpse of the underlying character, an Arkansas identity rooted in the land and in the people, the long range values many communities still hold.

Very few Volunteers were able to relate immediately to Arkansas' rural environment. One of a fortunate minority was Harry Conard, a Health Advocate Volunteer who helped establish the Lee County Co-operative Medical Clinic at Marianna. Facing substantial resistance from the white community to his work, Conard recalled an initial impression that contributed to his willingness to continue.

I drove into the area and saw a field of soybeans. Where I grew up in Illinois, the farmers also grew soybeans. I knew at that moment I could relate to a community that was in the south and was agriculturally oriented.

Most volunteers, however, found no such familiar symbols in their new environment. Instead, they often found themselves in a totally unfamiliar place, a location many of them had not even listed on their assignment preferences.

Compared to New Mexico, Oregon, or other western states, Arkansas held little attraction for Volunteers. Most could not specifically account for this negative attitude. Some of them recalled impressions of the school integration crisis at Little Rock's Central High School in 1957. Others based their negative impressions on a lack of information, assuming a state had little to offer if all they knew was that it was poor and southern. This was a common impression, and one stated by Pulaski County Volunteer Anna Gottlieb.

I wanted a New Mexico assignment. When I learned of Little Rock, I seriously thought of leaving but I didn't have any place to go back to. To me, Arkansas was the backwards of the backwards. I didn't think there was anything pretty here, just a place you're born and stuck in. I realized why they didn't tell where you'd go until you were into training. I wouldn't have gone.

Once on the scene, Volunteers had to relate as best they could to the sights that greeted them. Their training had been comprehensive, but facing poverty and isolation for the first time without training group security affected Volunteers' impressions. "Culture shock" is the term many of them use, recalling sights and experiences completely foreign to their backgrounds.

Some initial encounters were quite different from Conard's glimpse of green and friendly fields. Mike Watts, a Pulaski County Volunteer, described his first trip to Little Rock after being transferred from an unsuccessful and short-lived project in south Arkansas.

I arrived after dark late one night, trying to find a home in the East End where I was told a family would put me up. There were no lights on the streets or on the houses. I went up to the dark houses to feel for numbers on the porches. At a house that turned out to be the right one, I was standing on this dark porch, feeling for numbers on the wall, when I heard heavy snoring from just inside the door . . . The next morning, city police were waiting for me in the street with questions about my being in the neighborhood and checking if the car had been stolen.

Watts's story of feeling his way through the darkness, feeling for house numbers, can be seen as an allegory for the entire VISTA experience. He was the stranger searching for a receptive group he was told would take him in. The household, like the community itself, was absorbed in its own world of sleep, unaware of changes that were coming. The resonant snoring was evidence of the human presence that made up that world. Watts was awake while the others slept, separated from them by his newcomer's status, his awareness, and the physical wall between them. That separation was further revealed in the morning light when the police, representing the community structure, challenged his presence.

The Volunteers' perception of Arkansas home life was largely limited to poverty households, and the sights they witnessed there were indeed shocking. Adding to their amazement about home conditions was a passive acceptance by residents that seemed incomprehensible to the Volunteers. Barbara Conard was exposed to that tolerance on her second day in east Arkansas. As a new nurse at the Lee County Clinic, she had gone to a poverty home to give an injection for pain relief to a lady dying of cancer, Conard said.

We walked in this shabby, dirty house, and the lady was lying on the bed in just a white slip, and she was so thin and frail, and the house was filled with the smell of cancer, and there were kids yelling and screaming in the other room, and she just laid there and kept saying "Yes, ma'am" to everything we said. She was so submissive and so polite and thankful, and I was shocked at the state of her house, and that she was dying and we couldn't do anything more for her.

Gottlieb also mentioned a similar encounter early in her assignment. Following her visit to a one-room shack in Sweet Home where a young mother survived with three small children, Gottlieb said she stayed up that night thinking of the woman, her house, and the life she would have.

Many female Volunteers considered Arkansas a place where sexist roles had never seriously been challenged. Bringing feminist ideology to their assignments, the female Volunteers were amazed at social stereotypes, and the personal restrictions accepted by Arkansas women. Volunteer Carolyn Rose spoke of an early episode that brought her to this awareness.

> My first night in the old Grady Manning Hotel I was awakened to the sound of two men in the hall arguing over how much to pay a "lady of the evening." One of them wanted to give her only five dollars, saying she wasn't very good. The other argued she should get ten because she "did us both."
>
> I couldn't believe I had wanted to come to this state to see first hand what the South was like, having grown up in an area of rural New York where there were few members of ethnic groups, very little overt prejudice and no ladies of the evening.
>
> Unfortunately, I never got used to Arkansas, the southern belles and prominent families, the abject poverty on the other side of town, the religious fundamentalism, the prejudice and attitudes toward women among the good old boys who seemed to make up about 95 percent of the state.

VISTA administrators, particularly those brought in from out of state, were able to view Arkansas more objectively. Where Volunteers had made little gain through direct attacks, program officers could better analyze the problems and suggest alternative and more effective courses of action.

Richard First was a VISTA trainer with wide experience in community organizing. He came to Arkansas in 1968 and helped establish the Graduate School of Social Work at the University of Arkansas at Little Rock. Following involvement in North Carolina and exposure there to racial resistance to community organizing projects, First said he was surprised at Arkansas' relatively low level of resistance.

> I had expected more dangerous, life threatening situations in Arkansas than I saw. Organizing here was relatively easy if we could get sponsors to

place the right people into the communities. It was not difficult to be effective if we could get the people in.

With many unchallenged issues relating to the life of the people politically, First saw Arkansas as fertile ground for organizing. Few programs, both before and since the major VISTA efforts, have come in from the outside for this purpose, he added.

Before the development of community action agencies and the assignment of Volunteers, there was minimal black participation in state political life and few black professionals in positions of influence, First said. Based on his national exposure, he viewed Arkansas in 1969 as considerably behind other Southern states in black political involvement. This condition was directly affected by projects such as the Lee County Clinic where a service-based program used organizational strategies to change the social order.

This was a period of time in Arkansas history when outside influences were coming to bear. The influences had their impact either through the Rockefeller organization or the influx of outside people.

Resistance to these outside efforts was not well organized, and a highly centralized community power structure, usually the county judge, was the primary source of opposition, First said, and that the Rockefeller influence provided the leverage necessary to move the county judges.

Once you could make trade offs or get around the county judge, you could make progress. If we could manage the Volunteer work so they didn't make mistakes or threaten people, we could make inroads into the power structure easily.

Opportunities for rapid advancement were available, and Volunteers like architect Jim Mercado spoke of Arkansas as one of the least regulated places he had been. The absence of unions and well defined zoning or building codes gave him latitude in his work, but different problems had to be faced as a result of an extremely weak infrastructure, Mercado said.

An example of this was in Scott (Pulaski County) where Mercado's VISTA project, the Design Co-op, joined with other groups in

1975 to build eleven homes with a $100,000 grant. Moving people from sharecropper shacks to modern, insulated homes involved more than simply putting bricks and boards in the right places. Community consciousness also had to be raised, and so it was, Mercado reported, though not without difficulties.

> Scott came a long way in my years. The community was just making its first baby steps at that time. It came from being a bowed-head, insecure people to being an organized group able to articulate its needs despite a real cultural situation there.

The "situation" was arguments at community meetings and among local families concerning how the people should best control newly available resources. The Scott construction project illustrates the long range benefits of a physical project, yet it also reveals a potential for a rapid advancement that could at times surpass the community's level of organization.

While Arkansas VISTA projects were in no way limited to black poverty communities, the majority of state projects were directed toward that racial group because it had higher percentages in poverty than whites. As a result, racial issues and race relations are at the base of many Volunteer impressions.

Some Volunteers were shocked by overt displays of racism from the white community and the degree of humiliation Arkansas blacks accepted. Anna Gottlieb recalled sitting in a car with a Volunteer friend and the local black man her friend had begun dating and people screaming vulgarities at them as they passed by. She also recalls her project sponsor Goforth Coleman telling her that as a black man he felt it prudent to leave some north Arkansas mountain projects before dark. At first, Gottlieb said she thought he was joking.

The impressions of another white, female Volunteer were that black Arkansans never fully understood the Volunteers and never truly accepted them.

> I do not feel the blacks, who were not used to being treated nicely by whites in their community, ever completely trusted us . . . I don't think they could

believe we were for real. Sure, they let us in their homes, fed us, became our friends, but I still don't feel they trusted us . . . Our white skin was the enemy, no matter that our souls were all the same color.

Others involved in the program directly challenge these views. Rev. M. W. Williams spoke of the Volunteers as people who championed the black cause and rallied large numbers of blacks in some of the state's most controversial projects. Pat Jackson said her neighbors in Higgins (Pulaski County) immediately accepted the Volunteers and felt honored to have them doing things for the community. Volunteers were like members of the family, Mrs. Jackson said.

They would come in and live with you, eat with you, and not act like you weren't good enough. They would go to church with us. Because they mostly wore cut off jeans and tee shirts, we'd get them the proper clothes for church, our own kids or someone else's. That showed me they wanted to be part of where they were. They were totally involved with the people. They made us feel loved.

Volunteer and community race relations actually represent a secondary level of interaction. Race relations assume an enlarged position of importance only when human relations break down. When people can not deal directly with each other, when personal or social fears block a one-to-one understanding, then the masks of racial bias are put on and the problem shifts its focus.

W. L. "Sonny" Walker viewed Volunteer effectiveness as closely tied to community acceptance. Both were direct results of how well the two sides understood and got along with each other, Walker said.

Among the communities, those that didn't know them well or didn't understand them just saw the Volunteers as another white person. Those who knew them weren't adverse to the Volunteers. They were staunch supporters. Volunteers attempted to break down the barriers. No emphasis on education or advantages I have and you don't. You have to find a person's strengths and help them develop that without creating a paternalistic attitude.

Through the Volunteers, Arkansas communities were able to gain a better understanding of their ability to accomplish things and speak for themselves. For the most part, the opportunity to exhibit these strengths had not been offered prior to the VISTA program. Estella Morris commented on the community willingness to act.

> Poor people have always been the hardest workers. Once they know what they can do and what avenues to take, they are about as forceful a group as you'll find. Given the opportunity, the people in the situation are usually their own best spokesman.

VISTA gave poverty communities a chance to begin controlling their own destinies, but it was an opportunity not always taken. In some communities, the resistance to change was stronger than the will toward self improvement. Arkansas black communities had a national identity movement to support and encourage their efforts. White poverty communities, particularly the hill culture of the Ozark and Ouachita Mountains, had no such external support.

Allowing Volunteers to enter their lives and introduce alternatives violated two essential principles of the hill culture: The first was an admission of the need for help. The second was allowing an outsider to initiate the process of aid. According to Dr. Fred Morrow, resistance to change also related to high illiteracy and school drop out rates.

> A lot of the resistance and rejection of VISTA is a literacy problem. It is related to an educational level and the awareness of need. Hill people had a keen awareness, but the idea of letting someone come in and help was alien to their values. One did not turn to outside agencies for help. The Volunteers encountered a lot of that attitude.

Independence is revered by those familiar with the rugged pioneer lifestyle and the ethic of self-sufficiency in the face of overwhelming challenges. It was just such attitudes that allowed the early Arkansas settlers to survive in a sparsely populated wilderness.

VISTA Volunteers arrived in Arkansas more or less only one hundred years after the pioneer period. By this time, a typical family patriarch might be the son or grandson of the original pioneer who built his cabin from trees he felled and shaped, who fed his family from the game he hunted and trapped. In that past environment, there was no source of help beyond the resources nature offered and one's own ability to put them to use.

Volunteers who came from communities with a tradition of philanthropic agencies may have found it strange that hill people didn't take their efforts kindly, Morrow said. In social work, this was called a "relationship problem," and workers were encouraged to find a way, even a nonverbal one, to connect.

Morrow suggested that social work was an unknown phenomenon in Arkansas prior to the 1960s. That has clearly changed. Along with modern services such as better roads, public education, and greater exposure to the media, Arkansas' impoverished hill communities have entered an age where an acknowledged problem will no longer simply be ignored.

The Arkansas self-image is changing as state values and levels of culture change. As a barometer of that change, VISTA provided an accurate measurement during a period when initial efforts were being made. Resistance or acceptance of a VISTA project revealed a community's place in that changing environment.

Volunteer impressions of Arkansas are photographs in our state album. They illustrate the character and views of a given time and place. By reminding us of where Arkansas has been, they help provide a better understanding of where the state and its people are going.

BIBLIOGRAPHIES AND INDEX

Bibliography

ACTION. *VISTA Handbook for Volunteers and Sponsors.* Washington, D.C.: ACTION—Office of Domestic & Anti-Poverty Operations. 1984.

Alinsky, Saul. *Reveille for Radicals.* Chicago: University of Chicago Press. 1946.

Alinsky, Saul. *Rules for Radicals.* New York: Random House. 1971.

Arkansas Office of Community Services. *Poverty in Arkansas: The Crisis Challenged by Community Action, 1985 Annual Report.* Little Rock: Arkansas Office of Community Services. 1985.

Crook, William, and Ross Thomas. *Warriors for the Poor.* New York: Morrow. 1969.

Donovan, Timothy, and Willard B. Gatewood. *The Governors of Arkansas.* Fayetteville: University of Arkansas Press. 1981.

Foster, Alan S. *Goodbye, Bobby Thompson! Goodbye, John Wayne!* New York: Simon and Schuster. 1973.

Harrington, Michael. *The New American Poverty.* New York: Holt, Rinehart, and Winston. 1984.

Harrington, Michael. *The Other America.* New York: Macmillan. 1962.

Hough, John T. *A Peck of Salt.* Boston: Little Brown. 1970.

Legal Services Corporation, East Arkansas Legal Services, Legal Services of Arkansas. *Arkansas: State of Transition.* Little Rock. 1971.

Pass, David. *The Politics of VISTA in the War on Poverty: A Study of Ideological Conflict.* New York: Columbia University School of Social Work. 1976.

Ranchino, James. *From Faubus to Bumpers, Arkansas Votes, 1960–1970.* Arkadelphia, Arkansas: Action Research. 1972.

Sandford, Juanita. *Poverty in the Land of Opportunity.* Little Rock: Rose Publishing Company. 1978.

Seligman, Ben. *The Great Society's Poor Law: A New Approach to Poverty.* Baltimore: Johns Hopkins Press. 1969.

Seligman, Ben. *Permanent Poverty: An American Syndrome.* Chicago: Quadrangle Books. 1968.

VISTA. *VISTA—15th Anniversary Book.* Washington, D.C.: ACTION VISTA Office. 1980.

VISTA. *15 Years of Making a Good Place Better.* Little Rock: Arkansas ACTION. 1980.

Williams, C. Fred, ed. *A Documentary History of Arkansas.* Fayetteville: University of Arkansas Press. 1984.

Individuals Interviewed

VISTA Administration (with positions at time of service)

Bob Adkison—Director, Arkansas River Valley Area Council (Dardanelle)
Neal Blakley—Volunteer trainer and program coordinator
Esther Boswell—Volunteer supervisor, Pulaski County EOA
Joe Bruch—State & regional ACTION officer
Carol Cantrell—Ouachita Baptist University Summer Associate Program administrator
John Clark—Director, East Central Arkansas EOA (Forrest City)
Elijah Coleman—Director, Arkansas Council of Human Relations
Eddie Colen—Assistant Director, Southeast Arkansas Community Action Corporation (Warren)
Goforth Coleman—Volunteer supervisor, Pulaski County EOA
Jim Crawford—Volunteer supervisor, Pulaski County EOA, state program officer
George Ellis—National program counselor
Richard First—Director, UALR Graduate School of Social Work
Bill Green—State OEO public relations officer
Jerry Hornsby—Director, Health Advocates/General Electric project
George Ivory—Volunteer supervisor, Mississippi County EOA (Blytheville)
Jim Jansen—Director, Black River Area Development (Pocahontas)
Judge Charles Johnson—Director, Washington County EOA
Padraic Kennedy—National VISTA director
Diana London—Federal VISTA program officer
Mimi Mager—Director, Friends of VISTA, Washington DC
Freeman McKindra—VISTA and ACTION Program officer
Bobby Morgan—VISTA trainer
Veda Ranchino Morgan—OBU Summer Associate Program administrator
Alice Morganfield—Assistant administrator, Lee County Co-operative Clinic (Marianna)

Bob Morrison—Farm director, United Peoples Co-op
Tom McRae—Staff member for Gov. Dale Bumpers, director of Texarkana Model Cities program
Ollie Neal—Director, Lee County Co-operative Clinic (Marianna)
Ralph Nessan—Director, Washington County EOA
Rabbi Elijah Palnik—Board member, Pulaski County EOA
Thomas Pauken—National director of ACTION
Erma Dansby Pondexter—staff member, Southwest Arkansas Development Corp. (Texarkana)
Frances Rogers—Assistant to volunteer supervisor, East Central Ark. EOA (Forrest City)
Margaret Smith—Deputy director, Pulaski County EOA
Rev. H. D. Stewart—Project director, Watershed, Little Rock
Bob Torvestad—Director, State ACTION office
W. L. "Sonny" Walker—Volunteer trainer, Pulaski County EOA director, State OEO administrator
Gary Watkins—Project supervisor, Ozark Opportunities (Harrison)
Ted Wilson—Volunteer supervisor, East Central Ark. EOA (Forrest City)

Community Figures

Lyn Blackmon—Texarkana
Denzer Burke—Texarkana
Barbara Clayton—Texarkana
Martha Franklin—Garland City
Pat Jackson—Higgins
Robert Johnson—Birdsong
Lon Mann—Marianna
Vera MacAlister—Texarkana
Mrs. Zelma Miller—Sweet Home
Floyd Sexton—Texarkana
Rev. David Stephens—Texarkana
Lucille Warren—Birdsong
John Lee Wilson—Haynes

National Volunteers (by project)

LEE COUNTY CO-OPERATIVE CLINIC

Dr. Dan & Janet Blumenthal
Corrine Cass
Harry & Barbara Conard
Mike & Peggy McCarthy
Dr. Al Sartori
Dr. Robbie Wolf
Jan Wrede

EAST ARKANSAS HEALTH ADVOCATES

Earl & Cheri Anthes
Joel Camhi
Sue Christman
Charlie Deknatel
Barry Gaston
Charles Imhoff
Don Meaders
Gene Richards
Sandy Smegelsky

UNITED PEOPLES CO-OP

Christel Brellochs
Francis Woods

PULASKI COUNTY EOA

Tony Bozynski
Mike Fixler
Anna Gottlieb
John Lewis
Penny Lewis
Jim Mercado
Linda Patrick
Mary Potter

Bill Peters
Phil Quandt
Liz Roberts
Carolyn Rose
Joann Rose
Mark Sexton
Pam Sheen
Margaret Sokolsky
Karen Waldner
Mike Watts
Faye White

WASHINGTON COUNTY EOA

Steve Anderson
John Boyle
John & Donna Clark
Tracy Weir

SOUTHWEST ARKANSAS DEVELOPMENT CORPORATION (TEXARKANA)

Bob DeMarco
Jack Fleck
Frank Fuller
John & Carol Hoerster
Al Karlin
Bruce Neft
Tom & Joann Utterback

ARKANSAS RIVER VALLEY AREA COUNCIL

Greg Haag
Lou Vitale

SOUTH CENTRAL ARKANSAS COMMUNITY ACTION AUTHORITY

Jerry Cronin
Art Hoffman
Mrs. "Willie" Ferguson

SUMMER ASSOCIATE PROGRAMS:
OUACHITA BAPTIST UNIVERSITY & ARKANSAS COUNCIL OF HUMAN RELATIONS
Bill Meyers
Diana Ricou
Paul Williams
Teresa Young

OTHER PROJECT NATIONAL VOLUNTEERS
William Bookheim—Pocahontas, Little Rock
Berta Dargen—Harrison
Rex & Neva Erickson—Little Rock
Beverley Feinstein—Benton
Bob Frank—Little Rock
Bob Gorman—Newton County, Fayetteville
Bob Harrington—East Arkansas
Loren Ivener—Hot Springs
Larry Kressley—Warren

Local Volunteers

Linda Brown—Little Rock
Melvin Brown—Sweet Home
Katherine Knight—Little Rock
Estella Morris—Little Rock
Delcinia Robinson—Forrest City

Project Support & Endorsement

Dee Brown—author and historian
Sen. Dale Bumpers—former state governor
Susan Daggett—Marianna resident
Dr. Elaine Fox—University of Central Arkansas (project advisor)

Martha Ann Jones—Director, Arkansas Community Foundation (project fiscal agent)
Si Kahn—Grassroots Leadership Project, Charlotte, NC
Ms. Billie Meyer—Director, state Office of Volunteerism
Dr. Waddy Moore—University of Central Arkansas (project advisor)
Dr. Fred Morrow—University of Arkansas at Little Rock (project advisor)
Ted Parkhurst—Director, August House Press
David Pass—author and VISTA authority
Miss Lily Peter—project donor
Dr. Hampton Roy—project donor
Professor Juanita Sandford—Henderson State University (project advisor)

Arkansas VISTA *Project Files Reviewed*

Aldersgate
American Civil Liberties Union
Arkansas ABLE
Arkansas Community Education Development
Arkansas Community Organization for Reform Now
Arkansas Consumer Research
Arkansas Council on Human Relations
Arkansas Department of Energy
Arkansas Human Service Providers Association
Arkansas Land and Farm Development Corporation
Arkansas Legal Services
Arkansas Literary Council
Arkansas Louisiana Agricultural Research Corporation
Arkansas Nutrition Coalition
Arkansas Nutrition Project
Arkansas River Valley Area Council
Arkansas River Valley Crafts Co-operative
Arkansas Summer Associates Program
Arkansas Women's Training Project—United Methodist Church
Black River Area Development Corporation
Blinded Veterans Association
Boys, Girls, Adults Community Development Center
Central Arkansas Area Agency of Aging
Central Arkansas Development Council
City of Birdsong
Clark Institute
College Station Community Development Fund
Community Energy Futures
Community Resource Center
Criminal Justice Ministry
Crisis Center of Arkansas

Crowley's Ridge Development Council
Dermott Concerned Citizens Enterprise
Division of Community Services
Division of Human Services
East Central Arkansas EOA
Helping Hands
Housing Development Corporation of Arkansas
Human Service Providers Association
Inner City Alliance for Progress
Job Corps Conservation Centers
Korean American Association
Lonoke County Council on Human Resources
Luxora
Mari Spehar Health Education Project
Mid Delta Community Service
Mission Outreach
Mississippi County EOA
Morris Booker Memorial College
Neighbor to Neighbor
Newark Public Schools
Newton County Board of Education
North Arkansas Development Council
Northwest Arkansas Legal Services
Ozark Institute
Ozark Legal Services
Ozark Opportunities
Ozark Producers-Consumers Alliance
People & Awareness for Community Action
Pine Bluff Women's Center
Pulaski County Council on Aging
Pulaski County EOA
Southeast Arkansas Community Action Agency
South Central Arkansas Community Action Agency
South Madison County Home Improvement Project
Southwest Arkansas Development Corporation
Spring River Community Resource Council
UALR Graduate School of Social Work
Veterans Administration Social Services

Veterans Hospital Deinstitutionalization Project
Washington County EOA
Watershed
YMCA Carver Branch
Youth Home

Index

Abson Wynne Co-op, 227, 228
Academy Award, 12
ACORN, 24, 390
ACTION, 20–24, 51, 345, 350, 386, 395
Adams, Haskell, 244–246
Adkison, Bob, 63, 72, 108
Albany, NY, 411
Allentown, PA, 374
Alinsky, Saul, 38, 55, 91, 106
Alston, Rev. Bob, 217
Anderson, Steve, 397, 398
Anthes, Earl and Cheri, 40, 215, 216, 218, 219, 277, 425–427, 441
Apollo IX, 356
Appalachia, 63, 64, 85
Arkadelphia, 43, 291, 298, 356, 374
Arkansas Association of County Judges, 244
Arkansas Bar exam, 133
Arkansas Board of Education, 319
Arkansas Consumer Research, 390
Arkansas Council of Human Relations, 168, 291, 296, 297, 441
Arkansas Democrat, 357
Arkansas Department of Human Services, 108
Arkansas Department of Public Welfare, 419
Arkansas Division of Community Services, 389
Arkansas Division of Economic & Medical Services, 108
Arkansas Farm Bureau, 100, 244
Arkansas Gazette, 192
Arkansas Health Planning Commission, 201
Arkansas High School, 116
Arkansas History Commission, 48
Arkansas House of Representatives, 51
Arkansas Literacy Council, 389
Arkansas Nutrition Coalition, 389, 420
Arkansas Office of Community Services, 108
Arkansas OEO, 33, 139, 142, 145, 147
Arkansas River, 61, 63, 321
Arkansas River Valley Area Council, 61–88, 108, 439
Arkansas Supreme Court, 152
Arkansas Taxpayer's Guide, 334
Arkansas Tech, 78
Arkansas Women for Justice, 261
Arnett, Alvin, 51
ARVAC Housing Development Corp., 81
ARVAC Mental Health Program, 81
ARVAC Rural Folk Crafts, 5, 82, 84
Ashcroft, Bob, 81
Ashley County, 166
Ashdown, 131
Assembly of God Church, 180
Associate Volunteer, 13, 14, 43, 165–167, 180, 197, 291–302, 374
Association of Citizens Councils of Arkansas, 244
Atlanta, 164
Attorney General's Office, 9
Auden, W. H., 122
Augusta, 208, 209, 215
Austin, TX, 22, 47, 92, 202, 222, 229, 269, 277, 355, 373, 447

Back Bay Mission, 125
Baez, Joan, 245, 247
Bald Knob, 295, 301
Balzano, Michael, 23

Bankhead, Annie Mae, 312, 316
Barker, T. H., 192
Bay St. Louis, MS, 221
Bearden, 272
Bennet, Amos, 386
Berkeley, 174, 332
Bethel United Presbyterian Church, 115, 117, 121–125, 132, 137, 139, 142, 143, 145
Big Slough, 299, 300
Biloxi, MS, 125
Birdsong, 53, 229, 231, 235, 430, 443
Birmingham, AL, 220
Black Panthers, 164, 167
Black River Area Development Corp., 394–396, 399, 410, 412, 413
Black River Vo-Tech, 394
Black United Youth, 379
Blakely, Neal, 39, 45, 48, 55, 94, 442, 443
Blankenship, Leroy, 410
Blumenthal, Dr. Dan and Janet, 191, 196, 228, 237, 238–242, 248, 249
Blytheville, 233, 294, 298, 411
"BODS," 269
Bookheim, William, 394, 399, 407–414
Boone County, 105
Boston Mountain Co-op, 94, 397, 446
Boswell, Beverly, 318, 319
Boswell, Esther, 309
Boyle, John, 174, 434, 446, 447
Boy Scouts, 401
Bozynski, Tony, 333, 341, 347, 349, 430–432
Bradley County, 276, 374, 380
Bradley County Community Action Corp., 373–380
Brellochs, Christel, 40, 187, 202–204, 229–235, 256, 434, 448
Broadway Neighborhood Association, 334
Brooklyn, NY, 414
Bronx, The, 235, 448
Brown, Melvin, 43, 284, 350, 443
Brown, Rebecca, 318
Brown, Sam, 24, 37
Brown Shoe Co., 41
Bruch, Joe, 12, 21, 22, 42, 47, 48, 56, 92, 93, 100, 102, 106, 136, 173, 200, 204, 243, 281, 309, 361, 376, 377, 384, 385, 396, 409, 411, 440, 441
Brubeck, Dave, 413
Bumpers, Dale, 243, 247, 257
Burke, Denzer, 124, 143, 148, 149, 155
Burdette, 229
Burnett, Betty, 64
Burnley, James, 26

CABUN, 276
Calhoun County, 267, 276
Camden, 118, 166, 167, 272, 274, 296, 418–420
Camden Chamber of Commerce, 419
Camden News, 419
Camp Crajasett, 393
Cass, 390
CBS, 240, 241
Cantrell, Carol, 301
Caracen, 399
Carter, Jimmy, 23–25
Case, Rev. Travis, 217
Cass, Corrine, 200, 237, 242, 248, 255
Central Baptist Church, 217
Central High School, 296, 301, 375, 458
Centerville, 85, 86
CETA, 339
"Change," 129, 151
Chapel Hill, NC, 164
Chicago, IL, 117
"Chicago 8, The," 273
Cincinnati, OH, 413
Citizens Board of Inquiry into Hunger and Malnutrition, 384
Civil War, 115
Clark, John (administrator), 203, 204, 256, 262, 441
Clark, John (Volunteer), 431
Clarke, Rev. Lewis, 241
Clarksville, 360
"Class of 1969," 269
Clay County, 394, 395, 410, 412
Clayton, Barbara, 137, 153

Cleaver, Eldridge, 412
Clifton, Arthur, 323
Coleman, Elijah, 180, 441
Coleman, Goforth, 107, 314, 332–334, 345–347, 351, 352, 462
Colen, Eddie, 374, 380
Colfax, WA, 310
College City, 410
College City Volunteer Fire Department, 411
College of the Ozarks, 360
College Station, 312, 316, 317, 319, 400–403
College Station Progressive League, 312
College Station YMCA, 401
Columbia University School of Social Work, 409
Committee For Representative Government, 129, 151
Community Action Agency, 13, 99–108, 292, 295, 296, 386
Community Action Program, 14, 15, 19, 21, 22, 49, 50, 73, 74, 339
Community Energy Futures, 181, 435
Community School for Exceptional Children, 395
Community Service Award, 318
Community Workers Organization, 325
Conard, Harry and Barbara, 175, 248, 445, 457–459
Concerned Citizens of Lee County, 245
Cone, Rev. Cecil, 356
Congressional Record, 190
Conte, Silvio, 190
Conway County, 71, 374
Copeland, Ron, 126
CORAP, 390
Cornell University, 296
Counseling Associates, 81
Craighead County, 392, 393, 413
Crawford, Jim, 41, 51, 282, 312, 314, 334, 387
Crawfordsville, 227
Cress, Myrtle, 65–70
Crittenden County, 201, 227, 384, 441
Crockett, 166
Cronin, Jerry, 219, 267–278
Crook, William, 15, 446, 447
Cross County, 201, 259
Crowley's Ridge Development Council, 392–394
culture shock, 180
Cummins Prison, 272

Dallas Cowboys, 294
Dardanelle, 5, 64, 69, 386
Dardanelle Lock & Dam, 63
Darden, Bob, 92
Davis, Milton, 192
Deknatel, Charlie, 45, 103, 411
DeMarco, Bob, 123, 131
Democratic Convention of 1968, 117, 412
Denver, CO, 432
Department of Health, Education and Welfare, 19, 320
DeRousie, Mr. and Mrs. Charles, 259, 260
Design Cooperative of Arkansas, 330–341, 430, 432, 461
Dick Jeter Community, 334
Different Drummer, A, 140, 141
Disneyland, 430
Dixie Addition, 309
"Don't Get Sick in America," 240
Dooley, Dr. Tom, 174
Douglas, Bob, 151, 152
Douglas, Frederick, 294
Dublin, Ireland, 270
Dunwoody, Janet, 333

Earle, 218, 223
East Central Arkansas EOA/CAA, 100, 203, 237, 256, 262, 441
East Central Arkansas Legal Services, 207
East End, 458
East Fayetteville EOA, 165
East Texas Legal Services, 153
Easy Rider, 114
Economic Opportunity Act, 3, 10, 49, 101
Eisenhower, Dwight David, 357

Ellenbecker, Mary Ann, 333
Ellis, George, 55, 56, 426, 435
English, Margo, 227, 228
Entis, Christine, 333, 336
Erickson, Rex and Neva, 401–403
Eureka Springs, 417
Evans, Earl, 49

Family of Man, The, 413
Farmers Home Administration, 35, 64, 81
Faubus, Orville, 49, 167
Fayetteville, 67, 95, 161–169, 235, 396, 448
FBI, 92, 223
Federal Communications Commission, 148, 149
Federation of Southern Cooperatives, 24
Ferguson, Glen, 11
Ferguson, "Willie," 415–421
Few Comforts or Surprises: The Arkansas Delta, 209
Fields, Dr. Elizabeth C., 240
First Baptist Church of Marianna, 241
First, Richard, 101, 258, 383, 399, 414, 460, 461
First United Methodist Church of Little Rock, 357
Fixler, Mike, 368
Flat Rock Creek, 93
Fleck, Jack, 114, 118, 119, 122, 133, 135, 136, 147, 150, 151
Fleming, Robert, 374, 378
Frank, Bob, 180, 400, 447
Franklin, Aretha, 359, 360
Franklin County, 390
Franklin, Martha, 151
Freedom of Choice, 379
Freedom, Inc., 116, 143–145
Friends of VISTA, 15
food stamps, 417–421
Ford, Gerald, 23, 345
Ford Foundation Leadership Development Program, 164
Forrest City, 166, 193, 195, 197, 218, 224, 237, 260, 261
Fort Smith, 61
Fouke, 114
Fuller, Frank, 117, 123, 132, 138

Gaines House, 334
Garland, 150, 151
Garland County, 390
Gaylor Clinic, 429
Gehrig, Lou, 67
General Electric Corp., 18, 189, 201–203, 220–226
GE Management & Training Division, 93
Gilmore, 218
Girl Scouts, 287
Goldsby, Dean, 315, 347
Goldsmith, Aviv, 181
Gorman, Bob, 89–95
Gossett, Lilly Mae, 150
Gottlieb, Anna, 175, 342, 458–460, 462
Governor's Award for Volunteerism, 369
Graduate School of Social Work, 400, 409, 414, 460
Grady Manning Hotel, 460
Granite Mountain, 319
Gray, Dr. Dwight, 196, 243
"Great Society," 11, 49
Greene County, 392
Greensboro, NC, 164
Greer, Rev. and Mrs. Ezra, 218
Greer, Rosie, 294
Grey Rock, 72
Gullaksen, Gilbert, 332
Gursch, Wally, 176
Gyst House, 334

Haag, Greg, 81
Habitat for Humanity, 207
Hammerschmidt, John Paul, 93
Hampton, 267, 269–271, 273–277, 334
Hanger Hill, 310

Harrington, Michael, 9
Harrison, 93, 105, 385
Hart, Clyde, 202
Harvard School of Public Health, 386
Hatch Act, 15
Haynes, 241
Head Start, 10, 19, 56, 64, 99, 103, 108, 296, 316, 317, 321, 322, 367, 395, 427
Heald, Harry and Olive, 64
Health Advocates, 191, 200–204, 208, 215, 236–262, 384, 427, 457
Healy, Terry, 298
Hebrew Union College, 414
Hemlock Court, 309
Henderson State University, 298
Henry, Horace, 392
Hensley, 347
Higgins, 321, 322, 349, 442, 463
Higman, Howard, 45, 410
Highland Court, 318, 319
Highland Tenant Council, 319
Hilliard, N. H., 129, 151
Hoerster, John and Carol, 119, 133, 138, 142–144, 149, 152, 153
Hoffman, Art, 267, 271–274, 276
Hooper, Hazel, 143
Hope, 131, 356
Hornsby, Jerry, 189, 190, 191, 196, 202, 205, 220, 227, 433, 436, 444, 445
Hot Springs, 361, 390, 392
Housing and Urban Development, 35, 126
Howard, James, 333, 337, 345, 346
Hudman, Thomas, 142, 145, 147
Hughes, 190, 200
Human Rights Commission, 216
Human Service Providers Association, 389, 390
Hyde, Sharon, 68, 71

Imhoff, Charles, 46, 104, 215, 217
Independent Community Consultants, 219, 277
Indian Trails House, 398
Interaction, 323
"Invaders" of Memphis, 224
Iowa, 417–419
Ivener, Loren, 174, 391, 392
Ivory, George, 50, 102, 231–235, 296

Jackson County, 392, 393
Jackson, Jesse, 169
Jackson, Pat, 322, 442, 443, 463
Jacksonville, 313
Jansen, Jim, 395
Jasper, 94
Jaycees, 318, 413
J. C. Cooke School, 334
Jewett, David, 133
Job Corps, 10, 19, 67
Job Corps Conservation Center, 390, 392
Johns, Darcy, 309
Johnson, Charles, 396
Johnson County, 65, 81
Johnson, Lyndon Baines, 3, 10, 11
Johnson, Robert, 53, 182, 231, 235, 443
Jonesboro, 181, 298, 392, 413
Jonesboro Hot Line, 393
Justice Department, 9

Karlin, Al, 115, 117, 119, 120, 122, 128, 133, 139, 144, 154, 155
Kaul, Edward, 344
Kelly, Loraine, 343
Kennedy, John F., 9–11, 85
Kennedy, Lacey, 241
Kennedy, Padraic, 11, 18
Kennel, Lora, 348
Kensett, 295
Kinderman, Bob, 177
King, Rev. Martin Luther, 117, 168, 245, 312, 445
King, Sterling, 256
Kiwanis, 411
Knight, Katherine, 282, 286
Knoxville, TN, 269, 270
Kozinsky, Stanley, 332
Kressley, Larry, 374, 377–380, 446, 450

KTAL-TV, 148, 149
Ku Klux Klan, 152, 195, 207

Labor Department, 19
Lake Village, 334
"Land of Opportunity," 174
Lane, C. R., 19
Lawrence County, 394, 410
Lee County, 5, 175, 191, 192, 196, 200, 201, 218, 236–252, 259, 262, 384, 385
Lee County Citizens Council, 197
Lee County Cooperative Medical Clinic, 5, 56, 191, 236–252, 400, 442, 457, 459, 461
Lee County High School, 245
Lee County Farm Bureau, 192
Lee County Medical Society, 239, 240, 243
Lee County Memorial Hospital, 242, 244
Lee County Welfare Office, 384
Legal Services, 390
Lewis, John, 353–361
Lewis, Penny, 322, 324, 428
Literary Council of Jefferson County, 388
Little Rock, 41, 51, 61, 100, 138, 145, 165, 192, 200, 205, 224, 235, 277, 297, 301, 307, 313, 318, 321, 324, 332, 334, 355, 385, 389, 399, 414, 432, 458
Little Rock Air Force Base, 361
Little Rock Classroom Teachers Association, 287
Little Rock Housing Authority, 318
locally recruited Volunteer, 18, 22, 43, 281–287, 389
Lockhart, Tom, 147
London, Diana, 19, 27
Lone Star Munitions, 114
Longley, 355, 356, 359
Los Angeles, 188
Los Angeles Rams, 164
Lowndes County, AL, 445
Lynch, Dorothea, 217
Lynch, Kathy, 374, 376
Lynn, MA, 175

MacAlister, Vera, 152, 155, 156
Mackey, Frank, 328
Madison, 218
Madison County, 166
Mager, Mimi, 15, 26, 27
Malvern, 400
Mann, Lon, 218, 246
Many Voices, 209, 216, 218, 219
Maples, Mrs. Jesse, 218
Marche, 334
Marianna, 5, 191, 192, 197, 218, 228, 236–256, 258, 400, 412, 442, 457
Marianna Chamber of Commerce, 249
Mari Spehar Health Education Project, 397
Marked Tree, 294, 299, 393
Marshall, TX, 139
Martin, Donnie Peterson, 395
Martin Luther King Robert Kennedy Bald Knob National Memorial Park, 301
Mason, Tommy, 164
May, Martha, 395
McClellan, John, 239
McDermott, 334
McKindra, Freeman, 35, 47, 48, 56, 57, 103, 386
McLendon, Dr. Mac, 239
McRae, Tom, 127, 128
Memphis, TN, 92, 205, 207, 231
Memphis *Commercial Appeal,* 241
Menifee, 374
Mercado, Jim, 175, 179, 328, 333, 337, 346, 352, 369, 370, 431, 432, 448, 452, 461, 462
Mercedes, Frances, 337
Meyer, Ron, 250, 251
Meyers, Bill, 294, 298
Miller County, 5, 114, 131, 133, 138, 146, 150, 384

Miller, Zelma, 325, 328, 329, 363–370, 443
Mills, Roger, 295
Mills, Wilbur, 295
Minority Contractors Association, 335
Miss America, 359
Mississippi County, 36, 40, 50, 53, 107, 182, 191, 201, 229, 231, 294, 384, 430, 443
Mississippi County EOA/CAA, 102, 203, 232
Mississippi River, 189
Missouri, 413
Missouri Pacific Railroad, 240
Mitchell, Boss, 64
Model Cities program, 113, 115, 121, 123, 126–130, 139, 143, 152, 314
Monticello, 166
Mordhurst, Mary, 343
Morgan, Bobby, 161–169, 297
Morgan, Sherman, 161
Morgan, Veda Ranchino, 292
Morgenfield, Alice, 237, 246
Morrilton, 71
Morris, Estella, 284–286, 319, 320, 464
Morrow, Fred, 291, 464, 465
Mound Bayou, MS, 203

NAACP, 197, 225
Nashville, TN, 225, 444
National Advisory Committee on Child Nutrition, 261
National Demonstration Water Project, 248
National Service Corps, 9
National VISTA Alliance, 20
National Volunteer, 13, 104, 175, 179, 181, 281–287, 291, 295, 374
Neal, Ollie, 175, 242, 244, 246, 248, 253–258
Neighborhood Action Council/Committee, 237, 311
Neighborhood Youth Corps, 10, 92
Neighbor to Neighbor, 388, 389
Neft, Bruce and Gail, 117, 124, 135, 150
Negro Boys School, 356
Newman, Paul, 12
New Mexico, 47, 276
New Orleans, 181
New South Hope, 72
Newsweek, 297
Newton County, 92
New York Times, 148
Nixon, Richard, 19–22, 51, 106, 195, 200, 224, 314, 361, 432
Norman, OK, 374
North Carolina, 164
North Little Rock, 309
North Little Rock Stark Bend Water Commission, 334

Oark, 64, 65
Oberlin College, 409
Office of Economic Opportunity, 10, 14, 15, 17, 19–23, 49–51, 55, 57, 63, 94, 99, 101–103, 132, 165, 190, 192, 197, 202, 220–223, 225, 239, 241, 243, 244, 256, 257, 292, 296, 361, 386, 399, 411, 412
OEO Emergency Food & Medical Services, 201
OEO Training Program, 49
O'Kean, 396
Oklahoma City, 92
Ola, 65, 66, 68
Operation HOPE, 260, 261
Operation Robin Hood, 222, 224
Osceola, 191, 229
Other America, The, 9
Ouachita Baptist University, 43, 165, 291–294, 296, 301, 356, 374
Ouachita County, 418, 420
Ouachita Mountains, 61, 464
Ouachita National Forest, 392
Ozarka, 64
Ozark Mountains, 61, 161, 464
Ozark National Forest, 360, 392
Ozark Opportunities, 105
Ozark Regional Commission, 64

Palmers, Indulis, 92
Palnick, Rabbi Ezekial, 414
Page, Lurleen, 127, 131
Panama City, FL, 355
Paragould, 334
Pass, David, 20
Patrick, Linda, 310–311
Peace Corps, 4, 9, 12, 17, 281, 409
Pebble Project, The, 447
Pelkey, Jon, 76–79
Pentagon, 117
Penwell, Harold, 314
People for Awareness and Community Action, 397
People's Park, 174
Peters, Bill, 174, 332, 334, 351, 368
Pettus, Sharon, 342
Philander Smith College, 322
Phillips County Courthouse, 166
Pine Bluff, 311, 367, 388, 389
Pocahontas, 394, 395, 410
Poinsett County, 294, 392, 393
Pondexter, Erma, 131, 134, 142, 152, 156
Pope County, 76
Potter, Mary, 71, 310, 311, 452
Poverty In The Land Of Opportunity, 298
Pride In Education, 78
Princeton University, 132
Prescott, WI, 260
Press Argus, 421
Prestamon, Gregg, 435
Program Development Planner, 13, 45, 74–75, 81, 101–103, 132, 394, 410
Pulaski County, 5, 36, 43, 307–352, 400, 414, 432
Pulaski County Council on Aging, 343
Pulaski County EOA, 107, 287, 307–352, 400, 414, 432

Quandt, Phil, 339, 340, 350

Ramsey, Jack, 223
Ranchino, Jim, 43, 165, 291–296, 299, 301, 356
Randolph County, 394–396, 410, 412, 413
Reagan, Ronald, 25, 26, 181
Redlener, Dr. Irwin, 245
Red River, 150, 151
Red River Army Depot, 114, 124
Reid, Sharon, 343
Respect, Inc., 209, 215–219, 225
Reveille For Radicals, 38
Richards, Gene, 174, 176, 187, 197, 200, 208–215, 217, 218, 427, 428
Ricou, Diana, 295, 301
Riley, Bob, 292
Robert Kennedy Fellowship, 153
Roberts, Anne, 374
Roberts, Liz, 310, 313, 314
Robinson, Delcinia, 193, 260, 261, 283
Robinson, Litta, 259
Rockefeller, Winthrop, 139, 142–144, 191, 243, 245, 377
Rogers, James, 375, 378
Rose, Joann Violo, 40, 174, 321, 348, 349, 447, 450, 451
Royal, 390, 392
Rudzik, Frank, 74
Rules for Radicals, 106
Rural Electric Association, 93, 95
Rural Training Center, 101, 165
Russellville, 76, 78, 82, 93
Ruth, Babe, 67
Ryder, Barbara, 309

Saline County, 400
Salvation Army, 360
Samsel, Jim, 333
San Diego, CA, 407
Sandford, Juanita, 298, 299
Sandstead, Robert, 384
"Saturday party," 69
Schorr, Daniel, 240
Scott, 334, 342, 343, 461, 462
Second Harvest, 394
Selma Freedom March, 445
"Sesame Street," 148
Sexton, Floyd, 147

Sheen, Pam, 336, 350, 352
Shelton, Robert, 195
Sherman's Tavern, 161
Sherrod, Julia, 227
Shorter College, 309
Shreveport, LA, 148, 149, 275
Shriver, Sargent, 10, 22
"Sign of Jonah, The," 122
Smegelsky, Sandy, 174, 205–207, 429, 430, 448
Smith, Ellen, 374
Solgahachie, 71
Soul on Ice, 412
South Central Arkansas Community Action Agency, 271, 418
South Madison County Home Improvement Project, 51
South Texarkana Neighborhood Council, 128
Southwest Arkansas Development Council, 116, 119, 123, 131, 133, 138, 139, 142, 144–147, 153
State of the Union Address, 9
State Line Boulevard, 113, 145
St. Edwards University, 222
Stephens, Rev. David, 115, 121–125, 133, 136–139, 143, 144, 148, 153–155
Sterley, Bob, 339–340, 351
Sterling, 5, 10, 369
Stewart, David, 318
Stewart, Rev. H. D., 401, 403, 404
St. Francis County, 201, 262
St. Francis House, 400
St. Jude's Hospital, 430
St. Louis, 392
St. Mary of the Woods College, 400
St. Patrick's Church, 207
Stone County, 384
Success, 356
Super VISTAS, 410
Sweet Home, 70, 324–329, 333, 334, 350, 363–370, 442, 459
Sweet Home Community Center, 326, 328, 340, 365, 368
"Sweet Willie Wine," 224
Syracuse, NY, 205

Tabankin, Marge, 25
Tabernacle Baptist Academy, 217
Tabernacle Baptist Church, 217
Teapot Dome Scandal, 346
Teggatz, Pamela, 64
Temeyer, Pat, 68, 71
Tenant Landlord Organization, 397
Texarkana, 5, 100, 113–156, 384
Texarkana Boys Club, 124
Texarkana City Board of Directors (Arkansas), 128, 129
Texarkana City Council (Texas), 124, 139, 142, 144
Texarkana Community Chest, 124
Texarkana Gazette, 137
Texarkana Optimists, 124
Texas, 418
Texas High School, 118, 153
Texas School for the Blind, 124
Thompson, Roosevelt, 444, 445
Time, 114
Tin Cup, 161, 165
Toad Suck, 68–71
Torvestad, Bob, 21, 27, 52, 53, 57, 84, 388, 389
Tufts University-Delta Health Center, 203
Turrell, 218

umbrella agency, 24
Union AME Church, 356
Union Chapel, 72
Union County, 276
United Auto Workers, 241
United Church of Christ, 121, 125, 149
United People's Cooperative, 53, 191, 229–235
United Way, 22, 393, 394
University of Arkansas, 258, 297
University of Arkansas at Little Rock, 101, 291, 318, 399, 400

University of Iowa, 418
University of Maryland, 399
University of Oklahoma, 46, 92
University of Oregon, 46, 86
University of Tennessee, 269
Universal, Inc., 81
Upward Bound, 10, 93
US Army Judge Advocates Corps, 118
US Forestry Service, 390
Utterback, Tom and Joann, 116, 133, 143, 148–150, 152, 153

Van Buren, 421
VanLines, 261
Veterans Administration, 444
Veteran's Day, 360
Viet Nam, 114, 125, 173, 174, 195, 200, 297
VISTA Guidance Papers, 25
Vitale, Lou, 63, 71, 83–88, 93, 386
Volt Technical Corp., 18
Volunteers in Educational Work & Service, 94

Waldner, Karen, 325, 328, 367
Walker, Dora, 396
Walker, W. L. "Sonny," 33, 46, 142, 145, 147, 311, 315, 347, 350, 463
Walnut Ridge, 410
Walnut Ridge Chamber of Commerce, 413
Ware, Jesse, 268, 278
Warm Springs, 413
Warnock, Col. John, 118, 119
War on Poverty, 3, 10, 11, 15, 20, 21, 63, 291, 296
Warren, 373–380, 446
Warren High School, 379
Warren, Lucille, 191, 430
Warriors of the Poor, 446
Washington, DC, 20, 139, 149
Washington County, 165, 396, 431, 446
Washington County Courthouse, 161
Washington County EOA, 94, 168, 396–399
Watergate, 22, 345
Watershed, 400–403
Watkins, Gary, 105
Waters, J. W., 92
Watson, Lance, 224
Watts, Mike, 314, 315, 328, 458, 459
Weathermen, 164
West Helena, 166
Westinghouse Corp., 18, 201
West Memphis, 40, 189, 197, 202, 205, 206, 207, 209, 216, 217, 224, 225, 277, 433, 441, 444
West Memphis Central Baptist Church, 217
White County, 295
White House, 314
White House Conference on Hunger, 224
White, Frank, 181
White River, 208
Whitfield, Edward, 296, 297
Whitfield, Robert, 50
Wilbur Mills Freeway, 334
Williams, Paul, 297, 298
Williams, Rev. M. W., 50, 102, 103, 107, 176, 463
Williams, Roger, 412
Wilson, Ted, 35, 100, 104, 204, 220, 227, 228, 237, 241, 256, 261, 262, 283, 431, 449, 450
Wisconsin, 428
Wise, Suzanne, 26
Wolf, Dr. Robbie, 175, 242
Woodruff County, 201, 208
Woods, Frances, 187, 209, 229–235, 427, 428, 431, 432, 448
Woodson, 347
Wrede, Jan, 237, 242, 253–255, 412
Wrightsville, 346, 356
Wynne, 197, 209
Wynne Progress, 259

Yale University, 119
"Year Toward Tomorrow, A," 12
Yell County, 63–65, 86

Yell County Community Action Program, 64
Yell County Economic Opportunity Program, 63
Yopp, Bobby, 393, 394
Young America in Action, 68
Young, Dr. Mitch, 116, 117, 119, 127, 139, 143
Young, Teresa Jackman, 294, 298–300, 302
Youth Bridge, 397, 398